Safeguarding Childhood

Also by Nigel Parton:

The Political Dimensions of Social Work (edited with Bill Jordan)

*The Politics of Child Abuse**

*Governing the Family: Child Care, Child Protection and the State**

Social Work, the Media and Public Relations (edited with Bob Franklin)

Social Theory, Social Change and Social Work (edited)

Child Protection: Risk and the Moral Order (with David Thorpe and Corinne Wattam)*

Child Protection and Family Support: Tensions, Contradictions and Possibilities (edited)

Child Sexual Abuse: Responding to the Experiences of Children (edited with Corinne Wattam)

Constructive Social Work: Towards a New Practice (with Patrick O'Byrne)*

Constructing Clienthood in Social Work and Human Services: Interaction, Identities and Practices (edited with Chris Hall, Kirsi Juhila and Tarja Pösö)

* Published by Palgrave Macmillan

Safeguarding Childhood: Early Intervention and Surveillance in a Late Modern Society

Nigel Parton

palgrave
macmillan

First published 2006 by
PALGRAVE MACMILLAN
Houndmills, Basingstoke, Hampshire RG21 6XS and
175 Fifth Avenue, New York, N.Y. 10010
Companies and representatives throughout the world

PALGRAVE MACMILLAN is the global academic imprint of the Palgrave Macmillan division of St. Martin's Press LLC and of Palgrave Macmillan Ltd. Macmillan® is a registered trademark in the United States, United Kingdom and other countries. Palgrave is a registered trademark in the European Union and other countries.

ISBN–13: 978 1–4039–3332–4
ISBN–10: 1–4039–3332–4

This book is printed on paper suitable for recycling and made from fully managed and sustained forest sources.

A catalogue record for this book is available from the British Library.

A catalog record for this book is available from the Library of Congress.

Library of Congress Catalog Card Number : 2005044650

10   9   8   7   6   5   4   3   2
15   14   13   12   11   10   09   08   07   06

Printed in China

Dedication

For Chris, as always

Contents

List of Figures and Tables

Figures

Tables

Acknowledgements

I am indebted to many people who, over the years, have shared their ideas, experiences and concerns as well as their knowledge, expertise and critical reflections. Discussions with Linda Colclough, Nick Frost, Tara Gupta, Phil Holmes, Bill Jordan, Eileen Munro, Jim Laffer, Corinne May-Chahal, Phillip Noyes, Gillian Pugh, David Thorpe, Andrew Turnell and Martin Woodhead have been invaluable. More particularly, I would like to thank Terry Thomas who commented on Chapter 7 and, with Chas Critcher and Jenny Kitzinger, suggested a number of sources; and my colleagues in the Centre for Applied Childhood Studies, who provide such a supportive and stimulating environment in which to work, particularly Brid Featherstone and Helen Masson who offered considerable advice throughout and read and made suggestions on the draft manuscript, together with Sue Hanson whose considerable efforts in producing the final manuscript were invaluable. Julie Boffa and Chris Parton also read and commented on the manuscript and offered encouragement throughout. As in everything I have written over the years, Chris has helped in ways far too numerous to mention and it is with love and gratitude that I dedicate this book to her. Finally, I would like to thank the School of Human and Health Sciences at the University of Huddersfield for granting me sabbatical leave during 2003/4, as without that support the book would not have been possible. I am, of course, completely responsible for what follows.

The author and publisher would like to thank the following for permission to reproduce copyright material in the form of extracts, figures and tables: John Wiley & Sons Ltd for Table 4.1 from *Children and Society*, Vol. 9, No. 1, 1995; Palgrave Macmillan for Figures 4.2 and 4.3 from N. Parton et al: *Child Protection: Risk and the Moral Order* (1997); Sage for Figure 5.1 from 'Growing up in the Postmodern Age' by L. Dencik, in *Acta sociologica*, Vol. 32, No. 2, 1989. Crown copyright material is reproduced with the permission of the Controller of HMSO and the Queen's Printer for Scotland. Every effort has been made to trace all the copyright holders, but if any have been inadvertently overlooked, the publishers will be pleased to make the necessary arrangement at the first opportunity.

Introduction

The publication of the Green Paper *Every Child Matters* (Chief Secretary to the Treasury, 2003) and the passing of the Children Act 2004 marked a significant watershed in thinking about children's services in England and heralded a major period of reform and change. While the government presented the changes as a direct response to the public inquiry into the death of Victoria Climbié (Laming Report, 2003), it was much more than this. As Paul Boateng, the chief secretary to the Treasury, said in the introduction to the Green Paper:

> This is the beginning of a long journey which will present challenges for all of us, but from which we must not flinch ... underpinning this must be not just the resources but an attitude that reflects the value that our society places on *children and childhood*. Children are precious. The world they must learn to inhabit is one in which they will face hazards and obstacles alongside real and growing opportunities. They are entitled not just to the sentiment of adults but a strategy that *safeguards them as children* and realises their potential. (Chief Secretary to the Treasury, 2003, p. 4, emphases added)

The tragic death of Victoria Climbié, together with the murders of Sarah Payne, in July 2000, and Jessica Chapman and Holly Wells, in August 2002, dramatically demonstrated the failure of English society to safeguard not just individual children but the institution of childhood itself. Their deaths were seen as a terrible indictment of the current state of policy and practice and provided clear evidence that fundamental changes were required.

The problem of child abuse and failures to protect children had been a significant challenge since the early 1970s (Parton, 1985a, 1991). However, even though changes in policy and practice had been introduced, children had continued to die and, in many respects, the death of Victoria Climbié in February 2000 seemed all the more reprehensible because it was the latest in a long catalogue of similar scandals over the previous 30 years where professionals had failed to intervene.

England is not alone in trying to address these issues. Similar high-profile scandals and debates have been taking place in other parts of the UK (Scottish Executive, 2002), Australia (see, for example, Queensland Ombudsman, 2003), North America (Waldfogel, 2001) and other Western countries.

However, it is England which has embarked on the most radical and ambitious process of change. The pace and nature of change seems of a different order to elsewhere and is more self-consciously related to attempts to

'modernise' services and practices, in the context of the major social transformations of the previous 30 years, particularly in terms of the changes in the
family and the community more generally. However, as I will demonstrate,
the influences upon and rationale for the changes in England have been determined only in part by concerns about preventing the deaths and abuse of
children at the hands of their parents and other immediate carers. As Paul
Boateng argued, they were also influenced by the desire to ensure that all
children fulfil their potential. The changes were motivated as much, if not more
so, by the wish to ensure that children became skilled and productive members
of the *future* workforce and did not engage in criminal activity as they were in
protecting them from abuse and harm in the *present*. Where children were to be
the focus of protective interventions to prevent harm or abuse, the rationale for
this was, primarily, because such harm or abuse was likely to have a deleterious
impact on their health and development as *future citizens*. Thus, while the
political momentum for the changes being introduced in England was considerably strengthened by the government being seen to be actively responding to
the public inquiry into the death of Victoria Climbié, the government was also
provided with an opportunity to introduce wide-ranging and radical reform.
This would not only bring about major organisational change but would also
reconfigure the relationship between children, parents, professionals and the
state well beyond concerns about child abuse. The story whereby this has come
about is both fascinating and complex and provides the focus of this book.

A History of the Present

In order to unpack this story I am thus concerned with trying to understand and
explain what, following Paul Boateng, is meant by developing a strategy for
children that 'safeguards them as children'. What are the key elements of such a
strategy? Why is this important now? How does it differ from what has gone
before? Whereas previously the focus of policy and practice in England had been
'battered babies', 'non-accidental injury to children', 'child abuse' and, most
recently, 'significant harm and the likelihood of significant harm', the focus
now is 'safeguarding and promoting the welfare of the child'. What does the
term 'safeguarding' mean? How has it become the central focus for policy and
practice? How does it differ from the previous objects of concern? What are the
implications for policy and practice? These are the central questions I will be
addressing in this book.

My aim is to understand the historical conditions upon which the emergence
of contemporary policy and practice depends. I use historical inquiry as a means
to discover how the phenomena associated with attempts to safeguard children
and childhood in England have come to acquire their current characteristics.
The focus on the past is motivated by my concern to make sense of the present

and thereby engage with it. The primary approach is analytical and while there is a critical and normative dimension, I only make this explicit in the final chapter. The aim is to provide an analysis of how this emerging field of practice has been constituted and to make explicit the range of complexities, ambiguities and tensions that have fed into it.

Central Themes and Structure of the Book

In Chapters 1 and 2, I provide an analysis of developments up to the early 1990s. A central part of my argument is that for much of the twentieth century, and based on developments in the last quarter of the nineteenth century, the role of the state was essentially to support the family in the upbringing of children. In this respect the family became the prime instrument of government for ensuring the health and development of children. Essentially the patriarchal nuclear family had entrusted to it the responsibility for rearing children. At the same time, the definition of what constituted normal child development was increasingly informed by research, knowledge and expertise derived from the psychosocial sciences. The family was seen as functional to the overall development of modern society and as functioning in the interests of children in most instances. To carry out these functions it was important that the family be experienced, particularly by parents, as a private institution beyond the intervention of state agents. When the state did intervene, this would be with the full force of the law behind it and was reserved for the exceptional circumstances where particular families were seen as failing in their primary duty to care for their children. The family was seen as a benign and consensual institution where the interests of children were assumed to be coterminous with those of their parents. The model of the family which underpinned child welfare policy and practice was based on the institution of marriage, where parents lived in the same household as their biological children, often in close geographical proximity to other members of the extended family. Similarly, the community was deemed to be a practical and moral entity which had a knowledge about its members and would report any concerns about children to the authorities if and when the need arose.

Social work played a vital role in mediating the sometimes ambiguous relationship between the privacy of the family and the public responsibilities of the state to ensure that children did not suffer. While the family was seen as an essentially uncontested social good, acting in the interests of children, social work had a low profile. However, if any of the social and institutional arrangements supporting this rationale for social work were to change, its task of ensuring that children's welfare was adequately met was going to become more difficult.

This is precisely what started to happen from the early 1970s. The public inquiry into the death of Maria Colwell in 1973, when she was under the supervision of local authority social workers, received considerable media attention and political debate. Not only did it demonstrate that the family was not 'the haven' it had been assumed to be, but also that social workers were not competent in carrying out the responsibilities devolved to them. Over the next 14 years there were numerous high-profile cases of children dying in similar circumstances where professionals, primarily social workers, had failed to intervene. However, in 1987, the removal of over 100 children from their parents in Cleveland on the basis of dubious diagnoses of sexual abuse posed a very different challenge. By the late 1980s it seemed that the fine balance which was seen as so vital to the operation of child welfare practice was no longer working, for not only did it seem that children were not being protected but that social workers were also overintervening and thereby undermining the privacy of the family. The Children Act 1989 was introduced to try and ensure that such a balance could be re-established. However, worse was to follow, as there was increasing evidence that children who were living in children's homes, and were thereby the direct responsibility of the state, were also being abused. By the early 1990s it was clear that the consensus on child welfare policy and practice was considerably undermined.

However, it was also evident that the increasing crisis in child welfare from the early 1970s onwards coincided with a series of major social and economic changes evident in society more generally, changes which are the focus of Chapter 3. In particular, the increasing impact of globalisation and major changes in the structure of the family, the rise of electronic mass media and the introduction of new information and communication technology were all having major implications for the way day-to-day life was lived and experienced. I argue that these changes are very evident in a comparison of the Maria Colwell and Victoria Climbié cases. In effect, the patriarchal nuclear family began to change in fundamental ways and the position of children within it could no longer be taken for granted. By the 1990s the position of children and the institution of childhood were subject to increasing anxiety, to the point that childhood was seen as being 'in crisis'. This was most forcibly exemplified by the murder of James Bulger by Jon Venables and Robert Thompson in 1993. No longer were the family and the community seen as adequate in ensuring that children were reared according to the standards required. Not only were they 'victims' of child abuse, but they were also the perpetrators of murder, crime and antisocial behaviour more generally.

A new approach was required. As Chapter 4 demonstrates, a number of the key elements of what might contribute to such a new approach were developed in the mid-1990s. The 'refocusing' debate following the publication of *Child Protection: Messages from Research* (DH, 1995a), the development of the Looking After Children (LAC) project and the emergence of a growing interest in the importance of policies to enhance early child prevention strategies in order to forestall future problems such as crime and poor educational attainment were all key.

However, to take these ideas forward required a much broader and more interventionist role for the state in relation to children and this was to be a major priority for the New Labour government following its election in 1997. In Chapter 5 I analyse the New Labour approach to 'governing' childhood. No longer was the traditional patriarchal nuclear family seen as an adequate instrument of government. Increasingly the interests and identities of children and parents (both mothers and fathers) were disentangled and disaggregated. Not only were children and young people increasingly the focus for many reforms in both social policy and criminal justice, but parents were seen as carrying particular responsibilities. The New Labour emphasis on the need to combat social exclusion and investing in the future workforce placed children and childhood at the centre of its social programme. The rationale and practical implications of this new approach were well illustrated in the introduction of the Sure Start programme.

The way this new way of thinking was to impact on policies and practices previously concerned with the 'protection of children from abuse' is the focus of Chapter 6. The publication of government guidance in late 1999 explicitly reframed the issues to be addressed in terms of the 'safeguarding and promotion of children's welfare' (DH et al., 1999) and introduced a new form of assessment, whereby the focus was not so much the identification of child abuse and the risk of harm to children but the identification of a child's needs and possible impairment in the context of their development (DH et al., 2000b).

No longer, however, were concerns about children's safety only focused on what goes on inside the family. In many respects, as I discuss in Chapter 7, the period from the late 1980s is also characterised by a growing public anxiety about extra-familial abuse in a variety of institutional settings and the community more generally. The period witnessed the transformation of the paedophile into one of the most terrifying threats of contemporary times, and prompted the introduction of a range of new legal, policy and practice changes which aimed to 'protect the public' and children in particular. These have had particular implications for the police and probation service and the operation of the criminal justice system more generally and came to a head following the murder of Sarah Payne, in July 2000, and Jessica Chapman and Holly Wells, in August 2002. What becomes evident is that from the early 1990s, child protection has increasingly been seen as much as a criminal justice issue as a child welfare issue, with two distinct multi-agency systems established – the one organised around the long-standing operation of area child protection committees (ACPCs) and the other around the more recently established multi-agency public protection arrangements (MAPPAs). Not only have the various systems become increasingly complex but issues around the sharing of information have become crucial both in relation to children and potentially dangerous offenders (PDOs).

In Chapter 8, I discuss, in some detail, the Green Paper *Every Child Matters* and the Children Act 2004, together with the important policy initiatives and official reports which informed them, including the Laming Report. Underpinning the developments are two sets of assumptions concerning the nature of recent social change and the best way to respond. First, it is asserted that over the previous generation, children's lives have undergone profound change. While children now have more opportunities than ever before and have benefited from rising prosperity and better health, they have also been faced with more uncertainties and risks. They face earlier exposure to sexual activity, drugs and alcohol, and family patterns have changed significantly, making the position of children more precarious. Second, however, it is also asserted that these changes have come about at a time when we now have increased knowledge and expertise and are therefore in a better position to respond to these new uncertainties and risks.

In particular, it is argued that two areas of expertise are of particular significance. First, it is claimed that research has clearly established the importance of early influences on child development and that it is thus important to intervene at an earlier stage in order to forestall problems in later life. Second, the development of new information technologies, it is argued, can make a vital contribution to the reform and improvement of children's services. Not only do they provide the potential for identifying problems and enhancing attempts to intervene at an earlier stage, but they allow different organisations and professionals to share information in order to ensure that children's problems are not missed, so that, crucially, children do not fall through 'the net'. The introduction of new systems for collating, monitoring and sharing information are seen as providing a key contribution for safeguarding and promoting the welfare of children.

Finally, in Chapter 9, I bring the various threads of my argument together and consider their possible implications. I suggest that what we are witnessing is the emergence of the 'preventive state', where previous conceptions of prevention are fundamentally recast and are placed at the centre of public policy rather than at its periphery. The preventive state aims to intervene at a much earlier stage rather than simply being concerned with investigating and responding to crises once they have emerged. It aims to pre-empt problems before they occur and involves increasing restraints on the liberty of certain individuals, whether these be potentially dangerous offenders, parents or children themselves. A key element is the use of various systems of surveillance whereby the storage, analysis and sharing of information takes on a particular significance. It is these developments, I suggest, that help us to understand the nature and import of the development of policies and practices which have the 'safeguarding' of children and childhood as their central rationale. The development of policies which emphasise safeguarding are particularly protectionist in intent. *The*

Shorter Oxford English Dictionary (5th edition, 2002) defines *safeguard*, the noun, in terms of: 'protection, safety, security; custody, safe-keeping; guarantee of safety or safe passage given by a person in authority; anything that offers security from danger; a defence, protection'. *Safeguard*, the verb, is defined as: 'keep secure from danger or attach; guard, protect, defend; send or conduct in safety'; while *safety*, the noun, is defined as: 'the state of being protected from or guarded against hurt or injury; freedom from danger. Close custody or confinement. The quality of being unlikely to cause hurt or injury; the quality of not being dangerous or presenting a risk.' All these elements are evident in the recent policy developments which I analyse, where 'every child matters'.

A central part of my argument is that the social changes of the past 30 years, which I characterise as the move to a late modern society, which has seen an increasing individualisation of social relations, have also witnessed a growing recognition of children as persons in their own right and have placed them at the centre of political strategies in quite new ways. It is in this sense that the focus of policies and practices can be said to be 'child-centred', rather than 'family-centred' as before. In the process children are also seen to have the potential for greater autonomy and self-creation as well as being the subject of increased regulation. I conclude by arguing that the way current policies in England are being constructed is having the primary effect of regulating and constraining children's agency, and that a much greater emphasis needs to be placed upon the participation of children in decisions made about them and hearing their voices about what troubles them and what they want done about it. In this context issues around confidentiality and the way information is gathered, stored and shared and what control children have over this become key. I am particularly concerned that, in giving so much attention to the importance of maximising children's potential in the future, we are not giving enough attention to protecting children from harm in the present and developing policies and practices which are centrally concerned with reinforcing and developing their rights as citizens.

1

Child Welfare and Modern Society

Recent developments in England point to an important reconfiguration of relationships, responsibilities and lines of accountability with regard to a range of services whose prime focus is the child and childhood more generally. At the hub of this reconfiguration is the notion of *safeguarding* where the prime concern and object of intervention is *safeguarding and promoting the welfare of the child*. The central purpose of this book is to try and unpack the key elements which have made such developments possible and thereby make transparent what is meant by safeguarding and its implications for parents, professionals and children themselves. A key part of the argument is that, while this is related to quite specific conditions which have been particular to England from the late 1980s, it is also closely related to important changes in the nature of society more generally, what I refer to as the move to a late modern society. I will argue that the changes and reconfigurations I will be analysing point to the development of policy and practice along quite new trajectories which, in the process, are significantly shifting the relationships between the child, the family, professionals and the state.

In other ways, however, the changes can be seen as both a continuation and a refinement of governmental child welfare concerns and policies, which first came into existence in the second half of the nineteen century, were further consolidated and institutionalised during the twentieth century, and were particularly associated and interrelated with the development and professionalisation of social work. Rather than viewing current developments as simply a response to more recent crises, public inquiries and political debates about the best way to safeguard children and promote their welfare, I will be arguing that it is important to recognise that these issues have a much longer historical trajectory. The way we have addressed them previously not only has important implications for the way we are currently rethinking and reframing our response, but also for the nature of the problems they are aimed to address.

At one level, I am arguing that the current concerns with safeguarding and the safety of children in part arises from the shift from the modern to late modern society or, as Wagner (1992, 1994) argues, the move from 'organised' to 'extended liberal modernity'. The focus of this chapter is thus to provide a brief and schematic backcloth for understanding the nature of modern child welfare as this emerged in the late nineteenth century and was to be established in the twentieth century.[1]

Child Welfare and the First Crisis of Modernity

Although the history of the family and parent–child relations is shrouded in controversy (see, for example, Aries, 1962; Pollock, 1983; Frost and Stein, 1989; Archard, 1993), there is general agreement that, from the late seventeenth century onwards, a new attitude towards children began to manifest itself and this was closely related to social changes which had particular impacts on the nature of community and the role of the family. While there was considerable variation between the social classes, it seems that in traditional society work and home were not sharply separated, kinship shaded into community and any distinction between private and public life was very limited: 'Individual family members were part of a collectivity larger than the family' (Shorter, 1976). However, with increasing industrialisation and urbanisation, and the emergence of a capitalist economy based on commerce and intensive agriculture, this began to change (Thane, 1981).

Shorter (1976) suggests that 'modernisation' meant the dissolution of the structured, changeless, compact traditional order. Ties to the community were weakened and the ties binding members of a family were reinforced. In the process, the privacy of the family as a social and psychological form increased and awareness of children as a separate category developed. The 'egoism' that was established in the market became associated with the whole domain of cultural rules that regulated family behaviour and relationships. Because the bourgeoisie profited most from these economic changes, they were the first to modify their conceptions and practices towards children.

The family became an increasingly important social site as general sociability decreased (Barrett and McIntosh, 1982), so that from the eighteenth century people began to defend themselves against the vagaries of social life and became increasingly concerned to construct and protect the privacy of the family. At the same time, the emergence of schooling removed children from adult society, so that the distinction between adult autonomy and childhood dependence became more marked. Similarly, in the context of the emergence of secular views of children and childhood from the eighteenth century, the Industrial Revolution changed the character and context of child labour and produced conditions for the increased visibility of poor children, who became an object of concern for a variety of philanthropic organisations in the nineteenth century (Cunningham, 1995). No longer could the welfare of children be left to the vagaries of the traditional patriarchal family and the emerging market.

Equally as significant, however, was the undermining of the collaborative relationships between the traditional patriarchal family and the sovereign state, where, in essence, there was a contractual relationship between the sovereign and the head of the family. The state, in return for the provision of men for military service and generally keeping family members in line, granted to the head of a family virtually absolute power over family members. Surveying the situation in the late eighteenth and early nineteenth centuries, May (1978) has commented that there was a universal belief in the sanctity of parental rights, including the use of chastisement, so that physical punishment, often extreme, was part of the normal experience for most children. Foucault (1991) has argued that the absolutist repressive model of the family acted as a model of government. However, in the context of the major economic and social changes from the late eighteenth century onwards, this began to change so that rather than being a *model of government*, the role of the family was reconfigured as an *instrument of government*, whereby a range of new social problems evident in the population more generally could be addressed. The process whereby this came about was complex. At its heart, however, was the emergence of a range of concerns about the survival and growth of children, together with new techniques and forms of knowledge which aimed to improve the health of the population more generally.

With the move towards capitalist social formations, the factory and the growth of urban areas, the old methods of social regulation based on the traditional family and community were no longer adequate. The 1850s and 60s witnessed riots and famines which overwhelmed the capacities of the Poor Law to provide relief, while the fear of the mob and anxiety about the growth of rootless children and youth posed an increasing threat to social order (Stedman Jones, 1971). Thus the conceptions of the child that developed during the period, which have been at the heart of child welfare policy ever since, saw children as both innocent and vulnerable and in need of protection (the child as victim) and also as impulsive, undersocialised and thus in need of guidance and control (the child as threat or villain) (Foley et al., 2003). While in many respects these conceptions seem contradictory, and at different times in history one conception has been more dominant than the other in terms of influencing priorities and policies, one of my arguments is that both were at play from the mid-nineteenth century onwards and both lay at the core of child welfare practice as it has developed.

These issues took on a particular significance during the nineteenth century, when the population of England and Wales increased from under 10 million in 1801 to 14 million in 1837 and to over 32 million in 1901. Not only did the population increase dramatically, but those aged under 14 never fell below

30 per cent and for much of the period the figure was nearer 40 per cent. The proportions living in towns similarly increased from just over half in 1851 to three-quarters by 1901 (Walvin, 1982, p. 18). Thus the growth in concerns about childhood and the changing role of the family took place in a context of significant social and economic change where the growth, urbanisation and health of the population were key factors.

As James Walvin (1982) has argued, the death of the young was an inescapable and growing reality in nineteenth-century England. In 1839/40 the death rate for children under one was 153 per 1000 live births, in 1896 it was 156 and by 1899, the worst ever recorded, it was 163. Walvin commented that

> the new-born child's life was endangered by complex natural and social problems which nineteenth-century man seemed unable to counter. But the modern reader is struck by the fact that many of these dangers were eminently avoidable. Neglect, ill-treatment, dirt and ignorance – often interrelated – swept away large numbers of babies. (1982, pp. 21–2)

It is helpful to put these debates in the context of the analysis provided by Peter Wagner (1992, 1994) about the nature of modernity and how this developed during the period. Wagner argues that there was a central tension which lay at the core of the modern condition as it emerged from the seventeenth century onwards, namely that between the aspirations for individual liberty and self-creation and the need for social discipline. However, the nature of these tensions, and more particularly the balance between the two, varies in different historical periods. The post-Enlightenment project of a liberal society focused on the idea that human autonomy was in principle universal and without boundaries. Freedom was, in theory, utopian but in reality was more limited and restricted to an elite group, what Wagner (1994) calls *restricted liberal modernity*. However, as these freedoms were opened up to a wider population, together with the social transformations, such as urbanisation and industrialisation, which they both represented and made possible, the socially dangerous nature of liberal modernity was increasingly recognised, and a number of critical commentators argued that the liberal project – in its original form – was not feasible. From a variety of perspectives it was argued that nineteenth-century liberalism had failed, and was powerless in the face of the forces of social transformation evidenced by rates of death and crime – particularly in relation to children. It seemed that changes in economic relations and the impact of the laissez-faire market had profound social consequences. This fed into growing concerns about 'the social question' or, as Wagner (1994) calls it, *the crisis of liberal modernity*. In the last quarter of the nineteenth century, the political debate increasingly focused on the need to address a growing number of social problems, such as crime, vagrancy and disease, without reimposing a strong (sovereign) state on the wishes and activities of individuals. Although perhaps put differently, the same question was being asked in a number of Western European countries at the same time.

During the last quarter of the nineteenth century, political economy gradually relinquished its earlier explicit interlinking of economic and moral laws, and formulated itself as a distinctly economic doctrine, with its own internal laws. At the same time the domain of civil society became *socialised*. Statistical investigations gradually revealed the population as a domain with its own specificity. Statistical techniques and sociological investigations revealed the nation to be a set of aggregated statistics, with regular fluctuations and knowable processes, and their own laws and cycles (Abrams, 1968). Towns became the target of a variety of interventions – social, hygiene, police – which gave rise to further detailed statistical mapping of urban space. As the social body became subjected to new government norms, for example the registration of births, marriages, deaths, types and number of crimes, new realms of social visibility became the object of investigation (Hacking, 1991a). A *social* domain came into being that could be both the object of science – *social* science – and the territory for a variety of policies – *social* policies – and interventions. The primary technology that emerged for governing 'the social' was based on attempts to socialise risk, particularly by the introduction of a range of social insurance schemes (Swaan, 1988; Ewald, 1991). The *social way of governing* thus constituted a quite new departure in the context of trying to respond to key tensions which lay at the core of the emerging modern conditions of the nineteenth century.

While the dominant means of improving social security was via social insurance, another strategy involved the emergence of social work. The former was primarily concerned with the collectivity and thus attempted to be inclusive and solidaristic, while the latter was individualistic and responsibilising. Social work was concerned not so much with the community of citizens but with individual problem cases, and the private family was its key site of intervention. *Social insurance* and *social work* can be seen to exemplify this new formula of *social government* as it emerged in the late nineteenth century (Garland, 1985) and was to be refined and institutionalised during the twentieth century, in terms of the welfare state or, as Wagner (1994) calls it, *organised modernity*. To understand this further, however, it is important to say more, not just about how these arrangements were conceptualised but also how they were organised.

The way these issues were addressed was crucially informed by the emergence of a range of new scientific rationalities, calculations and interventions, which not only provided ways of responding to these emerging problems but informed the way they were conceived. It was not simply that there were new problems for which the new scientific approaches provided new answers, but that the way the problems were constituted as problems in the first place was qualitatively different from what had gone before. The traditional approaches were far more fatalistic and assumed that things occurred because they were 'God's will', and in that respect the 'Word of God', and the sovereign and the head of the household acting on 'His' behalf, was both absolute and final. There was little that humans could do to change their situation. The growth of scientific rationality was to have an enormous impact on this way of thinking.

The work of Michel Foucault has been particularly influential in providing insights into understanding the development, nature and impact of this way of thinking. He sees the emergence and exercise of 'biopolitical' power over life in the period from the mid-seventeenth to the end of the eighteenth century as being key. During this period, he argues, new forms of knowledge about concerns about the population began to be developed through statistical enquiry (Hacking, 1990), when the beginnings of modern medicine were being established (Foucault, 1973) and in which new forms of spatial arrangement, for example modern prisons, hospitals and schools (Foucault, 1977), would render individuals visible in new ways. What Foucault highlights here is the emergence of forms of 'knowledge-power' in which individuals are conceived as members of a population. Biopower can be seen to consist of two axes, the one centred on the body as a machine which is to be made useful through discipline, and the second focused on the supervision and regulation of the newly constituted population. Together these form two poles of the organisation of 'power over life' (Foucault, 1979, p. 139). The former has the effect of constituting the nature and dimensions of individuals, via the development of a range of new information in the form of reports and case files, while the latter has the effect of constituting the nature and key dimensions of a population, particularly via the development of statistics in relation to, for example, age, habits, activities, morbidity, mortality, health and crime, and most clearly represented by the development of epidemiology (see Hacking, 1991a). As Ashenden argues, following Foucault:

> This double focus of biopolitics is coterminous at the level of knowledge, with the development of the individual case history documenting the details of an individual's life, and with the development of statistics of population, documenting demographic patterns. (Ashendon, 2004, p. 111)

These individualising and totalising forms of knowledge are made possible and linked through the emergence of the social sciences and a variety of new technologies that provided institutional sites, initially via the hospital, the school and the prison, for the concerns of these 'sciences of man'. In the process, therefore, we are provided with a detailed knowledge of both the total population (and thus the nature of civil society), the individuals who make it up and possible ways to intervene. Perhaps, most crucially, the promulgation of statistics allowed for the possibility for locating individuals in relation to other individuals and their own life course and thereby making judgements about 'what is normal'.

The notion of 'normalcy' has since become one of the most powerful metaconcepts in human affairs. It only acquired its sense of 'usual' or 'typical' in the nineteenth century, originally in medical contexts where the opposite was seen as 'pathological'. While normalcy was originally measured by statistical methods to describe difference, increasingly it was also associated with being right or healthy (Hacking, 1990).

In this context the modern private family was to emerge as a key site for addressing the problems and health of individuals and the total population, particularly in relation to children. It is in this sense that the increasingly private family becomes an instrument of government. The social adjustment of the individual was to become the natural outcome of the child's development and the normal outcome of satisfactory family life. No longer, however, could the family be left to its own devices. Increasingly, in the last quarter of the nineteenth century, the family was seen as central for both the physical care and hygienic management of children and their moral and social education, what we might call their 'welfare'. Thus while the primary objective of intervention was to be the child, the instrument of this intervention was to be the parents – or, more specifically, the mother – via the family.

At the same time there was a central dilemma which lay at the core of this new relationship between the family and the state. If the state was to assume increasing responsibility for children, how could it discharge those responsibilities without undermining the privacy of the family? How could it devise a legal basis for the power to intervene into the private sphere of the family in order to protect children, but in a way which did not undermine the family and convert all families into clients of the state? And it is here that the knowledge claims and practices of the new human sciences – particularly medicine, psychiatry, criminology and, perhaps most crucially, social work – were to become important.

The original impetus for such developments was the growth of a variety of philanthropic organisations, the forerunners of social work, whose primary concern was the destitute child on the street, together with very young babies who were abandoned or subject to baby-farming.[2] The primary motivation was explicitly moral and concerned with 'child saving'. Such developments were particularly encouraged by economic changes, for as the bourgeoisie expanded and became more prosperous, the wife had more leisure time (Wilson, 1977). Charitable work not only provided an opportunity to display the success of her husband but also furthered the notion of the idealised mother and wife for working-class women to emulate. Philanthropists saw their duty not only in terms of rescuing children, but also in terms of articulating this new role and bringing souls to the kingdom of heaven. The more traditional Christian values of morality played a central role with regard to what made up the main elements of a 'proper' way of life (Walton, 1975).

Donzelot (1980) has suggested that two strategies were of particular signifi-cance in the relationships between the philanthropists and families, primarily with regard to children, what he calls 'moralization' and 'normalization'. 'Moralization' involved the use of financial and material assistance, which was used as a lever to encourage poor families to overcome their moral failure. It was used primarily for the deserving poor who could demonstrate that their problems arose from reasons beyond their control. 'Normalization' applied to attempts to spread specific norms of living via education, legislation and health, and involved a response to complaints, invariably from women about men, and hence provided a means of entry into the home. In return for this guidance and moral and minimal material support, philanthropic workers were given an insight into what was happening inside the home and leverage to bring about changes in behaviour and lifestyle. Clearly, however, there were problems if individuals did not cooperate or did not approach the worker in the first place, so that children were left to unbridled parental devices.

However, this was to change. The first Society for the Prevention of Cruelty to Children was established in 1883, modelled on the SPCCs being established in America. The National Society for the Prevention of Cruelty to Children (NSPCC) was formed in 1889 and was hugely successful in organising the public and political campaign which produced the first legislation specifically to outlaw child cruelty and give public agencies powers to protect children within their home – the Prevention of Cruelty to Children Act in 1889 (Behlmer, 1982; Parton, 1985a). Thus, while 'moralization' and 'normalization' were to be the primary forms of contact from the late nineteenth century, this was framed in legislation which would also give the possibility of coercive intervention for the removal of the child. 'Tutelage', as Donzelot (1980) calls it, based on the notion of preventive intervention, would combine a number of elements, although coercive intervention would be used for the exceptional circumstances where techniques of 'moralization' and 'normalization' had failed.

The activities of the NSPCC were of great significance in this period. Ferguson (1990, 2004) has analysed cases drawn from case files of the period and has shown how the new activity of child welfare was being conducted and thereby constructed. NSPCC inspectors worked in the homes of poor communities, describing, classifying and intervening in a variety of ways. Here were

> social workers actively constructing the foundations of modern forms of knowledge, of therapeutic and cultural practice: in short, a professional culture that would take child protection into the twentieth century. (Ferguson, 1990, p. 135)

Thus, what 70 years later would be called 'child abuse' provided a key focus for providing access into the family and for a new group of practitioners who, during the twentieth century, were to be explicitly identified as 'social workers'.

While the primary motivation had originally been moralistic, such activity was increasingly informed by the new social sciences, where the relationship between the worker and the mother and relationships between family members themselves were the focus of attention. Ashenden (2004, p. 25) has summarised the development:

> Thus we can say that the period between 1880 and 1914 saw the emergence and institutionalisation of a distinctly modern conception of childhood (Hendrick, 1994); the growth of laws concerning child protection combined with the medicalisation and psychologisation of childhood within schools, hospitals, children's homes and within families since the late nineteenth century has been important in producing a new domain of truth. It is in this context that modern social work developed as a practice within which child protection was to gain special significance.

The focus was the child, the role of social workers was to work with parents and thereby not undermine and, in many respects, strengthen the modern private family. There was a close interrelationship between the emergence of the modern notions of childhood, family and social work. However, it is also important to remember that the modern family was to be a site of perpetual ambivalence and tension for the modern liberal state, which was exercised about when and how to intervene so that its 'privacy' and 'naturalness' was not undermined. This tension was to be managed through expertise derived from law and increasingly science, particularly through the practice of social workers. It is not surprising, therefore, if the nature of child welfare social work was itself to be ambiguous and – potentially – contested (Parton, 1998). Even so, what becomes evident is that the establishment of this configuration of child welfare practice became ever more pervasive as the twentieth century developed. Child welfare social work was to provide a small, but key element of the welfare state in the twentieth century.

The Inter-war Period

And yet, after 1918, much of the activity concerned with saving children from the vagaries of the private family seemed to disappear from view. This is not to say that there is no evidence of physical and sexual abuse or child cruelty between the First World War and the 1960s (Smart, 2000) but that it received very little public or political attention. Parker (1995) suggests a number of reasons for this, including the decline of the women's movement following the granting of universal suffrage and changes to the NSPCC, to whom the government was happy to leave the responsibility for child cruelty, and which became more bureaucratic and less campaigning. Ferguson (1996, 1997, 2004) has argued that the general approach of the NSPCC to publicising child deaths shifted considerably during this period. In the nineteenth and early twentieth centuries, the NSPCC was not afraid to discuss publicly the deaths of children about whom they had direct knowledge and with whom they were working. The child death statistics were always included in its annual report. It seems that, paradoxically, the existence of child death was viewed as a sign that child protection was working well. It was highly publicised because it meant that increasing numbers of vulnerable children were being reached by its workers and hence it was fulfilling a valuable role (Ferguson, 2004). By the 1920s, Ferguson argues, this approach had been transformed so that death in child protection cases ceased to be made public, not because the problem was solved but because knowledge about it was, in effect, 'repressed' by the NSPCC and others. Disclosure of deaths, according to Ferguson, 'threatened the authority, optimism and trustworthiness of the expert system' (1997, p. 223).

What Ferguson is pointing to is that during the inter-war period we see developing a somewhat different conception of the family, together with changes in the nature of the problems which it was seen to engender and the forms of intervention which were seen as most appropriate. In effect, the more moralistic, neohygienist strategy of the beginning of the century was increasingly superseded by a more psychosocial strategy informed by the emerging science of human relationships. Increasingly, the objective of intervention was seen as the need to support and preserve the family, to get its emotional economy running along the right lines through acting on the inner feelings and interrelationships between family members (Dicks, 1970). The psychosocial family was 'naturalised'. The adjusted child was increasingly seen as the natural outcome of a 'normal' family. Hence the normal family could be specified in psychological terms and the 'normal' adapted child construed as its product. The family was to be reconstructed in terms of a set of psychological relations between mothers and fathers, parents and children, brothers and sisters. Similarly, the problems of children were to be conceived in terms spanning and linking both the dangerous and the endangered, the villains and the victims, along a single dimension of adjustment and maladjustment. The juvenile court, established after 1908, and the growing number of child guidance clinics acted as crucial nodes in a new network of powers and perceptions that was woven around the child and the family (see Rose, 1985, Chapter 7). I am not suggesting that this new approach was completely dominant in the inter-war period. However, after 1945, it was to become far more pervasive and much of the groundwork for this took place in the inter-war period.

In the post-war period, this new psychology was further revamped by a form of normalising psychoanalysis and ego-psychology. This increasingly took as its central concern not just the general state of emotional relations between family members but a specific focus on the relationship between mother and child (Holman, 1996; Rose, 1999a). The new psychology was also to act as a vehicle for the professionalisation of social work via its close association with the theory and practice of social casework (Timms, 1964; Payne, 1992). If the problems of the child lay in the wishes, feelings and actions of parents, it was the social worker who was most likely to be both in touch with these and able to do something about it. In the process, social workers could be more than collators and purveyors of information; they could take on a more therapeutic role via their relationship(s) with family members, particularly the mother. Such a way of thinking was to prove central in the development of children's departments after the Second World War. It is important to remember, however, that the responsibilities of these new local authority children's departments were originally restricted to children 'in care' – it was only children 'in care' who were to be the essential responsibility of the new children's departments and the new professionals employed to run them. It was children 'in care' who required normalising, rather than children in the general population.

The Children Act 1948 and the Post-war Settlement of 'Organised Modernity'

The Children Act 1948, which established the new children's departments, was seen as uncontroversial and received little public or political attention at the time (see Parton, 1999). However, while uncontroversial, the establishment of children's departments was significant as it provided the organisational framework for developments over the next 20 years. The new departments tried to lay to rest the Poor Law and embodied the revolutionary principle that the new agencies should seek the *best* development of children deprived of a *normal* home life. As Jean Packman (1981) has argued, children 'in care' were in future to be treated as individuals and not as an undifferentiated category of youngsters and should have access to the same range of facilities as any other children. Children not 'in care' were, by definition, normal. The new departments were to be staffed by a new kind of personnel who were professionally trained in the psychosocial sciences and had a thorough understanding of human relationships and needs. The new childcare officers were not drawn in any significant numbers either from Poor Law staff or the pre-war voluntary agencies. The establishment of children's departments was crucially informed by the experience of war itself, particularly the policy of evacuating children from the large metropolitan areas, particularly London, to the country. The policy had provided a new visibility for children separated from their parents and provided the proponents of the psychosocial approaches to mother–child relations with an opportunity to research and thereby demonstrate the importance of a *normal* family life to ensure that children developed appropriately and were well adjusted. Much of the pioneering work was undertaken by people like John Bowlby, the Winnicotts (1964) and others at the Tavistock Clinic (Dicks, 1970).[3]

Not only was the experience of war significant in influencing the nature and form of the post-war economic and social reconstruction but also the family was seen to play a central role in it. It is not surprising that the Children Act 1948, and the introduction of children's departments, was politically uncontroversial, in that it was thoroughly consistent with the central principles and approaches of that reconstruction.

Like other Western nations, Britain faced major political, social and economic challenges at the end of the war which were reinforced by popular demands that there should not be a return to the mass unemployment of the 1930s, and that 'a land fit for heroes' should be created. The issue for a capitalist society was how to combine a commitment to a free-market economy while maintaining social harmony. It was further evident that Britain's position as a world power was considerably weakened and was subordinated to the 'Western alliance' under the leadership of the USA, an alliance whose defining characteristics were increasingly determined by the opposition to the 'Eastern Communist bloc' and the growing Cold War. The creation of what came to be called 'the welfare state' was to play an important role in enhancing national prestige both at home and abroad and in compensating for the loss of world influence to the USA and imperial decline (Clarke and Langan, 1993; Hobsbawm, 1994).

The establishment of the welfare state is best understood not simply in terms of the growth of the interventionist state but as a particular form of government. The key innovations lay in the attempts to link the fiscal and economic capacities of the state to the government of social life. As a political rationality, 'welfarism' (Rose and Miller, 1992) was structured by the wish to encourage national growth and well-being through the promotion of social responsibility and the mutuality of social risk, and was premised on the notion of social solidarity (Donzelot, 1988). It rested on the twin and interrelated approaches derived from Keynes and Beveridge.

The Keynesian element stood for an increase in government in terms of attempts to manage economic demand through judicious state intervention, particularly by increased public expenditure during times of recession, with the aim of maximising production and maintaining full employment. The Depression of the inter-war years had demonstrated that, left to itself, the market economy could not function effectively. It led to a drastic fall in production, mass unemployment and fed social and political unrest. The Keynesian approach stood for state intervention from the demand side of the economy in order to ensure high levels of economic activity and full employment.

While Keynesianism provided the economic component of the welfare state approach, the ideas derived from Beveridge formed the social component and were based on the idea of social insurance, in its widest sense, against the hazards of the market economy. Unlike the Keynesian economic argument, the social arguments for welfarism were not new. Since the days of Bismarck in Germany and Lloyd George in Britain, most Western capitalist countries had developed forms of social protection underwritten and coordinated by the state. What was new in the post-war period was that the principle of state intervention was made explicit, and the institutional framework, which would make the state responsible for maintaining minimum standards, became far more of a reality.

A number of assumptions characterised the development of welfarism as it developed in the 25 years after the Second World War. The institutional framework of universal state welfare services, particularly in health, education and social security, was seen as the best way of maximising welfare and it was assumed that the state worked for the whole society and was the best way of coordinating this. State social services were instituted for benevolent purposes, meeting social needs, compensating socially caused 'diswelfares', such as unemployment, and promoting social justice. Their underlying functions were ameliorative, integrative and redistributive. Social progress would be achieved through the agency of the social (democratic) state and professional interventions. Increased public expenditure, the cumulative extension of statutory welfare provision and the proliferation of government regulations backed by expert administration represented the main guarantors of equity and efficiency. At the same time, social scientific knowledge was to play an important part in ordering the approach of the new social professions which were to make a significant contribution to developing individual and social welfare and were granted considerable authority and legitimacy as a result.[4] As Michael Sullivan (1992, p. 11) has concluded from his review of the literature and research on the post-war period:

> there is a widespread agreement amongst political analysts and commentators that there was a considerable political consensus on the principles and parameters of the mixed economy, full employment and the welfare state. Keynesian economic management and Beveridge's social philosophy had acted as midwives to a relatively durable form of welfare capitalism.

At the heart of this was a very particular elaboration of the ideal relationship between the state, the market and the family. For, apart from in health and education, it was clear that the role of the state was not to replace but to support and civilise the market and the family. It was assumed that needs would be met primarily through male waged work and the care of mothers in the family, and that sexual reproduction would take place within lifelong marriage. For example, the national insurance social security system was premised on the notion of the male breadwinner in lifelong, full-time employment, paying insurance contributions and thereby providing for his wife and children. Anyone who did not fit the model was excluded and had to call on the means-tested national assistance scheme.

Post-war welfare services were thus premised on a particular model of the patriarchal nuclear family (Pascall, 1986; Williams, 1989). The notion of 'the family wage' was central, linking the labour market to the distribution of social roles and dependency by age and gender within the family. Within the family, women were to trade housework, childbirth, child-rearing and physical and emotional caring as 'labours of love' in return for economic support (Finch and Groves, 1983). Thus, it was assumed that most child 'welfare work' was carried out within the family, either using the family wage to buy goods and services or by women caring for children. It was not simply that such a model of the family was seen as normal, but that it was based upon men and women's essential 'natures' (Clarke, 2004).

The model was key to the newly formed children's departments which were explicitly designed to provide a residual service for children deprived of a 'normal home life'. Clearly, however, they would be subject to a whole series of tensions and difficulties if any of the underlying assumptions were seriously questioned or there were to be significant changes in the key institutions which provided the context for their work, whether this be the labour market, the patriarchal nuclear family or the other more universal social services – particularly health, education and social security. Beyond this, further stresses would be created if the political consensus which underpinned the post-war welfare changes was itself put under strain. However, such severe strains did not seriously begin to show themselves until the 1970s.

Expansion, Rationalisation and the Establishment of 'the Family Service'

During the 1950s there was increasing evidence that the newly created children's departments were finding their role far too narrow and restrictive, as their statutory responsibilities were only for those who had already been received into care. While the emphasis was on the strength and formative power of the nuclear family, and the priority was with placing children with foster parents rather than in the large and often impersonal institutions as previously, this was felt to be doing too little, too late (Packman, 1981). Increasingly, there was an emphasis on trying to intervene with families before children came into care. Families were encouraged and helped to care for their own children, in their own homes, in the context of the importance of the psychosocial nature of childcare, with the relationship between the mother and her offspring seen as crucial if the possibility of the healthy development of children was to take place.

Such thinking was given a major boost in the 1950s when certain influential members of the Fabian Society, prominent academics and senior civil servants made explicit links between child neglect, deprivation and delinquency (see, for example, Donnison and Stewart, 1958), a thesis which was to receive its most explicit voice with the publication of the Ingleby Report in 1960. The central argument of the Ingleby Report was that those who were neglected in early life were the most likely to have problems later, particularly in terms of delinquency. Both the deprived child and the delinquent child were seen as arising because of maladaptive family and/or environmental circumstances. Thus intervening in family problems earlier would prevent children coming into care and forestall a range of unwanted problems in the future. In the context of the post-war welfare state, it was also assumed that growing affluence and employment and reduced poverty meant that such problems were small scale and primarily located within a small number of 'problem families' (Philp and Timms, 1962). The statutory power to intervene earlier to prevent children being received into care was provided in section 1 of the Children and Young Persons Act 1963. While the legislation was more cautious than the Ingleby Report recommended, much of the positive approach of the report was to have a profound effect upon the scale and future direction of local authority childcare services (Packman, 1993).

By the mid-1960s local authority childcare services were expanding their operations and reframing their responses. There was also an increasing conviction that better services could be provided by means of reorganisation, redrawing the boundaries between services and aiming to provide a rationalised and explicit *family* service. This ultimately led to the establishment of social services departments in 1971, following the Seebohm Report in 1968 on local authority personal social services (Hall, 1976; Clarke, 1980; Cooper, 1983) and the passage of the Children and Young Persons Act 1969, which aimed fundamentally to reorder the way delinquency was to be responded to in terms of a more explicit welfare approach, within which the role of social workers was seen as central.

Such developments took place in the context of a much more wide-ranging reappraisal of the full range of welfare services introduced in the post-war period. The introduction of social services departments in 1971 was a key element of this more overall reappraisal. However, these developments did not attempt to fundamentally change the principles and underlying assumptions of the post-war settlement. Rather, they were an attempt to update, in the context of important social changes and new challenges. There was a considerable consensus that welfare was a social good for all concerned and that social work with some families should play an increasingly central role.

The international post-war economic boom allowed a considerable expansion in the scope of welfare services throughout the West well into the 1970s. However, the welfare state in Britain increasingly came to occupy a distinctive political position because, while the British economy grew consistently at an average of 3 per cent a year, it was falling behind its major industrial competitors, whose average rates of growth were around 5 per cent a year. Between 1950 and 1975 the share of gross national product (GNP) taken by public expenditure increased steadily and it was spending on welfare services which accounted for the largest part of the growth. Spending on welfare services rose from a share of 11.3 per cent in 1939, to 16.3 per cent in 1955 and 28 per cent in 1975 (Gough, 1979; Sleeman, 1979). This expansion resulted primarily from changing patterns of need, and changing costs and patterns of welfare.[5]

The response of government to this complex and changing network of needs, costs and priorities was to try and modernise the organisational structures through which welfare was provided. Between the early 1960s and the mid-1970s, the British welfare state underwent a series of reorganisations affecting central and local government and the NHS. All were aimed at improving integration and efficiency via better coordination, management and cost-effectiveness.

The role for the new social services departments was not just to provide a range of services, including social work, but to coordinate aspects of other welfare services, thereby making services more responsive to need, including the functioning of a small number of families who were seen as causing a disproportionate number of problems. Social services departments were established as the 'fifth social service' (Townsend, 1970) with the family as its focus. They would provide the personalised, humanistic dimension to the welfare state, the primary tool being the professional worker's personality and understanding of human relationships. This perhaps marked the high point of the optimism and confidence in social work, which had been fostered by the development and approach of the children's departments and its key political and academic advocates. At the same time, the policy of preventing family breakdown meant that the institutionalised care of children was increasingly seen as a failure, thus reinforcing the ideal of the natural, biologically based, nuclear family.

Conclusion

We can also see such developments as further refining and consolidating what Wagner has called *organised modernity*, which he argues achieved something of a coherence or closure during the 1960s – in terms of the various institutions, their specific embodiments of collective agency, their interlinkages and respective reaches into society. It appeared as a 'naturally interlocking order'. Such a social configuration did not halt the dynamics of modernity, but channelled them into apparently controllable avenues, whereby the ambiguities and tensions related to liberty and discipline, while not completely expunged, seemed peripheral. More specifically for our purposes, it was as if the modern nuclear family had become almost completely functional to the requirements of the increasingly well-integrated economic, political and social order.

Jock Young (1999), following Hobsbawm (1994), has called the post-war period up until the late 1960s 'the Golden Age' where there was: full employment; steadily rising affluence; the gradual incorporation of the working class into some of the trappings of full employment; and the entry of women more fully into public life and the labour market. He argues it was an era of inclusion, affluence and conformity and was redolent of certainty and security:

> The Golden Age was one where the twin sectors of society, work and the family, fitted together like a functionalist dream: the site of production and the site of consumption, a Keynesian duality of supply and demand each necessary for the other, but underscored by an accepted division of labour between the sexes and all heavily underwritten by the ever-increasing collateral of affluence ... it was a consensual world with core values centring around work and the family. It was an inclusive world; a world at one with itself, where the accent was on assimilation whether of wider and wider swathes of society (lower working class, women or youth), or immigrants entering a monocultural society. It was a world where the modernist project was deemed within a breath of success. (Young, 1999, pp. 3–4)

An important dimension of this was the consensual politics of the period, where the nation state intervened to achieve a degree of social justice as part of a metanarrative of progress. It was assumed that the vast majority of citizens accepted the given social order, which simply required occasional fine-tuning as it was not only seen as relatively just and in the interests of all, but essentially 'natural'. The major institutions, particularly of work and the family, were accepted without much question. The family appeared stable and subject to its own well-established internal dynamics and rules and children had their clear place within it. More generally, the norms and rules were seen as essentially clear cut, taken for granted and uncontested. As a result, anyone who seemed on the edge of or outside the norms or rules did so primarily because they could not help it. Their behaviour was determined by their psychological and social circumstances. Such deviance was seen to occur because of problems located in the past rather than the present, and the conduit of causality was essentially individualised and located in the person or the psychosocial dynamics within the family. Both the cause and site of any problems were located primarily in the family, so that it was the family which should be the focus of adjustment. The role of the welfare state was to assimilate the deviant from the margins into the main body of society: 'To this end a corpus of experts builds up, skilled in the use of the therapeutic language of social work, of counselling, of clinical psychology and allied positivistic disciplines' (Young, 1999, p. 5).

However, and as I will argue, this was to change, because, as Eric Hobsbawm has suggested:

> The history of the twenty years after 1973 is that of a world which lost its bearings and slid into instability and crisis. And yet, until the 1980s it was not clear how irretrievably the foundations of the Golden Age had crumbled. (1994, p. 403)

As I discuss in the next two chapters, such an assessment applies equally to the major changes that were to take place in child welfare thinking, policy and practice from 1973 onwards. Two processes are seen by Hobsbawm as being central to these changes: the cultural revolution of individualism; and the economic crisis and restructuring of the labour markets arising from the growing globalisation of capitalist economic relations. Both have important implications for the role and functioning of the family and the way family life was experienced.

What emerged from the late 1960s onwards was what Wagner (1994) has called the second 'crisis of modernity', which has seen the move from 'organised' to 'extended liberal' modernity, but which I call 'late modernity'. Whatever we call it, the issue is that a number of the key assumptions and building blocks which underpinned the post-war state began to be severely challenged both culturally and economically. For example, by the early 1970s it was clear that the model of the family, which lay not just at the heart of the reorganised social services departments but also at the heart of the post-war welfare state, was considerably more complex than previously assumed and was changing in important ways. The changes included: a significant increase in married women's paid employment, although much of this was part time and casual in nature; a growing number of lone parents; a growing number of births outside marriage; and an increasing number of older people dependent upon public rather than familial care (Fox-Harding, 1996).

Young (1999) argues that one of the key features of the transition to late modernity is from an *inclusive* to an *exclusive* society, where the accent on assimilation and incorporation gives way to one that separates and excludes and that this poses qualitatively different problems, particularly around how to maintain social order, in its widest sense. Such a transition also provided new opportunities for those who had effectively been 'silenced' previously to have a 'voice' now, so that their views and interests could be taken into account. This has particular implications for the way we see the family and children in particular. As I will argue, the processes of increased individualisation helped to create the social conditions that made it possible for children to gain more protection, initially within the family and subsequently in other institutions. Increasingly, the processes of individualisation had the effect of not only disaggregating the family but recognising that children had a right to a life and a biography and autonomy of their own.

The inauguration of social service departments in 1971 can be seen to have come right at the end of the golden age, when the second crisis of modernity began to emerge. They were based on the assumption that social problems could be overcome via state intervention by professional experts with social scientific knowledge and skills in the use of relationships. They would provide a progressive, universal resource available to all and with wide community support. Its focus and rationale was the family. Interventions in the family were not conceived as a potential source of antagonism between social workers and individual family members whether mothers, fathers or children. Indeed, parents and children were not seen as having interests or rights distinct from the unitary family itself.[6] When a family required modification, this would be via social casework, help and advice and if a child did come into state care, this was assumed to be in their best interests. Contestation was not seen as important and when the law was drawn upon, this was seen primarily as a tool for more significant therapeutic goals. This was about to change and the year 1973, as Hobsbawm (1994) had argued, was to be significant.

2

Child Abuse and the Growing Crisis in Child Protection

The consensus which had been established, based on the family as the primary mechanism for ensuring the welfare of children, with social workers entrusted with primary responsibility for state child welfare, began to collapse during the 1970s. What became evident, from the mid-1980s onwards, was that the problems had become considerably more complex and high profile and were not amenable to easy resolution. In this chapter the key developments whereby this scenario unfolded are discussed. Initially, one issue dominated, which had been at the core of modern child welfare policy since the late nineteenth century: namely, how could a legal basis be devised for the power to intervene into the private family in order to protect children, which did not convert a sizeable proportion of families into clients of the state? Such a problem was posed by the demands, on the one hand, of ensuring that the family was experienced as a private institution and the primary sphere for rearing children, while recognising that there was a need for intervention in some families where they were seen as failing in this primary task and in a context where such laws were supposed to act as the general norms applicable to all (Parton, 1991).

Social work was seen as having a vital role to play in mediating this difficult and ambiguous relationship between the *privacy* of the family and the *public* responsibilities of the state. 'Private' here means beyond or outside the power or purview of the state in the sense of 'civil' liberties or 'civil' society. However, the relationship between the 'public' and the 'private' also has meaning in a quite different sense. In this second sense, 'public' means 'open', or what is observable, or 'made visible', what is performed in front of an audience, or is open for all or many to see or hear about. In contrast, what is 'private' refers to what is hidden from view, or what is said or done in secrecy or among a restricted and known circle of people. In this sense, the relationship between the public and the private is concerned with the relationship between what is visible and what is invisible.

A key part of my argument is that, beginning in the 1970s, state child welfare practice became increasingly subject to public scrutiny in this second sense, and that *public inquiries* and the media took on an increasingly central and pervasive role in raising the profile of issues which, for most of the twentieth century, had been hidden from view, while, in the process, having a considerable impact on how those issues were framed and responded to. The changes that led to the establishment of social services departments and the legitimation of social work in 1971 had received little public or even political attention (Hall, 1976). This was, however, to change dramatically with the public inquiry into the death of Maria Colwell in 1973/4 (Secretary of State for Social Services, 1974). As I argued over twenty years ago:

> The Public Inquiry into the death of Maria Colwell can be seen as a watershed in the contemporary history of social work, particularly in social service departments. Prior to this, social work practice was seen primarily as a private activity carried out between clients and professionals, the latter optimistically feeling that their skills and techniques could tackle, even solve, many social problems. The case of Maria Colwell and the numerous subsequent inquiries into cases of child abuse have quite changed all that. (Parton and Thomas, 1983, pp. 56–7)

This was explicitly stated by Jean Wall, an area director in the East Sussex social services department which was one of the departments placed under the microscope in the Maria Colwell inquiry, when she commented that the inquiry 'was beyond our experience, because at that time nothing had been more private than social work' (Shearer, 1979, p. 14).

What this chapter will demonstrate is that while much of the debate, criticism and reforms of policy and practice have been carried out in terms of how to respond to the (re)discovery of child abuse from the early 1970s onwards, the primary focus has been concerned with the nature, priorities and competence of a range of health, welfare and criminal justice professionals. While initially the focus was almost exclusively on social workers, increasingly a much wider range of professionals and their respective agencies have been opened up to scrutiny and modification. This process of change and sense of crisis has been almost perpetual since 1973, although, as I will argue, the focuses of concern shifted during the period. However, by the early twenty-first century, we have reached the point where the problems are seen as so fundamental and the proposals for change so significant that it is not an exaggeration to suggest that the current process of reconfiguration is explicitly transformational in intent so that few vestiges will remain of what was put in place in the early 1970s. In the process, the use of both social work and the family as the primary mechanisms for ensuring the welfare of children is changing.

As I will argue in subsequent chapters, this is primarily because the relationship between the child, the family, professionals and the state is itself being reconfigured in a way which no longer sees the need to preserve the privacy of the family in the same way as previously. New mechanisms and techniques for governing childhood are being established which, while they do not completely sideline either the family or social work, have the effect of dislodging them from their previous central positions and locates them in quite different relationships, both with each other and with the wider policy, practice and institutional arrangements that are being put in place.

Child Abuse Moves Centre Stage

It was the issue of child abuse and how to respond to it which had the effect of opening up for interrogation the modern system of child welfare policy and practice and the assumptions on which it was based. However, when the issue of child abuse exploded onto the professional, public and political agendas in the 1970s, this was initially informed by the way it had been conceptualised and identified in the 1960s. There are two important characteristics to note about the (re)discovery of child abuse. First, it was discovered in the USA in the early 1960s and then imported into England, particularly via the NSPCC and a number of other social work and health professionals (see Parton, 1985a, particularly Chapter 3). As a consequence, policy and practice in England, and most other English-speaking Western societies, were heavily influenced by developments and changes in knowledge, policy and practice in the USA.

Second, and perhaps most significantly, the initial (re)discovery took the form of the 'battered baby syndrome', following the publication of the highly influential paper by Henry Kempe and his colleagues (Kempe et al., 1962) in Denver, Colorado. Unlike developments in the nineteenth century, it was professionals, particularly medical professionals, rather than victims, survivors, community groups, or the women's movement, who not only brought it to, primarily, professional attention, but in the process also conceptualised it in certain ways. It was defined as a 'syndrome' or 'disease' and hence something which professionals, particularly doctors, were seen as the experts in.

It is clear that the term 'battered baby syndrome' was specifically chosen by Kempe and his colleagues, as opposed to 'physical abuse', in order to appeal to as wide an audience as possible, including conservative paediatricians. Kempe wanted no hint of legal, social or deviancy problems to compromise this essentially medical problem, for which various medical personnel and their medical technologies were seen as key in identifying and diagnosing.

The original article (Kempe et al., 1962) claimed that the syndrome characterised a clinical condition in young children, aged under three, who had received serious physical abuse, usually from a parent, and that it was a significant cause of childhood disability and death. It argued that the syndrome was often misdiagnosed and that it should be considered in any child showing evidence of possible trauma or neglect, or where there was a marked discrepancy between the clinical findings and the story presented by the parents. The use of X-rays to identify old or otherwise hidden injuries was stressed, and it was argued that the prime concern of the physician was to make the correct diagnosis and make certain that a similar event did not occur again. It was explicitly stated that the problem was not simply a result of poverty and that the characteristics of the parents were that 'they are immature, impulsive, self centred, hypersensitive and quick to react with poorly controlled aggression' (Kempe et al., 1962, p. 19).

Such an approach was to have a considerable influence on the NSPCC in the late 1960s and official government guidance in the early 1970s (DHSS, 1970, 1972) and, while it pointed to a new phenomenon requiring professional attention and vigilance, discursively it was thoroughly consistent with the professionalised child welfare model of the time. The approach is well illustrated in the early work of the NSPCC Battered Child Research Unit in London (Baher et al., 1976) in the treatment strategies adopted. The main objective was to form a 'consistent, professional relationship' (Okell and Butcher, 1969, p. 9). Intervention was based on a careful psychosocial diagnosis and aimed to provide a 'transfusion of mothering ... in the hope they will identify with us and eventually interject a less punitive self-image' (Court, 1969, p. 15). The main feature of such a 'nurturing model' was an emphasis on intrapsychic and social factors, particularly emotional and social deprivations, as determining family relationships. History was seen to dominate, therapy was restitutive and parental maturation, or rather maternal maturation, was the goal. It was assumed that parents were not responsible for their situation and, in effect, were powerless to do anything about it. As a result, social workers had to accept considerable responsibility on the parents' behalf for trying to bring about improvements.

While the battered baby syndrome proved to be the dominant underlying metaphor until 1987, it is also clear that the category of child abuse was quickly subject to various 'mouldings' (Hacking, 1988, 1991b, 1992) and 'diagnostic inflation' (Dingwall, 1989, p. 29) and this was reflected in various government guidance (DHSS, 1970, 1974, 1978). By the early 1980s, the phenomenon was officially called 'child abuse' and included emotional abuse, neglect, sexual abuse, as well as physical abuse, and was focused not only on young children but on everyone aged up to 18 years old. However, it was the public inquiry into the death of Maria Colwell which catapulted the issue of child abuse and the practices of health and welfare professionals, particularly social workers, into the centre of public, political and media attention.

Maria died on 7 January 1973 at the age of seven, in Hove, Brighton, in the south of England, being one of nine children born to her mother by that time. She spent over five years in local authority care being fostered by her aunt, but was returned to her mother and stepfather (William Kepple) at the age of six years and eight months, having been placed on a supervision order to the local authority from that date. The family was visited by a number of social workers from both the local authority and the NSPCC and concerns about Maria were expressed to both organisations by her schoolteacher and neighbours on numerous occasions. However, she died of 'extreme violence' at the hands of her stepfather, and was found to weigh only about three-quarters of what would be normal for a girl of her age. William Kepple was convicted of Maria's murder in April 1973, although, on appeal, the charge was reduced to manslaughter and he was sentenced to eight years' imprisonment.

The decision to establish a public inquiry was taken by Sir Keith Joseph, the secretary of state, in May 1973 and the public inquiry took place between 10 October and 7 December 1973, with the report published in September 1974 (Secretary of State, 1974). During the whole of the inquiry, and subsequent publication of the report, there was high-profile media reporting in the national press and television. Maria's death and the failure of the 'helping' agencies to prevent this made a tremendous impact (see Parton 1985a, Chapter 4), which was seen as a 'national scandal'. As Butler and Drakeford (2003) have argued, this was initially prompted by the strong feelings and demands from within the local community:

> It began in genuine popular sentiment that was firmly rooted in the particular and very local circumstances of Maria's death and where the struggle to make events public was itself a driving force. The scandal of Colwell was forced into the public imagination by a concerted effort, largely by those who might hitherto have had little claim on the attention of political, professional or wider national audiences. (p. 81)

While the report was critical of the work of individuals, particularly that of the social worker with responsibility for Maria's supervision order and the NSPCC inspector, its main conclusion was that 'the overall impression created by Maria's sad history is that while individuals made mistakes it was the "system", using the word in its widest sense, which failed her' (Secretary of State, 1974, p. 86). This was a theme reflected in the media coverage of its publication. It was recognised that there was no formalised inter-agency system for dealing with child abuse in most parts of the country and that much was left to the initiative of individual workers.

We cannot overestimate the impact the case had on both policy and professional practice nationally, as it prompted a mentality which tried to ensure that such a scenario was avoided in the future, both in terms of the consequences for the child and the vehement public opprobrium for the professionals. A new system of child abuse management was effectively inaugurated, with the issue of a DHSS circular (DHSS, 1974) in the wake of the death of Maria Colwell and refined in a series of further circulars throughout the decade (DHSS, 1976a, 1976b, 1978, 1980). The primary focus of the new system was to ensure that professionals were familiar with the signs of child abuse and that mechanisms were set up so that information was shared between professionals. Coordination between agencies was officially seen as the key to developing effective systems for dealing with the problem of child abuse, although social services departments were to be the 'lead agency'. However, there were no legal requirements imposed on professionals to either report abuse (as is the case in the USA and most states in Australia) or attend case conferences. Even so, it was assumed that child abuse, as with the battered baby syndrome, constituted a readily identifiable reality, which was often hidden from view. The task for policy and practice was to identify the signs and symptoms, share information, coordinate action and intervene to protect the child.

Following Maria Colwell, public inquiries became the primary vehicle for bringing about change in policy and practice in the UK. Between the publication of the Colwell inquiry report and 1985, there were 29 further inquiries into the deaths of children as a result of abuse (Corby et al., 1998). There was a remarkable similarity between the findings (see DHSS, 1982, for a summary). Most identified: a lack of interdisciplinary communication; a lack of properly trained and experienced frontline workers; inadequate supervision; and too little focus on the needs of the children as distinct from those of their parents and families as a whole. The overriding concern was the lack of coordination between the various agencies. However, it seems that the intense public and media interest in the area declined after it reached its peak in the mid-1970s (Hartley, 1985). The mid-1980s saw this quickly change with the inquiry into the death of Jasmine Beckford chaired by Louis Blom-Cooper QC.

Jasmine died on 5 July 1984 at the age of four and a half, at the home of Morris Beckford, her stepfather, and Beverley Lorrington, her mother, in northwest London. She died of cerebral contusions and a subdural haemorrhage, as a direct result of severe manual blows inflicted on the child's head. She and her sister Louise had been made the subject of care orders to the London borough of Brent in August 1981, after both children had been admitted to hospital with severe injuries, including a broken arm and broken femur. From September 1981 to April 1982 they had lived with foster parents but were returned 'home on trial' in April 1982, still subject to care orders. When Jasmine was discharged from hospital after being taken into care, she had weighed 18 lb 14 oz. Seven months later, when she was returned home after being fostered, she weighed 23 lb. Following Jasmine's death, Morris Beckford was convicted of manslaughter and sentenced to ten years' imprisonment, while Beverley Lorrington pleaded guilty to child neglect and was sentenced to eighteen month's imprisonment. At the trial, Judge Pigot said that the social worker, Gun Wahlstrom, had shown a 'naïveté almost beyond belief' and called the assistant director of social services to court to be examined on oath about the work of his department in relation to the case. A panel of inquiry was set up by Brent Borough Council and Brent Health Authority. The report was published on 4 December 1985.

The report (London Borough of Brent, 1985) was to prove a powerful event which made a significant impact upon thinking and responses to child abuse.

A major focus of the report was to locate social work in its statutory context (Parton, 1986). This emphasis on the law was not simply concerned with social workers' technical knowledge of the statutes but was also aimed at changing attitudes within social work and the direction of social work with children and families. In essence, social workers' approach to families was seen as being infused with a 'rule of optimism' and that this was misplaced. This meant that the most favourable interpretation was put upon the behaviour of parents and that anything that may question this was either discounted or redefined in a positive light.[1] As a consequence, social workers failed to put into practice their statutory responsibilities for the child and failed to use the authority inherent in their role which was seen as crucial in fulfilling their responsibilities. The report argued that these factors, which were identified in the Beckford case, were not uncharacteristic of social work practice generally. The other major failure highlighted was that the social workers had failed to identify a series of characteristics which marked it out as a clear child abuse case.

As Ashley Wroe (1988) has demonstrated, the Jasmine Beckford case thrust the issue of child abuse and the incompetence of social workers back into the media. Coverage of the trial, the inquiry and the publication of the report aroused a considerable amount of media disquiet, together with political discussion both within the London borough of Brent and Parliament. The inquiry conclusion that Jasmine's death was 'both a predictable and preventable homicide' (p. 28) received considerable coverage and social work and social services were presented in a negative and sometimes extremely negative light (Wroe, 1988, p. 30). Social workers came across as essentially 'naïve', 'gullible', 'incompetent (and negligent)', 'barely trained (and training misguided anyway)', as well as 'powerful, heartless bureaucrats' (Wroe, 1988, pp. 26–8).

The Beckford inquiry was quickly followed by two further public inquiries into the deaths of Tyra Henry (London Borough of Lambeth, 1987) and Kimberley Carlile (London Borough of Greenwich, 1987). While different in detail, the messages were remarkably similar to those in the Beckford inquiry.

Up until the mid-1980s, public inquiries had virtually all been concerned with the deaths of children at the hands of their parents or carers. The children had died as a result of physical abuse or neglect and had often suffered emotional neglect and failure to thrive. The childcare professionals, particularly social workers, were perceived as having failed to protect the children, with horrendous consequences. The deaths were viewed as particular instances of the current state of policy, practice, knowledge and skills and the way systems operated and interrelated (Hallett and Birchall, 1992). Crucially, professionals, particularly social workers, were seen as too naive and sentimental with parents, failing to concentrate on the interests of the children and to use the statutory authority vested in them. As a consequence, they did too little, too late. The emphasis in inquiry recommendations was to encourage social workers to use their legal mandate to intervene in families to protect children, rationalise the multidisciplinary framework to enhance coordination and improve practitioners' knowledge of the signs and symptoms of child abuse so that it could be spotted in day-to-day practice (see Parton, 1991, Chapter 3).

However, the Cleveland inquiry (Secretary of State for Social Services, 1988) produced a rather different set of concerns, and a different set of interpretations of what was wrong and how we should respond. The Cleveland 'affair' broke in early summer 1987 and was focused on the activities of two paediatricians and social workers in a hospital in Middlesbrough, a declining chemical and industrial town in the northeast of England. During a period of a few weeks, over a hundred children were removed from their families to an emergency place of safety (the hospital) on the basis of what was seen by the media (Franklin, 1989) and two local MPs (see Bell, 1988) as questionable diagnoses of child sexual abuse. As a result, a number of techniques for diagnosing and identifying sexual abuse developed by paediatricians and child psychiatrists (particularly the anal dilation test, the use of anatomically correct dolls and 'disclosure' work) were subjected to close scrutiny.

Not only was it the first scandal and public inquiry into possible overreaction by professionals, it was also the first on sexual abuse and the first where medical science, as well as social work, was put under scrutiny (see Parton, 1991, Chapter 4; Ashenden, 1996, 2004). Unlike most developments up until this point, which had carried the imprint of thinking in the USA, developments in Cleveland were a very British affair and had a history and impact, both in this country and abroad, of their own (Hacking, 1991b, 1992).

This time it seemed that professionals, including paediatricians as well as social workers, had failed to recognise the rights of parents and had intervened prematurely in families where there were concerns about sexual abuse. While the reasons for the crisis were again seen as residing primarily in inter-agency and interprofessional misunderstandings, poor coordination and communication and the legal context and content of child abuse work, the emphasis was different to that in previous inquiries. Now, not only did it appear that the law needed to be changed but there was a need to recognise that professionals should be much more careful and accountable in identifying the 'evidence', legally framed, for what constituted sexual abuse and child abuse more generally. It was not only a question of getting the right balance between family autonomy and state intervention but also between the power, discretion and responsibilities of the various judicial, social and medical experts and agencies.

There were other issues associated with Cleveland, however, which meant its impact and significance made it of a different order to the earlier public inquiries. Cleveland was about sexual abuse and touched a range of sensitivities which were rarely evident in earlier concerns about physical abuse and neglect: it reached the most intimate, hidden and private elements of family life and adult–child relations; it represented a major set of debates around patriarchy and male power and thereby opened up a range of political arguments around gender never evident in the official discourse previously; and, for the first time, the issue threatened middle-class and professional households. No longer could child abuse be seen as only associated with the marginalised and disreputable sections of society. It seemed to permeate 'normal' families.

Changing Political and Social Contexts

The issues articulated through the Beckford inquiry and the Cleveland affair resonated with a number of developments in the previous decade, and con- tributed to the increasing questioning of the welfare consensus around the family. From the 1960s onwards, with the growth of the women's movement and the increasing recognition of violence in the family, it was argued that not only might the family not be the 'haven in a heartless world' (Lasche, 1977) it was assumed to be but that women and children were suffering a range of abuses at the hands of men. While campaigning was initially directed to improv- ing the position of women, from the mid-1970s, with the growing concerns about sexual abuse, energy was also directed to the position of children (Rush, 1980; Nelson, 1987; Dominelli, 1986; Campbell, 1988; Parton, 1990) and this increasingly entered the mainstream of professional thinking (BASPCAN, 1981; Mrazek et al., 1981; Dominelli, 1989). Such critiques helped to disaggregate the interests of individual family members and supported the sometimes contradictory development during the period of the emerging children's rights movement (Freeman, 1983; Franklin, 1986, 1995).

The period also witnessed the emergence of a more obviously civil liberties critique which concentrated on the apparent growth of intervention into people's lives that was allowed, unchallenged, in the name of welfare (Morris et al., 1980; Taylor et al., 1980; Geach and Szwed, 1983). Increasingly, lawyers drew attention to the way the administration of justice was unjustly applied to various areas of child welfare and the need for a greater emphasis on individual rights. During the mid-1980s, the parents' lobby gained its most coherent voice with the establishment of Parent Against INjustice (PAIN). This small organisation was to prove influential in ensuring that the rights of parents and children to be left at home, free of state intervention and removal, were placed on political and professional agendas. It provided a vital support/advisory role for the parents in the Cleveland affair and subsequently in Orkney, and helped to frame the way the issues were articulated in the media. As a result, state intervention, via the practices of health and welfare professionals, as well as parental violence itself, were identified as being actively and potentially abusive.

Thus while quite different in their social location and their focus of concern, we can see a growing set of constituencies developing from the mid-1970s which were critical of the post-war consensus in child welfare. These were most forcefully articulated in and through the various child abuse inquiries. What emerged were arguments for an approach where there should be a greater emphasis on legalism. Within this emphasis, the rule of law, as ultimately judged by the courts, should take priority over those considerations which may be deemed, by the professional 'experts', as optimally therapeutic or 'in the best interests of the child'. By the late 1980s, therefore, we can identify a distinct shift in the discourse concerning child welfare to one which emphasised child protection and had a series of implications for the way policy and practice were to be framed and operated. Child protection was not only concerned with protecting children from danger but also protecting the privacy of the family from unwarrantable state interventions.

These developments need to be located in the context of the more wide-ranging changes that had been taking place in the political environment. During the 1970s an increasing disillusion was evident about the ability of the social democratic state to both manage the economy effectively and overcome a range of social problems through the use of wide-ranging welfare programmes. The growth of the New Right (Levitas, 1986) and the election of the Conservative government under Margaret Thatcher in 1979 proved particularly significant in shifting the nature of political discourse in the 1980s. For the New Right, the problems in the economic and social spheres were closely interrelated. They were seen to emanate from the establishment and increasing pervasiveness of the social democratic welfare state. The prime focus for change was the nature, priorities and boundaries of the state itself. The strategy consisted of a fusion of the economic and the social and was premised on the twin pillars of the 'free economy and the strong state' (Gamble, 1988). Such an approach stressed the importance of individual responsibility, choice and freedom; supported the disciplines of the market against the interference of the state urging reductions in taxation and public expenditure; and, while stressing the need for a reduced state, required a strong state to establish certain modes of family life and social discipline. It had its roots in an individualised conception of social relations, whereby the market was seen as the key institution for the economic sphere, while the family was the key institution for the social sphere. The family was seen as an essentially private domain from which the state should be excluded but which should be encouraged to take on its 'natural' caring responsibilities, particularly for children. The key role for the state should be reduced to ensuring that the family fulfilled these responsibilities, while ensuring that no one suffered at the hands of the violent and abusive.

Freedom, while central, was construed in negative terms – as freedom from interferences. Clearly, however, a fine balance had to be struck between protecting the innocent and weak, and protection from state interference. In such circumstances the law becomes crucial in defining and operationalising both 'natural' rights and 'natural' responsibilities. Not only must it provide the framework to underwrite contracts between individuals and between individuals and the state, it also needed to ensure that the rationale for intervention by state officials into the 'natural' sphere of the family was explicit and their actions accountable. In this context, the situation in 1987/8 seemed to fall down on both counts. It seemed that, while the state, in the guise of local authority social workers, was failing to protect the innocent (as in the Beckford case), it was – simultaneously – invading the privacy of the family on the basis of unclear and unaccountable criteria (as in Cleveland). The crucial balance which lay at the core of the liberal compromise in the late nineteenth century between the role of the state and the family in bringing up children seemed in disarray. There was thus a need to establish a new *balance* between the *public* authorities and the *private* family in the care and upbringing of children.

There was a need for a new set of practices, attitudes and priorities among professionals, particularly social workers, who carried the burden of responsibility in this highly sensitive and emotionally charged area. While it was unlikely to be sufficient in its own right, there was a need for a new legal framework, whereby these issues could be addressed.

The Children Act 1989: A New Statutory Framework

It is in this context that we can understand the significance of the Children Act 1989. As David Mellor, the minister of state at the Department of Health, said when introducing the Bill for its second reading into the House of Commons on 27 April 1989:

> we hope and believe that it will bring order, integration, relevance and a better balance to the law – a better balance not just between the rights and responsibilities of individuals and agencies, but most vitally, between the need to protect children and the need to enable parents to challenge intervention in the upbringing of their children. (Hansard, vol. 151, no. 94, col. 1107)

In many respects the Act was not consistent with other pieces of social legislation being introduced by the Thatcher government at the time (Packman and Jordan, 1991). Deakin characterises it as an example of 'consensus legislation' (Deakin, 1994, p. 22) which reflected that no politician or political party wanted to be seen as either anti-family or not having the interests of children at heart. The Act was informed not just by child abuse inquiries, but by research and a series of respected official reports during the 1980s which looked to update and rationalise childcare legislation, particularly the Short Report (Social Services Committee, 1984) and the *Review of Child Care Law* (DHSS, 1985). These reports received little or no media attention but were crucial in helping to frame the legislation both in terms of its key principles and its detailed clauses.

While it was child abuse inquiries which created the political momentum for the legislation, it was these childcare reports which were to prove crucial to the way the law was reformed. The legislation was also subject to careful civil service drafting, management and exhaustive consultation with a wide range of professional groups and interested parties to try and ensure that it received wide support (Parton, 1991).

Consequently, the central principles of the Act encouraged an approach to child welfare based on *negotiation* with families, and involving parents and children in agreed plans. The accompanying guidance and regulations encouraged professionals to work in *partnership* with parents and young people. Similarly the Act strongly encouraged the role of the state to *support* families with 'children in need' at an early stage, thus keeping the use of care proceedings and emergency interventions to a minimum.

Following the recommendations of the *Review of Child Care Law* (DHSS, 1985), the concept of *prevention* was elevated and broadened from simply the duty to prevent children coming into care, to include a broad power to provide services to promote the care and upbringing of children within their families. As a result, local authorities were placed under wide-ranging duties by s.17 of the Children Act 1989, as follows:

17(1)   It shall be the general duty of every local authority (in addition to the other duties on them by this Part) –

(a) to safeguard and promote the welfare of children within their area who are in need;
and
b) so far as is consistent with that duty, to promote the upbringing of such children by their families, by providing a range and level of services appropriate to those children's needs.

A child is taken to be in need if:

- the child is unlikely to achieve or maintain or to have the opportunity of achieving or maintaining a reasonable standard of health or development without the provision for him of services by a local authority
- the child's health or development is likely to be significantly impaired or further impaired without the provision for him of such services; or
- the child is disabled.

The definition of a 'child in need' was further expanded by reference to the concept of health, development and disability in s.17(11). Thus, 'development' meant physical, intellectual, emotional, social or behavioural development; 'health' meant physical or mental health; and a child was described as 'disabled' where s/he was blind, deaf or dumb or suffered from a mental disorder of any kind or was substantially and permanently handicapped by illness, injury or congenital deformity or such other disability as may be described.

In addition, new threshold criteria were introduced which had to be satisfied before state intervention into the family was warranted. The criterion was 'that the child concerned is suffering, or is likely to suffer significant harm' (s.31(92)(a)), where harm is defined by s.31(9) as meaning 'ill-treatment or the impairment of health or development'. For the first time the criterion for state intervention included a prediction of what may or 'is likely' to occur *in the future*. The harm, however, must be seen as 'significant' and, where this turned on issues of health or development, the child's health or development were to be compared with that which could be reasonably expected of a similar child (s.31(10)). Thus while it was not intended that minor shortcomings in health or development should give rise to compulsory intervention (unless they were likely to have serious and lasting effects on the child), it was clear that the responsibilities of local authorities were broadened, not only because of the much wider notion of prevention but also because they must try and anticipate what might happen in the future. The overall duty was to *safeguard and promote the welfare of children* who were 'in need'.

Section 47(1) laid a specific duty upon local authorities where they

> have reasonable cause to suspect that a child who lives, or is found, in their area is suffering, or is likely to suffer, significant harm, the authority should make, or cause to be made such enquiries as they consider necessary to enable them to decide whether they should take any action to *safeguard or promote the child's welfare*. (emphasis added)

Section 47(3) continued:

> the enquiries shall, in particular, be directed towards establishing: whether the authority should make any application to the court, or exercise any of their powers under the Act, with respect to the child.

It was section 47 that gave the responsibility to local authorities to enquire into cases of suspected child abuse in their area. The implications of this for practice were to become a major issue in the mid-1990s, which I discuss in Chapter 4.

The Children Act 1989 was welcomed on all sides as a progressive piece of legislation, although it was recognised that it was being introduced in a 'hostile climate', out of step with the philosophy and aims of most other social and economic policy at the time, and its success would be dependent on whether resources were going to be made available for the more extended family support provisions (Frost, 1992). But, while this new legal framework attempted to restore balance to policy and practice and could be seen to impose greater accountability upon professionals and local authorities to the courts, their responsibilities were broadened, not only in terms of the notion of what constitutes a 'child in need' but also in terms of having to anticipate 'likely significant harm'. In this respect the medical and human sciences were clearly embedded in the legislation, in terms of making judgements about what constituted 'the health, development and overall welfare of children' (White, 1998), particularly where these might be indicating 'significant harm'.

The Emergence of Institutional Abuse and the Paedophile

In the light of the Children Act 1989, which came into operation in October 1991, new guidance was issued as to what to do in cases of child abuse (Home Office et al., 1991). It was clear that government, in particular senior civil servants, were keen to keep the use of public inquiries into cases of child abuse to a minimum. They had proved costly in terms of both the amount of finance needed to fund such exercises and their high-profile nature, which was seen as increasingly counterproductive. It was important to try and remove child abuse away from the media spotlight. In Part 8 of the new *Working Together Under the Children Act 1989* (Home Office et al., 1991) a new system of area child protection committee (ACPC) 'case reviews' was introduced; these quickly became known as 'Part 8 reviews'.[2]

The guidance required that the Social Services Inspectorate (SSI) or the Welsh Office be notified immediately of such cases. Final reports were expected to be completed by ACPCs within two months of an incident occurring, and agencies within the area concerned were expected to implement any changes recommended by the review. There was no clear guidance as to when such review reports should be made public and decisions on this were to be left to individual ACPCs. In practice most have not been made public and where they have been, this has been because the media raised questions following or during a high-profile court case.[3]

It is clear that this new system had an important impact. Research carried out by Corby et al. (1998, 2001) indicates that prior to 1973 the only public inquiry was that into the death of Dennis O'Neill, who was killed by his foster father (Monckton, 1945), which was a key element that informed the work of the Curtis Committee (1946) and provided the basis for the 1948 Children Act.

Between 1973 and 1989 there were 45 public inquiries (an average of 2.6 per year) but between 1990 and 1999 there were 14 such inquiries (an average of 1.4 per year). This is not to say that the problems identified in the 1980s had gone away, as a reading of Part 8 reviews indicates, the same problems were evident concerning the failure to 'spot the signs' and the inadequacies of communication and coordination. It did mean, however, that the issues were much less in the public domain.

In some respects the furore over the Cleveland affair and some of the changes instituted by the Children Act 1989 indicate that there was something of a 'backlash' (Myers, 1994) against the growth of professional concern about child abuse in the family, particularly as this related to child sexual abuse (Campbell, 1988), and we can see the introduction of Part 8 reviews as a way of defusing this and managing the tensions.

However, the early 1990s saw a range of new concerns come to the fore – ritual, organised and institutional abuse. These new concerns had a different relationship to the family; they were increasingly focused on extra-familial abuse rather than intra-familial abuse and, by the middle of the decade, were focused not just on residential homes, but daycare settings, sports clubs, youth clubs and the church. Not only did it seem that the state was failing to protect children but it could be seen to be actively condoning and, in some cases, perpetrating abuse upon children for whom it was directly responsible.

Events in the Orkneys in 1991 and the subsequent public inquiry by Lord Clyde (1992), together with the high-profile media reporting of the case, provided something of a watershed in moving the focus of concerns from intra- to extra-familial abuse. While the Orkney inquiry was similar to Cleveland, in that much of the concern was about the manner in which the children had been removed by social workers from their families, much of the attention was also focused on whether there was evidence of 'ritual' or 'organised' abuse. Concerns about ritual and organised abuse were evident in the media throughout 1990 and early 1991 and the 1991 Working Together had a specific section allocated to what agencies should do in relation to 'organised abuse' (Home Office et al., 1991, sections 5–26). High-profile police and social services investigations had taken place in Canterbury, Manchester, Merseyside, Humberside and Nottingham[4] and the removal of children from their families in Rochdale had been subject to a special social services inspection (SSI, 1990). However, it was events in Orkney which brought these issues to a head.

Events in Orkney began on 27 February 1991, when nine children from four families were taken into care following allegations of organised sexual abuse. The children were taken into care under place of safety orders during 'early morning raids' to houses conducted jointly by police and social workers. The children were removed to be medically examined and interviewed, while the local Church of Scotland minister and the children's parents were questioned by the police. The allegations were that 'lewd and libidinous practices' (Clyde, 1992, para. 6.57, p. 101) had taken place between adults and children, the children having been sexually abused in organised acts carried out in a quarry in South Ronaldsay. The children were returned home on 4 April 1991, following a court hearing which judged the proceedings incompetent and dismissed the cases without hearing all the evidence. In May the case for the prosecution of the parents was dropped, and in July the children's names were removed from the child protection register. Throughout the five weeks of the children being in care, and after returning the children home, the Director of Social Services Paul Lee maintained that the children had been abused and continued to need protection. In opposition to this claim, the parents and their supporters had formed the South Ronaldsay Action Group, assisted by PAIN, to campaign for the return of the children and aiming to discredit the claims of the social workers. As Samantha Ashenden (2004) has argued, the press provided ample images of natural families and a God-fearing community, rallying together in support of the rights of parents. In contrast, the actions of social workers were depicted as being 'interfering, out of touch, crusading and illegitimate' (p. 172) and as being implicated in a 'witch-hunt and conspiracy' (p. 172). Even though the removal of the children from their families was a joint action between the police and social workers, the media were virtually silent about the role of the police and directed their criticisms almost exclusively at the social workers.

As in Cleveland, the question of what actually happened in Orkney and whether the children were abused was never addressed by the inquiry and remains unresolved. The focus of attention was on the way the allegations were handled and the actions of the professionals, in particular the extensive interviewing of children. The following year the Home Office and the Department of Health published a *Memorandum of Good Practice on Video Recorded Interviews with Child Witnesses for Criminal Proceedings* (1992) to establish procedures for joint police/social work investigations of allegations of child abuse where the case might go for criminal trial.[5] While concerns about satanic ritual abuse subsided (La Fontaine, 1998), this was not the case in relation to organised abuse or, more specifically, abuse in a variety of institutional settings, which became a dominant preoccupation in the 1990s.

The shift in official and public concern from intra- to extra-familial abuse is clearly illustrated in the research carried out by Corby et al. (1998, p. 383):

> Of the thirty-one inquiries held between 1973 and 1982, all but two were concerned with cases of individual physical abuse or neglect, nearly all resulting in child deaths. There were twenty-eight inquiries between 1983 and 1992. Nineteen of these dealt with individual cases of physical abuse and neglect, seven were investigations into abuse in residential care and two were concerned with allegations of sexual abuse of children in their own homes. The research project found a further nine inquiries since 1993, five of which were focused on abuse in residential care and nursery schools.

Their subsequent research (Corby et al., 2001) identified 18 public inquiry reports into abuse of children in residential care between 1967 and 2000. The first of these was in 1967 and was concerned with the excessive use of physical punishment by staff at Court Lees Approved School in Surrey (Home Office, 1967) and was followed some eighteen years later by two inquiries into allegations of sexual abuse of residents by staff at the Leeways Children's Home (London Borough of Lewisham, 1985) and Kincora Working Boys' Hostel

(Department of Health and Social Security (Northern Ireland), 1985). The late 1980s and early 1990s, however, saw a plethora of concerns being raised about the physical treatment of children in care (SSI, 1988, 1991a, 1991b; Gwent County Council, 1992; Lancashire County Council, 1992).

The most infamous was the inquiry into the 'pindown' regime, which was being practised in a number of children's homes in Staffordshire (Staffordshire County Council, 1991). Following a complaint by a 15-year-old girl to a solicitor representing her in care proceedings, Staffordshire County Council set up an inquiry into a practice, 'pindown', which had been established in a number of its children's homes. While established by one of the area residential managers, the practice had the support of senior management. 'Pindown' was based on a crude behaviourist regime which aimed at dealing with problematic and challenging behaviour from children and young people in residential care, in a context of resource constraint. It consisted of taking children who were not going to school to a poorly furnished room and confining them there, depriving them of daytime clothing and any amusements such as television, not speaking to them and requiring them to do basic copying tasks as homework. The regime operated from 1983 to 1989, during which 132 children, including some as young as nine years old, experienced pindown, some for a number of weeks. The media, particularly a Granada Television *World in Action* shown in June 1990, and the efforts of the two local MPs, were to prove significant in ensuring the latter 'scandal' took on a national profile (Butler and Drakeford, 2003, Chapter 9).

The government responded by commissioning a 'special review of residential care in England ... to concentrate particularly on arrangements for the monitoring and control of residential care', to be undertaken by Sir William Utting (1991). The pindown scandal had the effect of recognising that children in care had rights but they were often forgotten and neglected. The subsequent Utting report recommended that the profile of residential childcare work should be raised and there should be a much greater degree of participation by children and young people in decisions that affected their lives. Perhaps most significantly, it argued that there should be an improvement in the management of residential care through improved planning, better inspection and monitoring, and much stronger guidance from central government. Increased participation for children and young people, together with closer managerial oversight, were two key themes which were to grow in significance over the coming years. Between 1991 and 1994 there was a range of new initiatives to address problems in relation to residential childcare (Berridge and Brodie, 1996).

However, the focus of concern was to shift quickly from the physical treatment and abuse of children in care to sexual abuse. A series of scandals and revelations of sexual abuse going back to the 1970s and 80s were to shatter any remaining complacency there may have been that 'child welfare' services were (or ever had been) necessarily serving children and young people well. A catalogue of allegations from various parts of the country emerged about the sexual abuse of children in care and these were subject to police and social work investigations. There were inquiries in Shropshire (Brannan et al., 1993), Leicestershire (Kirkwood, 1993), Islington (White and Hart, 1995) and Northumberland (Kilgallon, 1995), all published by the middle of the decade, together with many other police/social work investigations and inquiries going on in other parts of the country.

However, it was the growing and widening of concerns in North Wales and Merseyside which were providing an ongoing and increasingly complex backcloth to developments. The first allegations were made in Gwynedd in 1986 and spread to include Clwyd in the early 1990s. Two inquiries were completed in September 1992 and March 1996 but the reports were never made public because of legal and insurance loopholes. Many, including those in the media, felt the latter report in particular was suppressed to protect officials and highprofile members of the community. On 13 June 1996, under increasing political and media pressure, particularly from the *Independent* newspaper, the Prime Minister John Major announced that the Cabinet had decided to set up two inquiries: the first, a tribunal of inquiry in relation to the abuse in children's homes in North Wales; and the second, a national review.[6]

The tribunal was a major operation costing £12.8 million, involving 575 witnesses, of whom 264 attended to give oral testimony. It sat for 201 days and delivered its 937-page report to the secretary of state for Wales in September 1999, although it was not published until 15 February 2000, when most of the cases in the criminal court were completed (Waterhouse, 2000; see Corby et al., 2001 for a detailed analysis of the tribunal).

However, many of the key issues had been clearly set out in the review, which was again chaired by Sir William Utting (1997). It quickly became known as the 'Safeguards Review'. This was to prove a crucial document in helping to frame future policy and practice. While it was concerned with making recommendations for change in relation to children living away from home, the concept of 'safeguarding' was, in the future, to have a much wider relevance:

> 'Safeguard' and 'promote' are equal partners in an overall concept of welfare. Safeguards are an indispensable component to the child's security, and should be the first consideration for any body providing or arranging accommodation for children. Safeguards form the basis for ensuring physical and emotional health, good education and sound social development. (Utting, 1997, p. 15)

The other key aspect of the report was that it not only drew attention to failures in providing and managing residential care, which had been at the centre of the earlier Utting report (1991), but also pointed to the fact that institutional care seemed to be a major site for the predatory practices of 'career paedophiles' (Stanley, 1999). As Butler and Drakeford (2003) suggest, a rather different policy agenda had begun to form and this was well represented by the comments within the Safeguards Review, which made it clear that the need for change was precipitated by the past activities of sexually and physically *abusive terrorists* in children's homes. Such persistent abusers may be a small proportion of all those who harm children, but they create havoc with their lives. A single perpetrator is likely in a lifetime's career to abuse hundreds of children, who suffer pain, humiliation and torment, and incur permanent emotional damage. (Utting, 1997, p. 5, emphasis added)

They are seen as 'very dangerous people', and 'even the best organisations are not immune to infiltration by determined abusers'. The review also argued that below this extreme level 'are large numbers of adults who fall into abusive behaviour in circumstances ranging from personal weakness to the influence of a malignant institutional culture' (p. 5). The spectre of the 'persistent paedophile' (p. 18) or 'abusive terrorist' had clearly arrived, a development which I analyse in more detail in Chapter 7.

Conclusion

In this chapter I have argued that the political and professional consensus around child welfare which seemed so well established by the late 1960s began to collapse from 1973 onwards. While there were various factors which fed into this, it was child abuse public inquiries which provided the catalyst. While initially it was concerns about professionals failing to protect children in the private family, where there was evidence of physical abuse and neglect, which were the focus, by 1987, via the Cleveland 'affair', there were also concerns about overintervention, primarily into suspicions about sexual abuse. A major rationale of the Children Act 1989 was to try to re-establish an appropriate balance in professional practice via a new legislative framework.

Subsequently, during the 1990s, the focus of concern shifted from intra- to extra-familial abuse, particularly in a variety of institutional settings. While initially this was concerned with inappropriate and abusive overchastisement, by 1996 it was almost exclusively about sexual abuse and the activities of a number of 'abusive terrorists' working in children's homes. By the late 1990s concerns about child abuse had not only broadened but they had been relocated outside the family, certainly as far as the media were concerned. No longer was the family seen as the exclusive site for both explaining and intervening in problems. Concerns seemed to have changed significantly from those brought to public and political attention through the public inquiry into the death of Maria Colwell in 1973/4.

However, this was to change when, on 12 January 2001, an Old Bailey jury convicted Marie Therese Kouao and Carl Manning of cruelty and the murder of 8-year-old (Victoria) Anna Climbié. Sentencing them to life imprisonment, Judge Richard Hawkins told the pair that Anna had 'died at both your hands a lonely drawn-out death', and added 'lessons must be learned about the failures of social services and police'.

Alan Milburn, the health secretary, led a wave of anguished reaction and said 'she was undoubtedly failed repeatedly by the child protection system'. The government immediately ordered an urgent statutory public inquiry.[7] The similarities and parallels with the death of Maria Colwell, and the deaths of numerous other children in the intervening years, seemed stark to all concerned. However, there were numerous important differences between the two cases. As I argue in the next chapter, the differences arise from and are indicative of the considerable social changes that had taken place in the intervening 30 years – the emergence of late modern society. It is the key characteristics of late modern society and their implications for children and childhood which are the central focus of the next chapter.

3

From Maria Colwell to Victoria Climbié: The Emergence of Late Modernity

Victoria Adjo Climbié was born near Abidjan in Ivory Coast on 2 November 1991 and was the fifth child of seven children. In November 1998 she travelled with her aunt Marie Therese Kouao to Paris where they stayed for approximately five months, arriving in London on 24 April 1999. On 26 April they visited Ealing's Homeless Persons' Unit as they needed somewhere to live. In the following eleven months, known as Anna, she was known to four social services departments, three housing authorities, two police child protection teams, two hospitals and an NSPCC family centre. Yet, when she died, aged eight years and three months, on 25 February 2000, the Home Office pathologist found the cause of death to be hypothermia, which had arisen in the context of mal-nourishment, a damp environment and restricted movement. He also found 128 separate injuries on her body as a result of being beaten by a range of sharp and blunt instruments. No part of her body had been spared. Marks on her wrists and ankles indicated that her arms and legs had been tied together. It was the worst case of deliberate harm to a child he said he had ever seen. Marie Therese Kouao and her boyfriend Carl Manning were charged with her murder and convicted on 12 January 2001. It was only after the conviction that it became known that Anna's real name was Victoria.

In his statement to the House of Commons when presenting Lord Laming's inquiry report into the death of Victoria Climbié, on 28 January 2003, the Secretary of State for Health Alan Milburn said:

> It is an all too familiar cry. In the past few decades there have been dozens of inquiries into awful cases of child abuse and neglect. Each has called on us to learn the lesson of what went wrong. *Indeed, there is a remarkable consistency in both what went wrong and what is advocated to put it right.* (Hansard, 28 January, col. 739, emphasis added)

This theme, of the failure to learn the lessons of the many public inquiries of the previous 30 years, and the need for fundamental change, was a central one which was picked up in the ensuing political debate and the media coverage of the Laming Report. The comment in the *Daily Mail* leader on 29 January 2003 was typical:

> Thirty years ago Britain was shocked when seven-year-old Maria Colwell was beaten to death by the stepfather. Then too, there was utter determination that such tragedies would never happen again. Yet despite other victims and countless inquiries since, have the fundamentals really been learned? Hardly.

There were many similarities between the two cases, not least of which were the terrible circumstances in which both children died and the horrendous injuries inflicted upon them, together with the neglect which they both experienced. They were of a similar age and, while both had been in contact with a range of health, welfare and criminal justice agencies, no one professional was able to intervene to save their lives. However, both reports argued that these failures resulted not only because of individual incompetence but also because of major inadequacies in the responses of the 'systems' in place at their respective times.

A number of common themes were evident in both inquiry reports. There was:

- considerable confusion and a failure to communicate key information, so that both children fell through the elaborate welfare nets

- poor and often confusing recording of basic information relating to visits, phone calls, conversations and messages passed between different professionals

- a general failure to use the case file in a productive and professional way

- a failure to engage and communicate directly with the children themselves about their feelings, experiences and circumstances

- considerable deceit on behalf of the primary carers and insufficient critical analysis and scepticism on behalf of the professionals as to what was being told and presented to them

- a severe lack of consistent and rigorous supervision.

It was this message of the similarities in the findings of child abuse inquiries and the failure to learn the lessons over the previous 30 years which, politically, was to provide the momentum for major organisational and policy change at the beginning of the twenty-first century and which I will analyse in detail in Chapter 8.

However, as I have argued elsewhere (Parton, 2004), an analysis of the Maria Colwell and Victoria Climbié reports that focuses on their differences rather than their similarities demonstrates, profoundly, the wide-ranging and dramatic social changes which had taken place during the intervening period. If the case of Maria Colwell marked the beginning of the crisis in modern child welfare, and the more wide-ranging crisis of organised modernity, the case of Victoria Climbié demonstrated not simply the depth of the crisis but many of the characteristics associated with a late modern society.

While both cases were subject to considerable media attention and demon-strated the importance of the media in both framing issues and influencing the political and policy agenda, the Victoria Climbié inquiry, in particular, took on the guise of a major media event which drew upon the most up-to-date and sophisticated technology. The inquiry was a *production*, with a plot and personalities, and took on the guise of a full drama which was made available to whoever wanted access to it. The evidence to the inquiry was made available in full on a website (www.victoria-climbie-inquiry.org.uk) within hours of it being presented. The site received around three million hits between 30 September 2001 and 30 September 2002 (Laming Report, 2003, para. 1.48). There was also a more personalised and emotive dimension to the report which was dedicated to the memory of Victoria. As Lord Laming stated:

> It has felt as if Victoria has attended every step of this inquiry, and it has been my good fortune to have had the assistance of colleagues whose abilities have been matched by their commitment to the task of doing justice to Victoria's memory and her enduring spirit, and to creating something positive from her suffering and ultimate death. (para. 1.66)

And earlier:

> The most lasting tribute to the memory of Victoria would be if her suffering and death resulted in an improvement of the quality of the management and leadership of these services. (para. 1.28)

However, the most significant differences between the two cases are in relation to issues of identity and global mobility. There was never any doubt in rela-tion to Maria Colwell that everybody, including the inquiry team and the professionals involved, knew who Maria was. While complicated and often highly charged, there was never any doubt that her mother was her mother, her stepfather was her stepfather, that she had both brothers and sisters and half-brothers and half-sisters and a wide extended family. They were well known on the estate where they lived, often for quite infamous reasons, and the neighbours were heavily involved in reporting concerns to the local social services department and the NSPCC. The community seemed to have a practical and moral existence but the agencies failed to respond to its concerns. Not only was Maria white and English speaking, this was also the case with everyone, including the workers, involved with her. The estate on which she lived was almost exclusively white and working class and this was one of the issues which exercised the inquiry. In many respects, the Colwell/Kepple household had all the characteristics associated with a 'problem family' which marked it out as troublesome in an essentially solid and respectable working-class community. What is clear is that Maria had a name, a known mother, an address, a school and a clear identity and location.

None of these characteristics was evident in relation to Victoria Climbié. It was only after her death that it became known that her name was Victoria, that Marie Therese Kouao was not her real mother but a 'great aunt' and that her parents lived in Ivory Coast. There were major issues about her national identity, the nature of her entry into the UK, whether she ever had a permanent address, the fact that she did not have a school or a GP, and the fact that on numerous occasions the various health and social services departments did not realise they were actually dealing with the same child. Who had 'parental responsibility' was particularly confusing and was never clearly addressed or resolved in the inquiry report.

In contrast to the Maria Colwell case, many of the workers in the Victoria Climbié case had recently moved to Britain from other countries. For example, all the social workers in the intake team when Victoria's case was being handled in Brent had received their training abroad and were on temporary contracts. What comes across in the report in relation to all the London boroughs involved were the high levels of poverty and deprivation, together with a widely diverse ethnic, linguistic and cultural makeup of the populations and the workers themselves. The growth in global mobility and the rapid increase in the numbers of asylum-seeking families had a particular impact on the nature of the demands made upon the social services departments and the cohesion and stability of local communities. It is notable that, compared to the Maria Colwell case, where there were over 60 referrals, no referrals were forthcoming from neighbours or the community, apart from the 'childminder' Mrs Cameron and Mrs Ackah, a distant relative of her 'aunt', Marie Therese Kouao.

The two processes which Hobsbawm (1994) saw as key to understanding and characterising the major social changes which became evident from 1973 and which gathered pace in the 1980s – globalisation and individualisation – were key elements in the Climbié report in ways which were not evident in relation to Maria Colwell. Comparing these two reports demonstrates that there had been major changes over the intervening 30-year period which had a considerable impact on the nature of the problems and how these were addressed. It is to an analysis of these social changes that I now turn. The transformations have been economic, social, cultural and political and are very interrelated.

The Globalisation of Production, Markets and Exchange

The economic conditions of social life began to change significantly during the 1970s. While not the cause, the oil crisis that began in 1973 ushered in a period of economic recession throughout the Western industrialised world. The growth of inflation and unemployment, an increase in industrial disputes and a decline in production and growth all pointed to the apparent failure of Keynesian demand management. The restructuring of the labour market saw the collapse of the British manufacturing industry and the rapid decline of full-time, unskilled male jobs. As international markets grew, capital became more mobile and less closely tied to nations and regions so that capital could move production to much cheaper parts of the globe. New jobs in Britain required either higher levels of skill and training or were lower paid, part time and in the service industries and usually for female workers. As a result, from the mid-1970s onwards, the labour market became increasingly stratified, with growing inequalities in income and wealth together with greater contrasts in working conditions and lifestyle.[1]

Globalisation entails a transformation of social institutions, with a growing importance and strength of economic organisations, such as banks, corporations and the broad financial sectors, which are international in their reach, and a corresponding decline in the power of nation states. Through international agencies, such as the International Monetary Fund, the World Bank and the World Trade Organisation, the programme for the new world order promotes forms of collective life based on competition in global markets, at the expense of forms based on political authority, informal organisation or communal sharing. This changes the ways individuals live, their identities, their affiliations and their strategies for improving their situations (Bauman, 1998). It is not simply that capital has become more mobile but that there is increased mobility between communities and countries, often in the search for jobs (Jordan and Düvell, 2003).

Mobility has also increased within cities and regions, as households group together in homogeneous districts, with populations of similar incomes and tastes, leaving the poorest and most marginalised in deprived concentrations, often with many social problems and including the most transient and recent arrivals from other countries (Jordan, 1996). One result of globalisation is that there is greater complexity in the ethnic backgrounds and racial identities of children, and 'societies' previously thought of as national have adopted increasingly high-profile attempts to control the flow of people across their borders. These issues have become particularly sharply focused in relation to 'asylum seekers' and 'immigrants'. Such children are usually from poorer families, and use both kin and non-kin links to move between countries as a route to social mobility. These changes, together with the growth in the use of the private car and mass transport, have seen a relaxation of the close proximity between home and work and reinforced the decline in the importance of locality and the number of settings where face-to-face interaction takes place.

Manuel Castells (1996, 2000) has called the emergent capitalist formation a *new economy*, which, he argues, has three fundamental features:

- it is *global*, in the sense that its core strategic activities have the capacity to work as a unit on a planetary scale in real or chosen time, particularly in relation to financial markets, communication media, skilled labour, many production firms and increasingly goods and services

- it is *informational*, in that the capacity to generate knowledge and process/ manage information determines the productivity, competitiveness and efficiency of all kinds of economic units, regions and countries

- it is *networked*, for at the heart of the connectivity of the global economy and the flexibility of informational production, there is a new form of organisa- tion, the *network enterprise*, made up of a variety of alliances for the purpose of particular projects.

In the process the nation state has undergone a dramatic transformation. On the one hand, it builds partnerships between nation states and shares sovereignty to retain influence, and on the other, it decentralises responsibilities and resources to regions and localities, while taking on a more enabling or 'steering' role where the 'centre' attempts to set the direction and hold everything together. It is less a nation state and more a *network state*, where the gathering and management of information takes on a central role.

The Rise of Electronic Mass Media

A second, and related, area of major change has been the growing significance of electronic mass media, which has had such a key role in both publicising and framing child abuse since the early 1970s. Mass circulation newspapers had been established as early as the nineteenth century, but it was not until the development of broadcast radio in the 1920s and 30s, and the spread of television in the post-war period, that the 'mass media' established itself as a central institution of modern life. In the UK the television viewing audience grew from nothing to virtually universal coverage in less than a generation (Thompson, 1990, 1996) and as television's viewing figures increased, its share of advertising revenue and its growing impact upon popular tastes forced newspapers to compete more and more on television's terms. The consequence was a greater concentration in newspaper ownership,[2] the advent of the tabloid newspaper and a growing tendency towards a general 'dumbing down' in quality, together with an imperceptible merging of news and entertainment (Franklin, 1997).

Consumption patterns and lifestyles that were once confined to the rich and famous now became open to everyone, while issues and problems which were previously localised were thrust into the living rooms of the whole population, as with child abuse from 1973 onwards. The visibility of events and individuals ceased to depend on a shared locale and direct experience, and came instead to depend on the media. Television news conveyed a sense of immediacy and intimacy and increasingly emphasised the personalities involved and the emotive and intimate aspects of events (Thompson, 1990, p. 228).

These developments have had a particular impact on politics where the media have become the primary space of politics. To an overwhelming extent, people receive their information, on the basis of which they form their political opinions and structure their behaviour, through the media and particularly television and radio. As a consequence the presentation of policy has become at least as significant as the substantive policy content, so that the facility with which policy options lend themselves to media presentation is now a crucial ingredient in policy making (Franklin, 1994). Representations of politics and policy in the media need to convey simple messages, where the simplest message is an image and the most individualised image is a person. Stories of sex, crime and scandal take centre stage as mechanisms for both grabbing the attention of the reader/viewer and communicating the key boundaries of what constitutes good and bad behaviour. Thus, while these changes have helped to create a greater level of transparency and accountability, they have also had a direct impact on the way we understand the boundaries between the public and the private. In effect, things which might be assumed at the time to be private matters can be transformed into public events at a future date by the media.

The media thus play a particularly important role in the construction of contemporary public scandals. The style of popular news, in particular, which is irreverent and sensationalist, tends to provoke and disrupt, can cultivate scepticism and reduces the complex to the simplistic. Scandals do not necessarily destroy reputation and trust, but they always have the potential to do so, and for this reason are of considerable significance in the political field, for individuals and institutions (Thompson, 2000). The media have the power to transform the private into the public as well as the power to undermine trust and reputation in the process.

The Individualisation of Social and Cultural Life

In some respects, changes in culture appeared about ten years before changes in the world economic situation and initially became explicit via various civil rights and emancipatory campaigns of the 1960s, in relation to black people, gay people, prisoners, mental health patients and, perhaps most profoundly, women. These changes had their roots in the struggles of various campaigners and groups, the changing economic conditions of late modern society and a growing cultural expectation that individuals should be freed from their 'traditional' ties and able to challenge authority, particularly if this authority was seen as arbitrary and unjust. This led to what Ralph Miliband (1978) called a growing 'desubordination', where there was a decline in the levels of respect for authority and tradition.

Perhaps the most profound consequence of these social and cultural changes has been the emergence of a more pronounced individualism, where individuals are less constrained by the influence of traditional social demands and absolutist moral codes. The grip of tradition, community, church and family on the individual has been reduced, in a culture that stresses individual rights and freedoms and which has increasingly dismantled the legal, economic and moral barriers that had previously kept men, women, children and young people 'in their place'. During the 1970s and 80s, the growing individualism was inter-related with the emphasis on consumerism, whereby the individual constructs an identity through active choices in the market, and success and fulfilment are associated with consumption and the display of a variety of material signs and artefacts.[3]

Pluralism of lifestyle and relativism of values, where scepticism and critique ferment, became increasingly prevalent in late modernity. Hobsbawm has argued that 'the institutions most severely undermined by the new moral individualism were the traditional family and traditional organized churches in the West, which collapsed dramatically in the last third of the century' (1994, p. 337).

Changes to the Structure of Family and Household

While it is arguable whether the traditional family 'collapsed', the fact that it changed is not. One of the major economic changes of the period was the (re)entry of women into the labour market, particularly married women.[4] Similarly the 'facts' of family change are very real. In one generation, the numbers of first marriages more than halved from 390,000 in 1975 to 175,000 in 1997, while remarriages made up two-thirds of the total. The number of divorces more than doubled between 1961 and 1997 when the total was 175,000, only slightly less than the number of first marriages (ONS, 1998). The proportion of children born outside marriage quadrupled and by the end of the 1980s fewer than 50 per cent of 18–24-year-olds thought it necessary to marry before having children (Kiernan and Estaugh, 1993). Two-thirds of first partnerships in the early 1990s were cohabitations, compared to one-third 20 years earlier, and 22 per cent of children were born into cohabiting unions, compared to 2 per cent 20 years earlier (Ermisch and Francesconi, 1998).

The rate of cohabitation among couples with children reached 13 per cent in 1998 and, among those in the lowest third of the income distribution scale, the rate was almost as high again. Among couples with children drawing benefits, it was more than two and a half times as high (Marsh et al., 2001). Lone parent households with dependent children increased from 2 per cent of the total of all households in 1961 to 7 per cent by 1998/9.

Another transition occurred over the same period and concerned the changing characteristics of households, with a steady decline in average household size and more and more people living alone or in small 'family' units. In 1961 just 11 per cent of households were people living alone but by 1998/9 this had reached 29 per cent. Similarly, average household size decreased from 3.4 persons to 2.5 persons over the same period. Such changes reflected the fact that people were living longer, had more income and were going into higher education away from home. There were also important changes brought about by the increased cultural differences and living patterns arising from immigration, particularly from the Indian subcontinent and the Caribbean, from the mid-1950s onwards.

What becomes apparent is that the major changes in the labour market were paralleled by those in domestic life; relationships, like work, became increasingly fragile and impermanent. The notion of lifelong marriage as the only sanctioned framework for sexual partnerships and parenthood had come to seem increasingly outmoded in the final quarter of the twentieth century. Drawing on simultaneous follow-up surveys tracking the lives of three large, representative cohort studies born in 1946, 1958 and 1970, Bynner et al. (2003) provide a picture which strikingly demonstrates the increasing diversity and impermanence of family structure and family life in Britain. Partnership breakdown was a more frequent experience of successive cohorts, as was lone parenthood – predominantly involving mothers raising children on their own. However, the failure of one relationship appeared not to be a deterrent to repartnering, and another increasingly common feature of family life in the younger cohorts was 'social parenting', in which children were being raised in homes in which one adult, usually the father figure, was not their biological parent. Ferri et al. (2003) argue that what underlies many of these trends in family life and personal relationships 'is the extent to which they are rooted in the changing position of women' (p. 302).

Manuel Castells (1997) refers to such changes as 'the end of patriarchalism'.[5] The emergence of contemporary feminism has been an important factor in opening up possibilities for rethinking what family means and doing family differently, and has contributed to and benefited from wider economic, technological and cultural changes (Featherstone, 2004). For example, women's increased participation in paid work has provided opportunities for avoiding or leaving relationships with men or doing relationships differently. In the process, expectations of intimate relationships have both altered the meanings attached to marriage and made possible the doing of intimate relationships differently (Jamieson, 1998). There have been important changes in the relationship between men and women, particularly in relation to marriage and child-bearing. These have been aided by the development of more sophisticated and effective contraception and new forms of genetic manipulation which have given women greater control over the timing and frequency of child-bearing.

A number of commentators (Giddens, 1991, 1992; Beck and Beck-Gernsheim, 1995; Smart and Neale, 1999) have argued that these changes have shifted the basis of interpersonal relationships from nuclei to networks, so that what is increasingly left of families are 'partnerships' which are seen as modes of partnering. In the process sexuality has been decoupled from marriage and increasingly becomes something to be discovered, moulded and altered. No longer are marriage and parenthood seen as being tied together, for having a child is increasingly a separate 'decision' to decisions about marriage for an increasing number of women. For the first time fertility rates are below the threshold for generational replacement and the number of children in the population has been reducing in both absolute and relative terms as people live longer. As a consequence, the value of each child, both emotionally and economically, is much greater than previously.

As a result of these various developments, the model of the 'normal' nuclear family, based on the institution of marriage and premised on the male bread-winner model, seems increasingly outmoded. Whilst questions about the effects of these changes are difficult to answer, there is little doubt that such issues have proved some of the most contentious during the past 30 years and have formed a central theme in political and cultural debate. Taken together, the changes can be seen to contribute to and reflect the much greater diversification, a characteristic of late modernity.

Pluralism, Ontological Insecurity and Social Anxiety

These various overlapping and interrelated changes arising from globalisation and individualisation can be seen to have had an enormous impact on the nature of social relationships and individuals' experience of the world. Whereas previously tradition (past-oriented belief and practice) acted as a means of connecting the present to our expectations of the future, and the community existed as a spatially and socially bounded place which provided a familiar milieu for its members, this no longer seems to be the case.

Anthony Giddens (1990, 1991) contends that we now inhabit a world where personal relationships of friendship or sexual intimacy act as the key means of stabilising social ties, instead of kinship; while abstract expert systems act as the means of stabilising relations across indefinite spans of time and space. He delineates late modern society as being characterised by:

● heightened choice (stemming both from the opportunities of consumption and flexible demands of work)

● a constant questioning of established beliefs and certainties

● an increased sense of reflexivity

● a lack of embedded biography and life trajectory

● an increased confrontation with the plurality of social worlds and beliefs.

While there are important differences in how far these are experienced and can be enacted according to social class, ethnicity and religion (Smart and Neale, 1999), and while the changes may not be as dramatic or recent as Giddens claims, it is certainly the case that the traditional roles and relationships evident in the 1950s and early 1960s can no longer be taken for granted.

Such developments also breed *ontological insecurity* and a growing sense of *social anxiety*, for no longer is self-identity straightforwardly embedded in our sense of biographical continuity and the protective cocoon, which filter out challenges and risks. Our sense of certainty becomes weakened and an absolute sense of one's normality becomes disorientated by the growing relativism of values. Individualisation, with its emphasis on existential choice and self-creation, can contribute considerably to a sense of insecurity. Giddens describes living in late modernity as being akin to 'riding a juggernaut' (1990, p. 151) – a runaway engine of enormous power which is always threatening to run out of control. In this sense, living in late modernity can be likened to living in a 'risk society', whereby we are continually confronted by both the positive and negative possibilities of action. As a consequence, the concerns of risk consciousness lie not in the present but in the future. Increasingly, we act today in order to take precautions against the problems of tomorrow; we try and bring the future into the present in order to control its consequences.

In the move from modern to late modern society, the quality and nature of communal concerns and values shift. According to Ulrich Beck (1992a, 1992b), in the former the focal concerns were with the substantive and positive goals of bringing about social change, attaining something good and trying to ensure that everyone had a stake and a fair share. Increasingly, he argues, the normative basis is safety and the utopia is negative and defensive – preventing the worst and protecting from harm.

Pervasive ontological insecurity brings about increased attempts to create a sense of certainty and existential security and, in the process, there is a greater possibility of both the displacement and projection of anxiety (Hollway and Jefferson, 1997). In this context, Jock Young (1999) suggests that there are increasing tendencies to essentialism, which can provide a basis for ontological security and the clarification of rules for day-to-day life in much more absolutist terms. Not only does essentialism assert the superiority of certain views and provide the basis for the absolution of responsibility, it provides a basis for blaming 'the other' and projecting onto the other a variety of uncomfortable and insecure parts of the self. Essentialism can take the form of asserting that there is either (or both) a biological or cultural set of factors which explain the differences. Essentialism is

> the necessary *prerequisite* for the demonization of parts of society. Demonization is important in that it allows the problems of society to be blamed upon 'others' usually perceived as being on the 'edge' of society. (Young, 1999, p. 110)[6]

As a consequence the monstrous is construed and experienced as 'outside us' and is thus a quality possessed by monstrous others. This process is reinforced by the popular media and also hardens the processes of social exclusion.

However, the processes which Young identifies as feeding into 'the manu-facture of monsters', if we reverse the valence, can be seen to run in parallel with the processes whereby individuals are beatified by the public and the media, whereby all flaws are forgotten and an image of perfection and purity is constructed. Of course such processes are evident throughout history and notions of 'good' and 'evil', the 'wicked witch' and the 'fairy princess', are deeply embedded in our culture. However, these processes are particularly prevalent at times of uncertainty, when there are major social changes and high levels of ontological insecurity and social anxiety. What I am arguing is that these are such times and our feelings and actions in relation to children and childhood are particularly significant in helping us make sense of this and, more impor-tantly, do something about it. As Ferguson (2004) argues, the processes of increased individualisation 'have both created the social conditions that make it more possible to gain more protection and for public outcry when they do not' (p. 131).

Social Anxiety, Late Modernity and Childhood

When I tried to account for the (re)emergence of child abuse as a problem 20 years ago (Parton, 1985a), I argued that the public inquiry into the death of Maria Colwell in 1973/4 was crucial and that in many respects the social reaction could be analysed, following Cohen (1973), in terms of a 'moral panic'.

Because of the exceptional nature of the social reaction, it seemed to provide a helpful framework for analysis. However, the notion of a moral panic assumes that the panic, while severe, subsides and is either solved or disappears from public and media view for other political reasons. As I have demonstrated in the previous two chapters, while child abuse has undergone a variety of 'mouldings' over the past 30 years, rarely has it disappeared from view and in many respects we have lived with an increasing sense of 'moral panic' ever since.

Critcher (2003) has concluded, from his analysis of a series of moral panics in the UK during the period, that the central discourse which connects them all is a variety of concerns about childhood, and as Buckingham (2000, p. 3) has argued, while

> The figure of the child has always been the focus of adult fears and fantasies ... in recent years, debates about childhood have become invested with a growing sense of anxiety and panic. Traditional certainties about the meaning and status of childhood have been steadily eroded and undermined.

It is not only children but the institution of childhood itself which is increasingly perceived and experienced as 'at risk'. It seems that childhood is being constructed as a precious realm which is under growing threat from those who would rob children of their childhoods, as well as being undermined by children themselves who refuse to remain childlike. Jackson and Scott (1999; see also Scott et al., 1998) suggest that such fears nearly always surface during periods of rapid change but in the past were thought to be located within particular sections of the community and were thus containable. They now suggest that this is changing:

> While some symptoms of social disorder continue to be associated with the rebarbative elements of an 'underclass' and the areas they inhabit, others are seen either as more ubiquitous or as less predictable, identifiable and locatable – as liable to disrupt social life at any time in any place. Threats to children's well-being are seen as coming from all-pervasive, global social 'ills' such as the 'pernicious' consequences of sex and violence in the media and also from the unforeseen (but constantly anticipated) danger from a specific 'monstrous' individual, the shadowy figure of the paedophile which haunts the popular imagination. (Jackson and Scott, 1999, p. 88)

A number of the developments I have discussed in relation to late modernity feed into this, for many of the issues relating to risk and uncertainty can be seen to coalesce around the figure of the child and our anxieties about childhood more generally. In many respects the child–parent relationship has become the most fundamental and 'natural' form of contemporary relationships. The trust that was previously anticipated from marriage and the family is now focused more on the child. Rather than being secondary to that of marriage, the parent–child relationship increasingly takes a primary significance:

The child is the source of the last remaining, irrevocable, unexchangeable primary relationship. Partners come and go. The child stays. Everything that is desired but not realizable in the relationship, is directed to the child ... here an anachronistic social experience is celebrated and cultivated which has become improbable and longed for precisely because of the individualization process. (Beck, 1992a, p. 18)

In this respect 'late modern society has re-adopted the child' (Jenks, 1996, p. 106), for the child has increasingly become the site of the relocation of discourses concerning stability, integration and the key signifier of the social bond, so that having and caring for a child 'can in fact become the very core of one's private existence' (Beck and Beck-Gernsheim, 1995, p. 107). The loss of traditional families embedded within secure communities and the growth of individualisation create a context in which there is a greater adult emotional investment in children in what seems a more uncertain and less safe world. Thus what happens to children increasingly seems to symbolise the key benchmark for the kind of society we have become and a primary focus for the aspirations, projections and longings on the part of adults. Children can thus be seen to envision a 'nostalgia' or longing for secure times now past (Jenks, 1996), together with a growing investment in the future in order to bring about a better world. It seems adults have become so concerned about the safety of children because 'children have become our principal concern, we have become their protectors and nurturers and they have become our primary love objects, our human capital and our future' (Jenks, 1996, p. 99).

Increased social anxiety about risk to children has been superimposed on the earlier 'protective discourse', where children are seen as vulnerable innocents who need to be shielded from the dangers of the wider adult social world as well as their own, on occasions, unsocialised natures. Such a development engenders a growing preoccupation with prevention, where it is argued there is a need for constant vigilance in order to anticipate and guard against potential threats to children's 'well-being'. Thus in a late modern society, where the experience of ontological insecurity and risk anxiety seem increasingly prevalent, children and childhood provide key sites for trying to bring about a better world, both now and in the future. The case of Victoria Climbié provided a major catalyst for expressing these anxieties. However, how these issues are made the subject of public policy depends on how they are understood, explained and made the subject of intervention. This is essentially a political and governmental process and the focus of my analysis in subsequent chapters.

Conclusion

In this chapter, taking my lead from Eric Hobsbawm, I have argued that the year 1973 was to prove crucial in opening up a series of major social and economic changes related to the growing impact of globalisation. The changes were particularly evident in relation to the family and the community and the increasingly individualised nature of social relationships and identity. The changes both prompted and were reflected in a growing sense of social anxiety which have often been projected onto concerns about children and childhood more generally. What is also evident is that, in the context of increasing globalisation, the power of the nation state has also changed. While its power in economic spheres has increasingly been limited, its responsibilities in relation to children have expanded. Again, this is well illustrated by comparing the cases of Maria Colwell and Victoria Climbié.

At the beginning of the 1982 DHSS study, *Child Abuse: A Study of Inquiry Reports* (DHSS, 1982, p. iii), there was a quotation which reads:

> a story unfolds in the report of small carelessnesses, pressures of other work, difficulties of staffing and human procrastinations and failure to cooperate, by which few workers, if they are honest, have not at times been tempted from their standards, but which collectively resulted in individual tragedy and public scandal (this quotation is taken from Jean Heywood, writing in 1958 about the Monckton Inquiry, which was set up in 1945 after the death of Dennis O'Neill whilst in care (Jean Heywood: *Children in Care*; Routledge & Kegan Paul, 1959).

In many respects this quotation could have been taken from either the Maria Colwell or Victoria Climbié inquiry reports. At a superficial reading the issues are remarkably similar; however, there are some major differences. Dennis O'Neill was literally in the care of the local authority and had been 'boarded out' with foster carers in South Wales and killed by his foster father; Maria Colwell had been in the care of the local authority, and 'boarded out' with foster carers who were relatives, but had subsequently had the care order removed and was placed on a supervision order, to the local authority; Victoria Climbié was none of these. There was a brief period when she was on a police protection order but otherwise issues in the report were centrally concerned with trying to discuss whether the case was handled appropriately as a 'child in need' or a 'child protection' case. Put at its crudest, the legislative context in 1945 was such that Victoria Climbié would not have been seen as the responsibility of the local authority. Similarly, it is unlikely that she would have been seen as the responsibility of the local authority in 1973 either. However, as we saw in the previous chapter, following the 1989 Children Act the responsibilities of local authorities changed significantly, particularly via section 17 of the Act which gave statutory responsibilities in relation to 'children in need'. It seems in the post-war period that the relationships between children, parents, professionals and the state have been changing in significant ways.

In the context of the various changes in kinship, family and community relationships evident in the last quarter of the twentieth century, no longer could the traditional nuclear family be relied upon to provide the main *instrument of government* whereby the normal health and development of children could be assured. New arrangements and forms of accountability and authority needed to be put in place. This is a theme which will become of increasing significance in the remainder of the book. In the next chapter, however, I look at the debates that were opening up in the mid-1990s about the relationships between 'child protection' and 'family support'.

4

Rethinking Child Protection and Family Support

As I will argue in Chapter 5, the election of the New Labour government in 1997 witnessed a significant policy shift in relation to children and welfare more generally. It began a programme of major reform which was to change the balance of responsibilities between parents, professionals and the state in relation to children, and was prompted by many of the social changes summarised in the Chapter 3. However, much of the thinking which was to inform the New Labour approach had been developing in the years prior to it coming into office, and it is to this that I turn in this chapter.

As I argued in Chapter 2, the 1989 Children Act was not consistent with the Conservative government's broad approach to social policy and its attempts to refashion the social democratic welfare state and the economy more generally. However, it was becoming increasingly evident that the policies were being introduced in a hostile economic and political environment which was having a deleterious impact on the material circumstances of children and, more specifically, how far local authorities were able to respond to their wider responsibilities for children 'in need' (Frost, 1992). Government figures showed that by 1992/3 there were 4.3 million children (33 per cent) living on less than half the average income, compared to 1.4 million (10 per cent) in 1979 when the Conservatives had come to power. The proportion of children living in poverty had more than trebled, the increase being considerably greater than for the population as a whole (Oppenheim and Lister, 1996). This deterioration in the life chances of many children could be seen, in many respects, to be a direct result of the Conservative government's social and economic policies and its failure to protect children from the vagaries of the increasingly globalised market.[1]

The policies placed a particular emphasis on the market and urged reductions in taxation and public expenditure, while stressing the role of the 'natural' family in taking responsibility for its members, particularly children. When it was seen as failing in these responsibilities, state agents, such as social workers, were to intervene authoritatively on behalf of children. A fine balance, therefore, had to be drawn between not undermining the privacy of the family and the authority of parents, on the one hand, and failing to protect children from abuse and neglect on the other. In the light of the 'Cleveland affair' and the series of public inquiries into child deaths where professionals had failed to intervene, the central focus of the 1989 Children Act had aimed to establish an appropriate balance between these two potentially contradictory requirements. As a result, I have previously argued that, by the early 1990s, the child protection system in England could be characterised in terms of the need to identify 'high risk', in a context where notions of 'working together' were set out in increasingly complex yet detailed procedural guidelines, and where the work was informed by a narrow emphasis on legalism and the need for professionals to identify forensic evidence (Parton, 1991). Increasingly, child protection work was concerned with trying to identify 'high-risk' cases and differentiate these from the rest, so that children could be protected, family privacy was not undermined and scarce resources could be directed to where, in theory, they were most needed but in an overall context where an increasing proportion of children were living in poverty (Parton, 1992).

The 'Refocusing' of Children's Services

However, as the 1990s progressed, this rationale for intra-familial child protection policy and practice was increasingly seen as inadequate and subject to a wide-ranging and authoritative critique, and a major debate opened up about the future direction of policy and practice. The central issue was how policies and practices in child protection integrated with support for children 'in need' which lay at the heart of the 1989 Children Act. The two catalysts for the debate were the publication of the Audit Commission report (1994) *Seen But Not Heard: Coordinating Community Child Health and Social Services for Children in Need*, and the launch by the Department of Health of *Child Protection: Messages from Research* (DH, 1995a).

The Audit Commission report argued that the aspirations and central aims of the Children Act were not being achieved because local authority and community child health services were poorly planned and coordinated, resulting in a large part of the £2 billion expenditure being wasted on families who did not need support. The focus should be on assessing need, with a much greater emphasis placed on prevention and less on reactive interventions.

Many of the central themes were echoed in *Messages from Research*, which was the report summarising over twenty research studies into the process and outcomes of child protection interventions in England in the early 1990s. Thirteen of the studies had been funded by the Department of Health following the fallout from the Cleveland inquiry and the apparent confusion in the reactions of the investigating agencies (Parton, 1996a, 1997).

Messages from Research was to prove crucial in rethinking the nature and priorities of child protection policy and practice and in helping to integrate child protection into the mainstream of childcare policy more generally. In particular, it highlighted a number of key themes which helped to connect thinking about child protection with a number of other developments at the time and which were to prove crucial in informing the approach of the New Labour government when it came to power in 1997.

The report argued that any *'incident* [of abuse] had to be seen in *context* before the extent of its harm can be assessed and appropriate intervention can be agreed' (1995, p. 53), and that the research demonstrated that 'with the exception of a few severe assaults and some sexual maltreatment' (p. 53), long-term difficulties for children seldom followed from a single abusive event or incident – rather they were more likely to be a consequence of living in an unfavourable environment, particularly one which is *low in warmth and high in criticism*. In only a small proportion of cases in the research projects was abuse seen as extreme and warranting more immediate and formal child protection interventions.

It was argued that 'if we put to one side the severe cases' (p. 19), the most deleterious situations in terms of longer term outcomes for children were those of *emotional neglect* (p. 20) and the primary concern should be the *parenting style* that fails to compensate for the inevitable deficiencies that become manifest in the course of the twenty years or so it take to bring up a child. Unfortunately, the research suggested, these were just the situations where the child protection system was least effective. The report argued that while there was little evidence that children were being missed and suffering harm unnecessarily at the hands of their parents, as implied by most child abuse inquiries, and therefore the system was 'successful', according to a narrow definition of child protection, this was at a cost. Many of the children and parents involved felt alienated and angry, there was an overemphasis on forensic concerns and there was far too much time and resources spent on investigations and not enough on developing longer term coordinated treatment and preventive strategies.

Both the Audit Commission report and *Messages from Research* were considerably influenced by the study carried out by Gibbons et al. (1995). This research, based on eight local authorities and carried out over a 16-week period in 1992, identified all children referred for a new child protection investigation (1888 cases) and tracked their progress through the child protection system for up to 26 weeks via social work records and minutes of case conferences (see Figure 4.1). What was seen as particularly significant was the way a series of *filters* and *funnels* operated. At the first level, 26 per cent of referrals were filtered out by social work staff at the duty stage after initial checks without any direct contact with the child or family. At the second, the investigation itself, another 50 per cent were filtered out and never reached an initial case conference. Of the remainder, just 15 per cent were placed on a child protection register. Thus, six

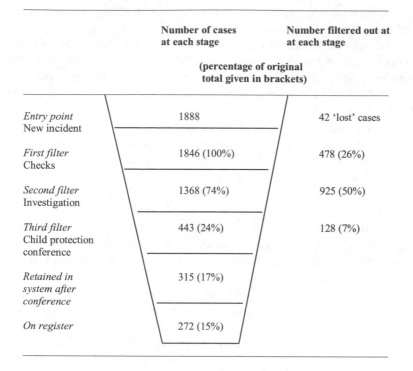

	Number of cases at each stage	Number filtered out at each stage
	(percentage of original total given in brackets)	
Entry point New incident	1888	42 'lost' cases
First filter Checks	1846 (100%)	478 (26%)
Second filter Investigation	1368 (74%)	925 (50%)
Third filter Child protection conference	443 (24%)	128 (7%)
Retained in system after conference	315 (17%)	
On register	272 (15%)	

Figure 4.1   Operation of filters in the English child protection system
Source: Gibbons et al., 1995

out of every seven children who entered the child protection system at referral were filtered out without their names being placed on the register. In a high proportion (44 per cent of those actually investigated), the investigation led to no further action at all. There were no interventions to protect the child nor were any services provided. In only 4 per cent of all cases referred were children removed from home under a statutory order at any time during the study.

The study also found that over a third (36 per cent) of the total referrals were headed by a lone parent and in only 30 per cent of cases were both natural parents resident in the household. Nearly three-fifths (57 per cent) lacked a wage earner and over half (54 per cent) were dependent on income support. Domestic violence (27 per cent) and mental illness (13 per cent) within the family also featured prominently. One in seven parents under suspicion was known to have been abused as a child. Most (65 per cent) of the children had been previously known to social services and a previous investigation had been undertaken in almost half (45 per cent) of the 1888 cases that Gibbons and her colleagues scrutinised. It was clearly the most vulnerable sections of the population who were most likely to become the object of the child protection system.

It was notable that the findings from this research reflected similar findings derived from research being carried out in other English-speaking Western societies who had borrowed from the American approach to child protection policy and practice in the 1970s and 80s. Increasingly, concerns were being expressed that far too many cases were being dragged into the child protection 'net', that the numbers involved had gone up inexorably over the previous 20 years, while the overall proportion of cases that were 'substantiated' had reduced (see Besharov, 1991; Lindsey, 1994; Parton et al., 1997). Crucially, the broader child welfare responsibilities and resources were seen as being dominated by a forensically driven and crisis-oriented child protection system (Kamerman and Khan, 1990). In particular, research carried out by David Thorpe in Western Australia and South Wales, published just prior to *Messages from Research*, painted a similar picture (Thorpe, 1994).

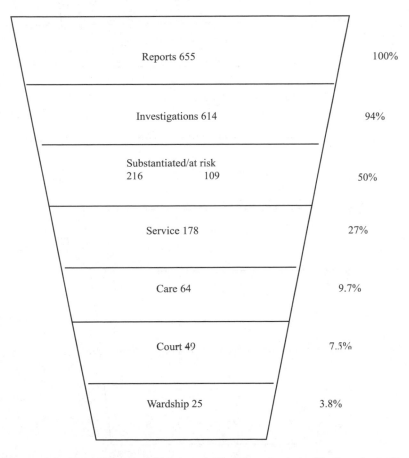

Figure 4.2 Funnelling and filtering child abuse reports in Western Australia
Source: Parton et al., 1997

Thorpe collected data on a 100 per cent sample of reports of abused and neglected children in Western Australia in 1987 (655 reports). After investigation, only 33 per cent (216) of the reports were considered to concern abused children, while a further 16.6 per cent (109) were judged to be 'at risk' of abuse or neglect (see Figure 4.2). Despite these assessments, just 27 per cent (178) cases received a service, of which 9.7 per cent (64) were taken into care. The proportion of the original 655 reports taken to the Children's Court on 'care

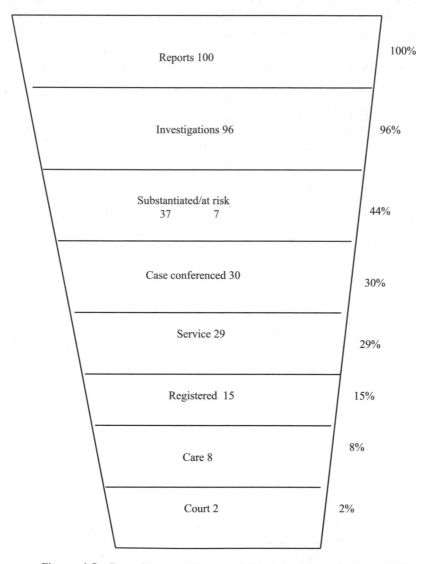

Figure 4.3 Funnelling and filtering child abuse reports in South Wales
Source: Parton et al., 1997

and protection' grounds was less than 10 per cent, while only 3.8 per cent (25 children) were made state wards.

Although the child protection laws and procedures in England and Wales were quite different from those in Western Australia, as Figure 4.3 demonstrates, the process of filtering in the South Wales social services department was very similar. The research also showed that 48 per cent of all referrals involved single parents and that they were caring for children in a context of financial difficulty. The research by Thorpe and that by Gibbons et al. demonstrated that the child protection system was least able to respond to referrals concerning *emotional neglect* – just the sorts of cases which *Messages from Research* suggested posed the major threat to a child's overall development and welfare. The findings of Gibbons et al. were particularly powerful in this respect (Parton, 1995). Of the 392 (100 per cent) referrals for suspected neglect, 40 per cent were filtered out at the first filter stage after checks with other agencies and some indirect work; 46 per cent were filtered out at the second filter after further investigation; so that just 14 per cent reached a case conference; with just 6 per cent being placed on the register (see Table 4.1). In 65 per cent of all the neglect cases, the researchers could not identify any protective actions taken or any mobilisation of support. Yet the researchers felt that the children had the highest number of poverty indicators and 'just as many indicators of vulnerability as those referred for physical or sexual abuse. Thus the commonest picture was of children not reaching the threshold for child protection proceedings, but not getting any preventive help either' (Parton, 1995, p. 85).[2]

In the light of the research reviewed in the report, *Messages from Research* (DH, 1995a) made a number of suggestions as to how 'children's safety' could be improved. It emphasised:

- the importance of sensitive and informed professional/client relationships, where honesty and reliability were valued

- the need for an appropriate balance of power between participants where serious attempts were made at partnerships

Table 4.1 Operation of filters in child protection systems: cases of neglect

	% removed by each filter	*Total*
Entry point: new incident	–	0%
First filter: checks	40%	40%
Second filter: further investigation	46%	86%
Third filter: child protection conference	8%	94%

Source: Parton, 1995

- a wide perspective on child protection, concerned not only with investigating forensic evidence but also with notions of welfare, prevention and treatment

- that priority should be afforded to effective supervision and the training of social workers

- that, generally, the most effective protection from abuse was brought about by 'enhancing children's quality of life'.

More specifically, it called for a 'rebalancing' of child protection work which prioritised section 17 and Part 3 of the Children Act 1989 in terms of supporting families with 'children in need', and thereby keeping notions of policing and coercive intervention to a minimum. It similarly suggested that section 47 of the Act should be understood as a duty to *enquire*, rather than simply a forensically determined power to investigate.

These conclusions had been spelt out in greater detail in September 1994 in a significant paper presented by Wendy Rose (1994), the then assistant chief inspector at the Department of Health, in which she shared some of the thinking within the Department of Health on the relationship between child protection and family support and the intentions of the Children Act 1989. She made it clear that the ideas were informed by the reports of the child protection research studies, the Audit Commission report and studies into the implementation of section 17 of the Children Act which were being carried out at the time (Aldgate and Tunstill, 1995). There were two themes which provided the core of her argument. First, Rose felt that current practices tended to polarise family support and child protection services as distinct and even contrasting activities. She argued that 'we should be promoting one integrated approach to the local authority's duties under Part 3 and Part 5 of the Act' (1994, p. 5). Second, she questioned whether the current balance between investigation/ assessment processes and the provision of support services best served 'children in need'.

Wendy Rose's discussion of section 47 of the Children Act 1989 was not only central to her argument, but is key to understanding the way thinking, policy and practice were going to develop over subsequent years. She pointed out that section 47 was in itself no more or less statutory than section 17. Family support should not be seen as non-statutory, discretionary and hence less important. Section 47 and section 17 were intimately interrelated. Under s. 47(1) the local authority was required to make or cause to be made 'such enquiries as they consider necessary to enable them to decide whether they should take any action to safeguard or promote the child's welfare'. Section 47(3) continues: 'the enquiries shall, in particular, be directed towards establishing: whether the authority should make an application to the court, or exercise any of their other powers, under this Act, with respect to the child'.

Rose argued that in the course of making *enquiries*, the local authority must consider providing services under Part 3 and she expressed the view that this link in the legislation appeared to be underemphasised. The *enquiry* was to decide whether to provide a service under Part 3; either a plan of social work intervention should be agreed with the family or, if necessary, an application made to the court. The primary focus is not to find out whether a child has been abused or whether a criminal offence has occurred. Essentially, Wendy Rose was arguing that it was important to develop a more *balanced* and *integrated* childcare system encompassing both family support and child protection. This was subsequently to be called the *refocusing* of children's services based on a *continuum* of provision. Rose (1994, p. 24) argued that it was important to

> intervene with a lighter, less bureaucratic touch in a number of cases, integrate family support services both practically and conceptually more with child protection, and thereby release more resources from investigation and assessment into family support and treatment services.

Extrapolating from the Gibbons et al. research, *Messages from Research* developed a *map* of the child protection system in England for 1992. In doing so, not only did it identify where and how many cases were filtered out in the decision-making process, but it also provided a representation of how child welfare, child protection and family support could be seen as related to each other along a continuum (see Figure 4.4). For the first time it was possible to map and represent child protection processes and begin to see their impact and interrelationships with other state child welfare services. But, while it was not yet possible to measure in any way the size and nature of family support provided for 'children in need' in the community, this was now seen as an important and key statutory responsibility.

While *Messages from Research* received much publicity, had wide dissemination and a foreword written by John Bowis, the parliamentary under-secretary of state, the Conservative government did not take a strong lead in attempts to 'refocus' children's services. This was seen as the responsibility of local authorities and few extra resources were made available.[3] However, it was evident that local authorities were struggling to respond positively to this new agenda. The problems were clear in research (Colton et al., 1995; Aldgate and Tunstill, 1995) and explicitly identified by the *Children Act Report 1993* (DH, 1994, para. 239) which noted that:

> A broadly consistent and somewhat worrying picture is emerging. In general, progress towards full implementation of Section 17 of the Children Act has been slow. Further work is still needed to provide across the country a range of family services aimed at preventing families reaching the point of breakdown. Some authorities are still finding it difficult to move from a reactive social policing role to a more proactive partnership role with families.

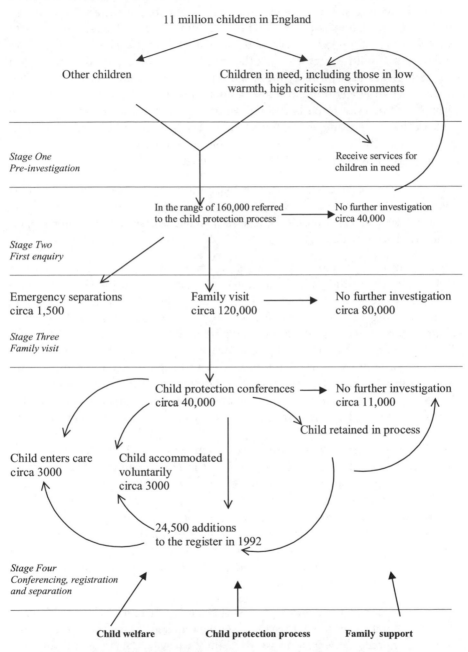

Figure 4.4 The child welfare, child protection, family support continuum
Source: DH, 1995a

It was clear that few authorities were going to prioritise services for children unless they had clearly defined responsibilities for them, as in the case of children 'looked after'. It was still the case that children were unlikely to be offered services unless they were seen to be at risk of child abuse.

Further research evaluating the Children Act (DH, 2001) looked at the period in the middle of the decade, immediately prior to the election of the New Labour government in May 1997. The studies showed that changes in the operational definition of need and the development of a wider range of services were beginning to take place in some areas; but while there was some evidence of a response to the 'refocusing' initiative, a preoccupation with 'risk' still dominated intervention at the point of access. It seemed that in the initial screening of families, the identification of the risk of child abuse continued to be the key criterion for accessing resources (Brandon et al., 1999; Thoburn et al., 2000; Tunstill and Aldgate, 2000). Jane Aldgate summarised the situation as follows:

> The conclusions from the research which has evaluated the implementation of Section 17 over the first eight or so years, suggest that progress has not been straightforward. The Children Act was implemented at a time when investigation of child abuse dominated practice. The concept of identifying children in need based on the impact of impairment or harm was some distance away from an approach which was focusing on identifying risk and the commission of abuse or neglect. With hindsight, the aim of allowing social services and other agencies to identify children in need and set local priorities for service provision was too complex for the primitive technical infrastructure of the time. It was also difficult to shift the attitudes of local authorities to the broader perspective of family support. (Aldgate, 2002, pp. 164–5)

The research overview of the Children Act studies argued that 'the balance between safeguarding and promoting welfare for children in need who are living with their families' (DH, 2001, p. 46) had not yet been achieved. It seemed that families who required help, where children were 'in need' for reasons other than 'child maltreatment', were not always gaining access to services. The research studies pointed to the value of integrating different routes to accessing services, and showed that the system of separating child protection inquiries and family support assessment was ineffective and counterproductive to meeting the needs of children and families. By separating the two systems, some children had missed out on the benefits of early intervention which would prevent more intrusive and intensive activity at a later stage. Conversely, some children who needed safeguarding because of neglect were slipping through the 'net' of family support services because these services failed to address the importance of safeguarding children's welfare (Brandon et al., 1999). The studies revealed the need for a more discriminatory matching of children's needs to services, and planning to be linked to welfare outcomes for all children in need (Statham and Aldgate, 2003).

If 'refocusing' was to be achieved and the central principles of the Children Act thoroughly implemented in practice, the research indicated that central government should take a much stronger lead and there was a 'need for a wider system of assessment that could lead to differential and well-planned patterns of intervention' (DH, 2001, p. 46).

The 'Looking After Children' Project

In 1987 the Department of Health and Social Security established a working party made up of senior civil servants in the department, together with a number of well-established academic childcare researchers, to consider the development of a practical scheme for assessing outcomes for children who were 'looked after' or 'supervised' by local authorities. The impetus for the initiative was the recognition that the climate and context of practice had changed so that it was no longer appropriate to assume that social work assessment and intervention could be taken for granted:

> Recently, research into modern social conditions, the emergence of theories about prevention, the weakening of confidence in the public care of children following a number of well-documented tragedies, the attention given to consumer views and the emphasis on cost-effectiveness have all served to produce a climate in which the development of reliable means of assessing outcome is increasingly seen as a necessity. (Parker, 1991, pp. 16–17)

The work focused on the small group of children whose unmet needs were considered the greatest and who had, therefore, been in receipt of the most extensive level of service – being 'looked after' away from home. The aim of the working party 'was to introduce ideas about developmental outcomes into everyday social work practice' (Ward, 1998, p. 208). The report of the working party (Parker et al., 1991) became the first stage of what became known as the 'Looking After Children' (LAC) project. The working party identified seven 'developmental dimensions' along which children should achieve long-term well-being in adulthood:

- health
- education
- identity
- family and peer relationships
- emotional and behavioural development
- self-care and competence
- identity and social presentation.

It was argued that children would only make satisfactory progress if their needs were adequately met in each of these seven dimensions, and that parents at a private level and children's welfare services at a public level should both be held accountable for the extent to which they attempted to meet children's needs. The outcome of their efforts could then be measured with reference to both children's experience of parenting and their progress (Parker et al., 1991).

Such an initiative took on an even greater significance in the light of the growing political concerns about residential care for children and the scandals that received wide media coverage in the late 1980s and early 1990s. It was vital that local authorities fulfilled their responsibilities as 'corporate parents to the children and young people they looked after' (Jackson and Kilroe, 1996). Much of the evidence suggested that 'looked after' young people did not succeed educationally and also their health, mental health, general well-being and integration into mainstream society was poor. It seemed that those who had been 'looked after' made up a disproportionate number of the unemployed, homeless and criminal population and accounted for a variety of other problem groups later in life. At the heart of the LAC project was an attempt to make explicit what 'good parenting means in practice' (DH, 1995b, p. 22) so that local authorities could fulfil their responsibilities.

The key components of the LAC system were a series of six, age-related assessment and action records (AARs) which set specific, age-related objectives for children's progress within the seven developmental dimensions. The AARs posed two types of question: first, how far children were progressing towards recognised developmental objectives; and second, whether they were being given the experiences or services necessary for their attainment.

The AARs were set within a system for gathering information and reviewing children's cases that aimed to provide baseline information about the specific needs of individual children, the situation of their families and the purpose of providing the service. The AARs were implemented initially as a practice tool, designed to set an agenda for social work encounters with individual children 'looked after' away from home. The information was collected on a face-to-face basis by social workers, carers, parents, children and young people and encouraged the discussion of issues which otherwise might not be addressed. By 1997 AARs were being implemented in 92 per cent of local authorities in England (Ward, 1998). However, the use of the AARs in setting agendas for direct work with children, determining responsibilities and improving care planning was secondary to their original purpose, which was to provide local authorities with a systematic means of gathering information that would enable them to assess the outcomes of 'looking after' children away from home. The information on individual children could be aggregated to assess the effectiveness of the service as a whole.

Increasingly, local authorities and researchers began to examine how far the thinking behind LAC and more specifically the AARs could be used to develop similar tools for assessing outcomes for other children's services. This was specifically discussed by Roger Bullock, one of the principal authors of *Messages from Research* (DH, 1995a). As we have seen, *Messages from Research* estimated the number of children in England and Wales who entered the child protection process and charted what happened to them (see Figure 4.4). It showed that although there were 160,000 referrals each year, only 6000 of those needed to be 'looked after'. Moreover, half of these separated children were 'looked after' by relatives and many of the remainder quickly returned home. The large number of children in need of protection who were supported at home marked one of the major changes in childcare over the previous 20 years. Numbers 'looked after' had halved and those receiving family support now outnumbered them by an estimated six or seven to one. Bullock posed the question in the following terms:

> A small proportion of abused children will need to be looked after for a long period. These are likely to be grossly maltreated, neglected and rejected children, some of whom will be adopted. For them, the state is in *loco parentis* and the value of using the *Looking After Children* materials is self-evident. But as they form a minority of child protection cases, the question arises of what measures of service delivery and progress are relevant to the rest. (Bullock, 1998, p. 23)

As we have noted, *Messages from Research* recommended adopting a broad perspective on needs and that child protection should be seen in the wider context of child and family support. Bullock argued that it was a major achievement of LAC that a method was now available – which had not been available ten years previously – for assessing outcomes in childcare, but 'while the overall approach can be used to monitor the development of children everywhere, clarification is required about which details should apply to children with particular needs who receive services but are not looked after or whose separations are short' (Bullock, 1998, p. 235). This was because, in situations where children are supported at home, but where specific and targeted services are provided and parents are encouraged to work in partnership, the nature of the responsibilities placed on local authorities was much less clear cut.

A number of commentators have provided critical analyses of the LAC materials and the assumptions on which they are based (Knight and Caveney, 1998; Garrett, 1999a, 1999b, 2002, 2003). The approach has been criticised for: being overly normative and white and middle class in orientation; reducing practice to a checklist mentality and thereby increasing bureaucratic demands on practitioners, parents, children and young people; and being overly concerned with regulating the behaviour of children, young people, parents and frontline professionals. My purpose here is more mundane. I am trying to demonstrate that the LAC system was being developed and operationalised at the same time as the 'refocusing' debate was taking place and that the former provided an opportunity for taking forward the latter. The LAC system, suitably adapted and broadened, provided an opportunity for addressing some of the issues which were at the centre of the refocusing debate in terms of the need to rationalise and improve assessments of children in need. A number of the same key researchers and childcare research units, together with the same senior civil servants at the Department of Health, were involved in both developments. It is not surprising, therefore, that it was the LAC system that was to provide the basis for the wider system of assessment which was seen as so important in progressing and broadening the refocusing initiative.

However, attempting to develop materials to assess the outcomes of public services for 'children in need', which were intended to complement the private activities of parents, raised a number of ethical as well as theoretical and practical questions. Because local authorities acquired, to a greater or lesser extent, parental responsibilities for the children they 'looked after', monitoring 'corporate parenting' standards and assessing their relationship to children's progress could be justified on the grounds of accountability. There were no similar grounds for requiring parents to offer evidence of the standards of care they provided, with or without assistance from public services, except where there might be grounds for considering care proceedings. However, as Harriet Ward (1998) argued, it seemed that the point had been reached where serious consideration needed to be given to monitoring progress where families were receiving ongoing assistance from public services more generally. As Ward (1998, p. 210) put it: 'is it, for instance, justifiable to offer extensive social work support to a family without asking whether there has been any improvement in the children's school attendance?'

In looking to widen the scope and application of formalised assessment and monitoring procedures beyond 'looked after' children to those where family support was being provided for 'children in need', the traditionally understood relationship between the responsibilities and accountabilities of the 'private' family and the 'public' authority would be made far more blurred. As Ward noted, 'these are far-reaching ethical questions concerning issues of control, authority and the relationship between public and private responsibilities for children' (Ward, 1998, p. 211). However, the possibility of using assessment and monitoring tools developed specifically for children 'looked after' in 'public' care seemed to provide the basis for the assessment and monitoring of children living at home but where the family was receiving some form of 'family support' service. The importance and influence of the LAC project in subsequent developments under New Labour will become apparent when I discuss the Assessment Framework (DH, 2000a) in Chapter 6, and the development of the Common Assessment Framework (DfES, 2004b), which followed the publication of the Green Paper *Every Child Matters* (Chief Secretary to the Treasury, 2003), in Chapter 8.

Early Childhood Prevention

As we have seen, the idea of prevention in relation to childcare services had been considerably broadened and reframed by the 1989 Children Act. The 1963 Children Act had for the first time given local authorities preventive powers but this was restricted to providing minimal resources and carrying out work to prevent children entering public care. The 1989 Act had extended these responsibilities to providing family support for 'children in need', whether or not there was a possibility of the child being 'accommodated'. However, as the research evidence about the development of family support in the 1990s demonstrated, this was being done in a piecemeal and restricted way.

However, interest in prevention in childcare was also being developed in a rather different quarter in the early/mid-1990s and this was to provide considerable momentum for arguments and interests which were sympathetic to what was increasingly called 'early intervention' (Bright, 1997). The Family Policy Studies Centre (Utting et al., 1993), the Joseph Rowntree Foundation (Utting, 1995), and the National Children's Bureau (Sinclair et al., 1997; Utting, 1998a) all played important roles in making the case for prevention, articulating some of its policy and practice implications and placing it on political agendas. Perhaps most crucially, the case was made that early intervention could play a significant role in developing new policies for crime and delinquency reduction, which was to become a key area for the New Labour Party under Tony Blair.

The case for prevention was firmly rooted in the realities of family and household change which I have outlined in Chapter 3. Those supportive of such a development also recognised that a dominant view in the Conservative government was that the 'collapse of the traditional family' – identified as two married parents and their 'natural' children – could be blamed for a whole range of social ills, including the emergence of a benefit-dependent 'underclass', increased homelessness and rising crime. Rather than seeing changes in the family as resulting from, or at least being a part of, the wide-ranging economic, social and cultural changes of the previous 30 years, they were seen by many in the Conservative government as the cause. In contrast, others on the political left construed parents and children as the 'victims' of these social and economic changes and thus quite unable to act independently. Between these perspectives, it was argued that there was a growing consensus which was far more positive, proactive and pragmatic. It recognised that turning the clock back to the 1950s was neither a serious nor a desirable option and that policies to 'strengthen families' and 'help parents' needed development. Family change should be managed not anathematised, with a firm policy emphasis on supporting parents, not stigmatising them. The case for prevention was clearly put by David Utting (1995, p. 8):

While believing that relationships and choice of lifestyle within families should normally be a private matter, it accepts that this cannot always be the case. The welfare and safety of children, in particular, are viewed as a collective responsibility which can be met through the public provision of preventive services and intervention where necessary. Parents, too, may be unable to cope without help from the state, or the arbitration of law, at times of conflict within the family. Indeed, the financial and social costs which fall to the community as a result of family malfunction and breakdown are reason in themselves to justify the essential contribution of public policy involvement.

The way that children grow up – their attitudes, behaviour and achieve-ments – was seen as being crucially 'conditioned by their relationships with parents and other members of their families' (Utting, 1995, p. 32), but 'parent-ing' could not be considered in isolation from a wide range of economic and environmental influences, and the growth in poverty in particular. At the same time, changes in family and household and the growing 'moral uncertainty' and fluidity of family relationships provided further complexities and potential stresses. In this changing world the role of parents or 'parenting' was seen as playing an important mediator between the stresses of adult life and the way children develop. Parental attitudes and behaviour affected the lives of children from the time of conception, and research, which built on the 'attach-ment' theories of John Bowlby (1951, 1973, 1979, 1980), was seen as particularly important in demonstrating how the neglect of infants' emotional needs played a crucial role in whether they became passively withdrawn or aggressive and antisocial (Rutter, 1981; Goldberg et al., 1996).

The importance of prevention for pre-empting future crime was underlined. For example, John Graham and David Utting (1996) argued that criminological studies over many years in different Western societies had consistently identified a range of family-based factors linked to an increased risk of offending. They quoted a meta-analysis of these studies in America, Britain and Scandinavia by Loeber and Stouthamer-Loeber (1986) which identified clusters of such influences in terms of:

- *neglect* – where parents spend little time interacting with and supervising children

- *conflict* – where parents exert inconsistent or inappropriate discipline and one party rejects the other

- *deviant* – where parents are themselves involved in offending and/or condone law breaking

- *disruption* – where neglect and conflict arise from marital discord and the breakup of the marriage, with the subsequent absence of one parent, usually the father.

In ranking the strength of the four clusters, neglect was found to be the strongest and disruption the weakest. The key factor seemed to be the quality and consistency of relationships between children and their parents, and, where there were two parents, between the parents themselves.

A body of evidence seemed to show that children who began their offending careers at an early age were more likely to commit serious crimes and persist in criminal activities than those who started later (for example, LeBlanc and Frechette, 1989; Patterson, 1994). Other research showed that the early onset of offending was strongly related to troublesome behaviour during childhood (West, 1982), which in turn was strongly related to early childhood behavioural problems and poor parenting (Farrington and West, 1990). The justification for early intervention was further reinforced by the finding that the same clusters of risk factors predicted a range of different problems encountered by young people. Overlapping personal and environmental risk factors had been identified not only for drug abuse, criminal behaviour and violence, but also for educational failure, unsafe sexual behaviour and poor mental health (Dryfoos, 1990; Mrazek and Haggerty, 1994).

However, it was recognised that not all children who might be deemed by research findings to be 'at risk' would develop problems, as there were 'protective' as well as 'risk' factors (Rutter, 1985; Farrington, 1996; Catalano and Hawkins, 1996). In this respect it was argued that a 'public health' approach to policy provided a powerful and versatile tool for ensuring policy intentions could be realised in practice:

> Like successful campaigns to lower the incidence of heart disease, it argues that even when chains of causation cannot be incontrovertibly established, successful efforts to reduce known risk factors and increase protective factors across a broad population can achieve a desirable, preventive effort. (Utting, 1998b, p. 9)

Sinclair et al. (1997) likened the passage through childhood, from birth to eighteen years, as a journey through territory that was akin to a snakes and ladders board; where the ladders represented positive supports and enablers, while the snakes were the mishaps, mistreatment and miseries along the way. The role of preventive services was to provide more ladders and remove or minimise the snakes and their impact.

Clearly, then, the role of prevention was not simply to combat the negatives (risks/snakes) but to enhance the positives (opportunities/ladders) via maximising the protective factors and processes. Rutter (1990) conceived of risk and protection as processes rather than fixed states and saw protectors as the basis for opening up opportunities. The timing of interventions was crucial, because if they were to have the most impact, the 'early years' were key and success depended on recruiting parents – usually mothers – into the role of educators. This notion of protection thus took a much wider span than simply protection from harm or abuse, in the sense usually understood in terms of 'child protection' and the child protection system and as criticised in the 'refocusing debate'. This idea of protection was more positive and placed it alongside approaches which emphasised childhood resilience and strengths, and was thoroughly consistent with the central principal of the 1989 Children Act in terms of 'promoting and safeguarding children's welfare'. Prevention and protection were not in tension or conflict but were thoroughly consistent with each other. Crucially, an emphasis on prevention and protection was seen as providing a major contribution to policies which aimed to reduce crime and antisocial behaviour. It argued that:

> the purpose of prevention is to reduce the risk factors associated with criminality and other 'problem behaviours', such as drug misuse, to strengthen the factors which protect against them and to reduce opportunities for crime. It notes that many preventive measures have multiple benefits of which the prevention of crime and criminality is but one (Bright, 1997, p. 14)

and that the three key elements of policy should be: early childhood services; opportunities for young people; and safer neighbourhoods. While the link with crime was explicitly made, the purpose of developing early childhood services was not simply to reduce criminality per se but to 'enhance physical, intellectual and emotional development, to reduce child abuse and to improve family functioning' (Bright, 1997, p. 45). It had much wider and positive implications. Crucially, it was claimed that evaluations of early childhood services for 'disadvantaged children' could improve parenting and family functioning, reduce family breakdown as well as improve the developmental and educational performance of young children.

Conclusion

This growing and powerful consensus about the importance of early intervention to prevent a whole range of social ills clearly had much in common with many of the central themes articulated in the 'refocusing' debate about the importance of family support for 'children in need', with its emphasis on the significance of 'parenting style' and the deleterious longer term consequences of 'contexts' for child-rearing which were 'low in warmth and high in criticism' and the importance of overcoming 'emotional neglect'. Perhaps most crucially, 'protection' was reframed in positive terms and emphasised the importance of combating risks and enhancing resilience and strengths so that opportunities for 'normal' child development could be maximised.[4] In the process it provided a rationale for a broadening of the role of prevention well beyond the 'prevention' of children coming into public care. For this to be achieved, however, assessment would need to take a much more proactive and all-encompassing role and in this respect the development of the LAC initiative was to prove vital. For these developments to be taken forward, however, required a quite new role for the central state, as it had been demonstrated that local authorities, left to their own initiative, were unable to do so in any consistent and coherent way.

What I have done in this chapter is argue that during the 1990s thinking about child protection policy and practice had moved in quite new directions, but that these had only been partially taken forward by the Conservative government. With the arrival of New Labour this was about to change. What became clear soon after New Labour came into power was that the government was keen to broaden the 'refocusing initiative' beyond simply rebalancing family support and child protection, to embrace concerns about parenting, early intervention, supporting the family and regenerating the community more generally. This was to be a key responsibility for local authorities generally, rather than just social service departments, and was to reposition the role of health trusts, education authorities and non-government agencies, who were encouraged to develop accessible, non-stigmatising, preventive approaches, where the role of early years services was seen as key. The future direction of public policy in this area was outlined in a statement from Paul Boateng at a conference in March 1998 when he was parliamentary under-secretary of state for health:

> This government is committed to ensuring we support families, especially in their parenting role, so as to give children the best start of life. We are committed to supporting families when they seek help, and before they reach crisis point, and to making the best use of scarce public resources. It is because of that we see the importance of early intervention. The evidence is that early intervention works. (Boateng, 1999, p. 14)

And in a news release from the Treasury in January 1998, Tessa Jowell, when minister for public health, stated:

> We want services to be flexible and responsive to the needs of each child so that everyone can get the best possible start to life. If government departments work together, not only can we give best value to the children but we can also get value for money by cutting the costs of crime and unemployment which can so easily follow if children do not get help at an early age.

Taken together, these two statements capture many of the key elements of the New Labour approach. New Labour came into power with a quite distinctive political agenda which not only attempted to reframe how 'family support' should be delivered but had fundamental implications for policy more generally.

This was made explicit with the publication of the Green Paper, *Supporting Families: A Consultation Document* (Home Office, 1998b), by the ministerial group on the family chaired by the home secretary. While presented as providing a coherent framework for the development of social policies relating to the family, it was less concerned with promoting a particular family form than in ensuring that children, particularly poor children, were better supported and developing a new balance between the state and parents in the care, control and upbringing of children (Featherstone, 2004; James and James, 2004). The Green Paper sprang primarily from the government's interest in developing a new strategy for combating juvenile delinquency and both supporting and disciplining parents in this key task (Maclean, 2002). Childhood was identified as a key site for overcoming current and future social problems so that children were 'defined in terms of their future, rather than being recognised in their own right' (James and James, 2004, p. 193).

5

Governing Childhood under New Labour

As I argued in Chapter 3, one of the key social changes brought about by late modernity has been the shift in the environments of both trust and risk and the growth of ontological insecurity. I argued that the changes can be seen to have undermined the salience of kinship ties, fractured the hold of the local community and undermined the traditional authority of the family and religion. In this chapter I aim to analyse how such changes have not simply provided the context for policy development but, crucially, demonstrate how they have been interpreted and responded to in the formulation and content of policy. Essentially I will be looking at the way politics itself has been reformulated, particularly in terms of the New Labour project and how attempts to govern childhood lie at its core. A key element in the transformation of the Labour Party was its response to crime and social disorder, and much of this was developed in the wake of the huge social and media reaction to the death of James Bulger.

The Death of Childhood Innocence

On 12 February 1993 two-year-old James Bulger was abducted from a shopping centre in Bootle, Merseyside, by two ten-year-old boys, Jon Venables and Robert Thompson. He was taken to a nearby canal and then to a railway track, where he was beaten to death and his body left on the rails to be cut in half by a passing train. The abduction from the shopping centre was captured on CCTV and the hazy images broadcast across the globe. The case attracted enormous media attention, both during the police investigation and again during the trial.

The media took its cue from the judge's summary observation that 'the killing of James Bulger was an act of unparalleled evil and barbarity' (Morrison, 1997, p. 228). The 'demonising' of Robert Thompson and Jon Venables by the British media was so relentless that Michael King (1995, p. 8) described it as 'the kind of outbreak of moral condemnation that is usually reserved for the enemy in times of war'. However, journalists moved beyond their attack on the two boys to encompass general assertions about the current state of childhood and the general moral decline in society, where liberal permissiveness, the collapse of family life and the failings of schools were all seen as culpable. Feature articles and editorials addressed the case in terms of moral and social disintegration, the threat of delinquency to the whole social fabric, the hidden evil within children, the vulnerability and corruptibility of childhood and the need for a new sense of community responsibility. There were high-profile contributions from various experts, politicians and religious leaders, all pursuing similar themes. If the dominant theme arising from child abuse inquiries and media coverage from 1973 onwards, which lay at the heart of the 1989 Children Act, had been one of 'childhood innocence', where children are seen as in need of protection from evil or misguided adults, the effect of the Bulger case was very different. It is notable that the death of James Bulger was never constructed by the media or politicians as a child abuse case. The overriding impression was that this was an evil crime, which had enormous symbolic and emotional resonance with wide-ranging anxieties about contemporary British society, and the state of childhood was deemed to be in crisis and in need of serious attention (Scraton, 1997).

As Franklin and Petley (1996) have argued, media and political responses had the effect of 'killing the age of innocence', for it was clear that media coverage signalled a phenomenon with a significance which extended beyond the tragic death of an individual child. Just prior to the death of James Bulger, there had been a growth in media coverage of children and young people which had become almost wholly focused on crime. This had been prompted by the urban disturbances of 1991 (Campbell, 1993) and emergent concerns about 'persistent young offenders' who were said to account for a high proportion of the spiralling crime figures (Newburn, 1996).

The Bulger case helped to ventilate a political backlash characterised as 'authoritarian populism' (Bottoms, 1995). The immediate policy response was 'back to basics', which was summarised by the injunction of the Prime Minister John Major that 'we should understand a little less and condemn a little more' and the announcement by the Home Secretary Michael Howard, to the 1994 Conservative Party conference, of a new law and order package, which had at its core the pronouncement that 'prison works'. In the wake of the Bulger case, politicians were keen to address public and media anxieties with the promise of ever tougher and more repressive legislation to police what appeared to be a generation of children who were 'out of control' in a context of growing social disorder. Michael Howard's period in office marked a key moment of transition in the English criminal justice system in general, and youth justice in particular. The issue of crime, particularly youth crime (Pitts, 2001, 2003; Smith, 2003) became a central political issue. The victim, not the perpetrator, emerged as the central object of penal policy, so that being for the victim meant being against the offender.

We can also trace the origins of the New Labour project for reforming the welfare state and remodelling society to the notion of being 'tough on crime and tough on the causes of crime', which was developed at the time of the death of James Bulger (Jordan, 1999). The phrase was first coined by Tony Blair soon after he became shadow home secretary in an article, 'Why Crime is a Socialist Issue', published in the *New Statesman* in 1993. It had the effect of seizing the initiative on law and order from the Conservative government and demonstrated that Labour took such issues seriously. The article contained all the seeds of the subsequent New Labour approach, both in terms of the analysis of the problems to be addressed and the policy implications. At its core were particular notions of responsibility, obligation and community, where the relationship between the state, the child and the parents was seen as in need of realignment (Jordan, 1998).

In his *New Statesman* article, Tony Blair argued that crime and disorder had become an everyday and serious problem for traditional Labour Party voters in both the inner city and the suburbs, causing considerable anger, fear and anxiety. The possessive individualism of the Conservative government had failed but the Labour Party was seen as responding only with 'patronizing sympathy or indifference' (Blair, 1993, p. 27). He called for the party to make crime a genuine 'people's issue' and the subject of a campaign for 'better and safer communities'. He articulated the need for a 'Third Way' because 'we are moving the debate beyond the choice between personal and social responsibility, those who want to punish the criminal and those who point to the poor social conditions in which crime breeds'. He argued that people had a right, and society a duty, to punish offenders who violated the rights of other citizens that properly reflected the seriousness of the crime, while recognising that 'poor education and housing, inadequate or cruel family backgrounds, low employment prospects and drug use will affect the likelihood of young people turning to crime' (p. 27). It was here that he introduced the notion of 'social exclusion' which was to become the centrepiece of New Labour's approach to social policy, because 'if these young people are placed outside mainstream culture, offered no hope or opportunity, shown no respect for themselves, there is a great chance that they will go wrong' (p. 27). People thus had the *right* to security, job opportunities and a stable community; but against this they had the *responsibility* to act honestly, not violate the rights of other citizens and actively participate in the workforce. There was an explicit merging of the boundaries between the realms of social welfare and penal policy (Stenson, 2001; Matthews and Young, 2003), particularly in relation to children and young people in the light of the James Bulger case.

New Labour, the 'Third Way' and 'Tough Love'

The 'Third Way' was the name given by the New Labour leadership to its political philosophy and strategy when it came to power in May 1997. It was also the title of texts written by Tony Blair (1998) and Anthony Giddens (1998), one of his key advisors. The approach aimed to transcend the Thatcherite free-market model of the neoliberal state and the old style socialism of both the Soviet command economy and the 'Old Labour' variety, with its emphasis on a universalist, collectivist welfare state. The globalised nature of the market economy was accepted as a given, together with the assumption that the nation state could have very little influence upon it. Rather than intervene in the economy from the demand side, as with the Keynesian approach, the emphasis should therefore be on the supply side. In particular, the Third Way argued that national competitiveness and prosperity were crucially dependent on the skills and knowledge of the workforce, which needed to be flexible, adaptable and educated. Instead of job security, the new aim was 'employability', which would aid both economic performance and social cohesion. Social security would be refashioned to maximise workers' willingness and ability to enter the labour market. A strong work ethic would also benefit the whole of society, for hard work and personal discipline would not only benefit the individual but the whole economy and social cohesion and thereby attack the causes of crime. In effect, the work ethic was to be placed at the centre of the welfare state. In the process, the character as well as the behaviour of certain sections of the population would need to change, thus doing away with the 'dependency culture' which was seen to afflict many of those in receipt of welfare benefits.

At the centre of the New Labour project was its emphasis on the need to articulate and establish a new set of values appropriate for the time: 'The Third Way is a serious reappraisal of social democracy, reaching deep into the values of the Left to develop radically new approaches' (Blair, 1998, p. 3). Along with the mantra 'tough on crime, tough on the causes of crime', the other key catchphrase was 'no rights without responsibilities' (Giddens, 1998, p. 65). One of the strongest moral themes in the new orthodoxy was the insistence that rights implied responsibilities, and benefits entailed contributions. It was asserted that the social citizenship created by the post-war welfare state had a one-sided emphasis on rights. The key conditions built into the Beveridge insurance benefits for unemployment, widowhood, disability and sickness were seen as too weak and were to be replaced by much stricter tests of availability for work. For example, the Jobseeker's Agreement was to turn conditional social rights into individual obligations sanctioned by an individual contractual agreement. Collective protection was to be replaced by individualised compulsion and training. A number of key themes have informed the New Labour approach to government and all have informed its policies in relation to children and childhood.

Communitarianism

New Labour has drawn on a version of communitarianism espoused by the American sociologist Amitai Etzioni (1993, 1997) which has been explicitly expressed by the leadership (Blair, 1995, 1996) and was advanced by the left-of-centre think tank Demos (Leadbeater, 1996). Appeals to community are seen as a focus for moral renewal, asserting the need to restore to communities their moral voices and requiring a greater emphasis on individuals' responsibilities towards, rather than rights over, their communities. As such, communitarianism attempts to reactivate the institutions of civil society, notably schools and families, into vibrant forms of social regulation and opportunity. The approach is premised on the idea that our initial moral commitments are derived from the families and communities into which we are born, and are reinforced by other forms of community membership. It is argued that no longer should 'the social' constitute the prime focus of government action, because 'society, as a community of communities, should encourage the moral expectation that attending to welfare is the responsibility of the local community' (Etzioni, 1993, p. 146).

Communitarianism is not simply concerned with replacing 'the social' with 'the community', but is premised on the idea that the hold of 'the social' over our political imagination, particularly via the nation (welfare) state, has been weakening. The solution proposed is no longer through a reinvention of 'the social' but through the regeneration of responsible communities prepared to invest in themselves. The community is conceptualised as the key site for explaining and intervening in a range of social problems: 'Community thus emerges as the ideal territory for the administration of individual and collective existence, the plane or surface upon which micro-moral relations amongst persons are conceptualized and administered' (Rose, 1999b, p. 136).

As a result, issues are problematised in terms of the strengths, cultures and pathologies of communities, and strategies are developed to act on the dynamics of communities and enhance the bonds that link individuals to their communities. Central to these strategies are attempts to enhance the connections to the labour market and ensure that the control and discipline of parents in relation to children is strengthened so that they are brought up appropriately.

But as Bill Jordan (1999) has argued, the New Labour approach, while appealing to the spirit of an idealised working-class community, in practice substituted state officials for the informal controls that such communities supplied. Because community was rediscovered in a moral context of panic about the collapse of order and the growing lawlessness of the young, it could not be entrusted with the responsibility for the regeneration of local economies and social support systems. There was a need for top-down authoritarian methods carried out by 'a new brand of bureau-motivator' (Jordan, 1999, p. 202) to stimulate the active, participative yet dutiful claimant or service user to re-establish the common good. Social workers were no longer seen as adequate for the task, being too tarnished by previous failures. It was no coincidence that, during the debate about the Bulger case, the journalist Melanie Phillips (1993), a conservative communitarian in the Etzioni mould, formulated the concept of 'tough love', which was quickly seized upon by a number of politicians. This phrase captures the mixture of charisma and authority required by the new breed of public servants who were to play a key role in the programmes introduced by New Labour. 'Tough love' could be seen to combine the high levels of support needed to lift individuals out of social exclusion, together with the refusal to accept excuses or evasions, in a way which was to become a hallmark of the New Labour approach.

We should also note a central tension, for while New Labour has introduced a range of intensive inclusionary strategies, it has also promulgated strong exclusionary strategies for some, and this is most explicit in relation to its approach to crime. While crime is seen as being primarily caused by processes of social exclusion which must be attacked, crime in the present also disintegrates communities and undermines the forces of inclusion; it must therefore be combated strongly where it arises. We therefore need 'tough' criminal justice and welfare systems which are authoritative and strong on enforcement. The state should provide a role model of what constitutes good parental behaviour. In the process, for those in the community who are seen to pose a particular threat to safety, we should not be afraid to use exceptional measures.

Managerialism and Modernisation

There is both an explicit and implicit managerialism at the heart of New Labour. In many ways, the changes introduced have intensified the new public management approach (Horton and Farnham, 1999) introduced by the Conservative administration from the mid-1980s. Originally, under the Conservatives, the primary impetus was to rein in public expenditure and introduce some of the disciplines of the private sector, via the quasi-market and the introduction of the contract culture. However, the Conservative changes were not simply concerned with trying to improve 'economy, efficiency and effectiveness', but also emphasised the need to make the actions of professionals and the services they provided more 'transparent' and 'accountable' (Power, 1997). What occurred was a significant shift towards giving managers the right to manage, instituting systems of regulation to achieve value for money and thereby producing accountability to the taxpayer and the paymaster, on the one hand, and the customer and the user on the other (Clarke et al., 2000). Under New Labour, the changes have been even more rapid and intensive and have been introduced under the general banner of 'modernising government' (Cabinet Office, 1999; DH, 1998a), where there is a much greater emphasis on the promulgation of a range of new performance targets, inspection regimes and league tables, with the avowed attempt to maximise 'best value' and ensure ongoing effectiveness.

However, New Labour 'modernisation' also has a clear normative inflection, as it has been used to designate ways in which the institutions of government and public services themselves must change to respond to the social changes prompted by globalisation and the increasing demands of the individualised, sceptical citizen-consumer. In doing so, however, the approach has emphasised the importance of rational and scientific approaches in order to get rid of the 'traditional, old-fashioned' practices of the past, which went unquestioned, were associated with the activities of certain vested interests and professional groups and did not put the citizen-consumer at the centre of what they did. Rather than base practices on dogma and tradition, they should be based on evidence and 'what works'. In the process, research and evaluation should aid measurement, audit and thereby contribute to the new form of managerialism (Newman, 2001).

Partnerships, Networks and Joined-up Government

Closely associated with the ideas of managerialism and modernisation has been the notion of 'joined-up' government through partnerships with cross-cutting approaches to solving particularly 'wicked problems'. This has implications for both government departmentalism and assumptions about the state–civil society divide: 'to improve the way we provide services, we need all parts of government to work together better. We need joined-up government. We need integrated government' (Cabinet Office, 1999, p. 5). The notion of 'partnership' has emerged as a central theme for New Labour, both rhetorically and practically, in that it exemplifies the drive to move beyond the old politics of organising public services and is seen to exemplify the pursuit of pragmatic solutions to policy problems which are becoming increasingly complex (Glendinning et al., 2002).

The importance of partnership working and inter-agency coordination had been a key recommendation of all child abuse inquiries since 1973 and had been at the centre of the Children Act 1989; however, New Labour saw such approaches as being fundamental to its whole approach to government more generally, and a key element which made its approach politically distinctive:

> The Third Way recognises the limits of government in the social sphere, but also the need for government within those limits, to forge new partnerships with the voluntary sector. Whether in education, health, social work, crime prevention or the care of children, 'enabling' government strengthens civil society rather than weakening it, and helps families and communities improve their own performance ... New Labour's task is to strengthen the range and quality of such partnerships. (Blair, 1998, p. 14)

Networks of a variety of agencies drawn from the public, private and voluntary sectors have been heralded as alternatives to approaches based on either bureaucracies or markets and are seen as the bedrock of a new form of governance (Clarke and Glendinning, 2002). Thus while partnership can be seen to exemplify an approach which aims for pragmatic solutions to practical policy problems, partnerships are also intrinsically associated with networked forms of governance, where there is an attempt to draw on the new forms of information technology and ideas about ways of 'ordering' the complexities involved in contemporary social and governmental systems (Rhodes, 1997, 2000).

Positive Prevention and Early Intervention

A critique developed by Third Way thinking of the welfare state was that it had been organised on a social insurance principle whereby society insured itself, collectively, against certain risks such as sickness, unemployment and old age. In the process, most health and welfare provision had been established to address problems after the event rather than at their source. The emphasis was on treatment and cure rather than prevention. However, New Labour argued that a much more proactive approach should be adopted in order to address problems before they occurred, and that increasing knowledge of a whole range of individual and social problems meant that actions could be taken before these problems became chronic. Not only would this be better for the people concerned, but also the financial savings to society over the longer term would be considerable.

This emphasis could take a variety of forms. Giddens (1994, 2000) has argued strongly for the notion of *positive welfare*, which attempts to move beyond the Beveridge plan, which aimed to tackle the negative problems of 'want, disease, ignorance, squalor and idleness', and see welfare as a crucial component in promoting both economic growth and individual well-being: 'More generally, we should recognise that the reconstruction of welfare provision has to be integrated with programmes for the active development of civil society' (Giddens, 1998, p. 118).

Another version of prevention is more concerned with identifying 'at risk' groups in the population before the onset of problems and engaging in 'early intervention' before the problems get worse. Such an approach borrows many of its concepts and technologies of calculation and intervention from the public health model of illness, with its emphasis on primary, secondary and tertiary prevention (Freeman, 1999) and its implications for policy and practice, whether in the area of social welfare or crime (Pease, 2002). This approach suggests that there are certain sections of the population or individuals who are at risk and therefore require special attention. Simply treating everyone the same and waiting for the exceptional/crisis situation to occur is simply not adequate; targeting at risk populations with scarce resources via early intervention becomes a key strategy for improving individual and social health in the future.

Combating Social Exclusion

Initially, the most significant way these ideas came together in influencing the New Labour project for social policy was via its approach to social exclusion, a core theme which resonated throughout both its first and second terms of office. One of the first acts of the new government in December 1997 was to set up the Social Exclusion Unit with a strategic relationship to all government departments. It was located in the Cabinet Office, 'putting it at the heart of government'. It has since produced reports on a wide range of issues, for example truancy, deprived neighbourhoods, unemployment, drug use, teenage pregnancy and the reintegration of ex-offenders into society.

There are a number of underlying assumptions which inform New Labour's approach to social exclusion. Firstly, it is seen as emerging from the huge changes arising from global economic and social change, which have impacted considerably on certain communities:

> We came into office determined to tackle a deep social crisis. We had a poor record in this country in adapting to social and economic change. The result was sharp income inequality, a third of children growing up in poverty, a host of social problems such as homelessness and drug abuse, and divisions in society typified by deprived neighbourhoods that had become no go areas for some and no exit zones for others. All of us bore the cost of social breakdown directly, or through the costs to society and public finances. And we were never going to have a successful economy while we continued to waste the talents of so many. (Blair, 2001, p. 1)

Secondly, social exclusion is seen as a series of linked problems. It is a shorthand term for what can happen when 'people or areas suffer from a combination of problems such as unemployment, poor skills, low income, poor housing, high crime, bad health and family breakdown' (Social Exclusion Unit, 2001, p. 11). Thirdly, it is assumed that because of the nature of the problem(s) it is necessary to respond in a joined-up way. Finally, social exclusion is addressed in the context of rights and responsibilities, whereby government makes 'help available but requires a contribution from the individual and the community' (Social Exclusion Unit, 2001, p. 3). As a result, benefits can be withdrawn if job opportunities are not taken up, educational maintenance depends on regular attendance, neighbourhood funding depends on community involvement and so on.

Two key and interrelated elements are seen as indicative of and crucial contributors to social exclusion – unemployment and crime – so that policies which aim to address social exclusion are believed to have a positive impact on both, particularly in the medium and longer term. A variety of factors associated with certain individuals, families, schools and communities are seen as putting certain people 'at risk' of suffering social exclusion: poor parenting; truancy; drug abuse; lack of facilities; homelessness; unemployment; low income and economic recession. While it is recognised that it is difficult to distinguish between risk factors which are causes and those which are effects, the primary and original cause of many problems associated with crime, education and employment is seen to reside with poor parenting. The notion of 'developmental prevention', derived from, among others, the work of David Farrington and Donald West's ongoing study of 411 south London boys between 1961 and 1985 (West and Farrington, 1973; Farrington, 1995), has become a key strategy for addressing the causes of crime and a range of other antisocial behaviour. While the family was to continue as a key site for social intervention, this was reconfigured in quite new ways in terms of a much closer focus on parents and their responsibilities towards children. The New Labour government delineated a three-pronged strategy for countering social exclusion: the *prevention* of social exclusion, the *reintegration* of the excluded and the delivery of *basic minimum standards* available to all. The strategy extends across a wide variety of policies and – as I will demonstrate – has particular implications for policies for children and families.

What we have, therefore, is a particular model of social exclusion which sees the problems of globalisation as resulting in problems of social cohesion brought about by those who have been left behind by economic change:

> It presents 'society' as experiencing a rising standard of living by defining those who have not done so, who have become poorer, as excluded from society, as 'outside it'. (Levitas, 1996, p. 7)

As a result, policy is not concerned with redistribution to aid social and material equality but with integration, where the solutions lie in altering the behaviour and characteristics of the excluded in order to enhance their integration into society or they will be subject to increased regulation and discipline (Levitas, 1998; Veit-Wilson, 1998; Byrne, 1999). The emphasis is on equality of opportunity not outcome.

Children and young people are seen as particularly 'at risk' of social exclusion and are, therefore, identified as in need of special attention. Not only had the numbers of children in poverty trebled between 1979 and the mid-1990s, but they were potentially vulnerable to the effects of divorce, single parenthood and the increasing violence and malaise in communities, and often accounted for a high proportion of crime and disorder. As Giddens (1998, p. 94) argued, 'the protection and care of children is the single most important thread that should guide family policy'.

Promoting Social Investment

This focus on children at the core of welfare reform has been further prompted by an emphasis on social investment at the centre of New Labour policy. Various social policy commentators have recently pointed to the importance of the idea of the 'social investment state' as a helpful means for understanding New Labour's approach to social policy, where concepts more traditionally associated with economics and business are applied to social welfare (Esping-Anderson, 1999; Midgeley, 1999; Jenson and Saint-Martin, 2001, 2002; Esping-Anderson et al., 2002; Hendrick, 2003; Lister, 2003; Fawcett et al., 2004; Featherstone, 2004). Social spending in the past is characterised as having been too passive, too present-oriented and insufficiently focused on anticipated returns on investment. The term 'social investment state' was coined by Anthony Giddens when he argued that welfare provision should focus less on protection against the negative consequences of the market and the life course and more on positive wealth creation and the integration of the individual into the market:

> The guideline is investment in *human capital* wherever possible, rather than the direct provision of economic maintenance. In place of the welfare state we should put the *social investment state*, operating in the context of a positive welfare society. (Giddens, 1998, p. 117)

While calling for a new partnership between families, markets and states, Giddens also challenged the state to develop an entrepreneurship approach which would encourage positive risk taking. Thus security would come from the capacity of the individual to change, which required investing in human capital and lifelong learning. The role of social investment was to encourage a level of skill and flexibility more suited to the labour markets of global capitalism and an ability to withstand and negotiate positively the increasing stresses and complexities of daily life. For social spending to be effective, therefore, it should not be consumed by current needs but should focus on *future* benefits. Where the focus was on present needs, this should be targeted on sections of the population who were marginalised and thus posed a threat to social cohesion and the total social *enterprise*. A focus on social exclusion was thus a necessary current expenditure. However, policies for the socially excluded should be located in a rationale for state welfare spending which was primarily concerned with investments in the future. The balance of welfare spending should therefore shift from a concentration on services which encourage passivity to those which encourage individual responsibility and active, positive risk taking. The priorities should shift from social security benefits to services which are explicitly preventive, promotional and positive, particularly health and education.

In this scenario, the section of the population which would most benefit from investment is children, particularly very young children. As Tony Blair argued in his Beveridge lecture, where he made a commitment to abolish child poverty within 20 years, there needed to be a refocusing of the objectives and operation of the welfare state:

> If the knowledge economy is an aim, then work, skill and above all investing in children become essential aims of welfare ... we have made children our top priority because, as the Chancellor memorably said in his Budget, 'they are 20% of the population, but they are 100% of the future'. (Blair, 1999, p. 16)

Policies for children, therefore, lie at the heart of the New Labour project to refashion the welfare state. In a context where social investment for the future becomes the prime objective, it is not surprising that the Treasury has been the major driving force for introducing many of the changes in children's services, and Gordon Brown, the chancellor of the exchequer, has consistently articulated these themes and made resources available. For example, in his foreword to the 2002 pre-budget report, he wrote that 'our children are our future and the most important investment that we can make as a nation is in developing the potential of all our country's children' (Brown, 2001, p. iv).

Since New Labour came to power, it has introduced a plethora of new policies and made significant changes to long-established ones (see Millar and Ridge, 2002; Skinner, 2003; Pugh and Parton, 2003; Fawcett et al., 2004). These cover:

- *General support for all parents with children*, including increasing the value of child benefit, the introduction of a children's tax to replace the married couples' tax allowance, the introduction of a national childcare strategy, improving maternity and paternity leave.

- *Specific and targeted support for poor families with children*, including the introduction of the working tax credit, the child tax credit and the childcare tax credit; and the special services to aid welfare-to-work under the New Deal initiatives where personal advisors give practical advice and support and there is considerable encouragement and finances available to enter the labour market or take up training.

- A range of initiatives specifically *targeted at disadvantaged children who are 'at risk' of being socially excluded*, particularly Sure Start, Connexions and the Children's Fund.

Investing in children has become a central feature of New Labour's social programme and Ruth Lister (2003) has estimated that, between 1997 and 2002, the real financial value of assistance for children under the age of eleven virtually doubled.

Sure Start

Perhaps the clearest overall exemplar of New Labour's strategy has been the introduction of the Sure Start programme designed for parents and children

under four, announced in July 1998 as part of the government's first comprehensive spending review.[1]

While local programmes were to be universally available for those living in
the Sure Start localities, the localities were to be selected to cover geographical
areas with the greatest need and were eventually to cover 20 per cent of the child
population. The aim of Sure Start was to work with disadvantaged parents and
children to promote the physical, intellectual, social and emotional development of children, in order that they could thrive when they went to school.
It was intended to achieve long-term results, such as better educational performance, lower unemployment, less criminality and reduced levels of teenage
pregnancy.

The programme emerged from one of the government's cross-cutting reviews
as part of the first comprehensive spending review and reflected concerns that
current services for young children appeared to be failing those in greatest
need. A steering group of officials representing eleven different departments,
plus the No. 10 Policy Unit, the newly established Social Exclusion Unit, the
Women's Unit and the Efficiency Unit, was established and was led by Norman
Glass, a senior civil servant at the Treasury. The ministerial steering group
was chaired by Tessa Jowell, the minister for public health but acting in her
own right, rather than as a departmental minister. The steering group com-
missioned a review of research evidence from the Thomas Coram Research Unit
and held a series of seminars, initially hosted by the Treasury, and attended
by researchers and experts in the broad childcare field (see Comprehensive
Spending Review: *Cross Departmental Review of Provision for Young Children:
Supporting Papers Vol 1 and 2*, 1998). The third seminar was attended by the
ministerial group and the report presented by Tessa Jowell to the Cabinet
committee overseeing the comprehensive spending review contained a wide-
ranging review of the state of services and made a number of recommendations.
Norman Glass has summarised the most important conclusions to emerge from
the review as follows:

• The earliest years in life were the most important for child development, and
  very early development was much more vulnerable to environmental influences than had previously been realised.

• Multiple disadvantage for young children was a severe and growing problem,
  with such disadvantage greatly enhancing the chances of social exclusion
  later in life.

• The quality of service provision for young children and their families varied
  enormously across localities and districts, with uncoordinated and patchy
  services being the norm in many areas. Services were particularly dislocated
  for the under-fours – an age group who tended to get missed out from other
  government programmes.

- The provision of a comprehensive community-based programme of early intervention and family support which built on existing services could have positive and persistent effects and lead to significant long-term gain to the Exchequer (Glass, 1999, p. 261).

The steering group accordingly proposed a programme to be called 'Sure Start', which would provide an upgraded level of services to young children and their parents, with an initial expenditure of £200 million a year. The programme was approved by Cabinet to be ring-fenced as part of the budget of the Department for Education and Skills.[2]

We should not underestimate the significance of this development. Not only has the financial commitment grown considerably so that there will be a combined budget for Sure Start, early years and childcare that will be around £1.5 billion by 2005/6 (HM Treasury et al., 2004), with a huge growth in the number of Sure Start and related projects, but it provides a clear insight into the New Labour approach.

The Sure Start programme represented a new way of doing things, both in the development of policy and its delivery. It was a serious attempt to put into practice joined-up thinking, together with emphasis on evidence-based policy making. As Polly Toynbee and David Walker (2001, p. 15) have argued: 'Sure Start became an administrative model for other Labour interventions: a small central unit setting targets for local committees, often made up from but not led by councils.' In addition, the emphasis on the importance of early child development and the impact of multiple disadvantages and their relationship with social exclusion later in life was key. Because of the way the programme was set up and because it received such strong backing from the Cabinet, the chancellor and the prime minister, as well as senior civil servants in a number of government departments, the impact and influence on thinking was much more wide ranging than simply providing the political impetus that established Sure Start itself. It could be seen to both reflect and feed into the heart of the New Labour government.

Speaking in November 2003 at the launch of a Labour Party consultation document setting out the biggest challenges facing Britain following the invasion of Iraq earlier in the year, the prime minister stated that if he had an extra £1 billion to spend, he would spend it on under-fives:

to give them a good chance in life when the evidence is very clear that investment in early years learning is of huge benefit to them both as individuals and to their social responsibility in life. (White and Wintour, 2003)

He said that he had been struck by figures showing that every £4500 invested in a preschool child can produce benefits of over £40,000 to society later, in terms of better school results and greater social responsibility. He argued that, with the traditional bonds of community life eroded, the government needed to think through how it could regenerate a sense of neighbourhood and added 'we have to develop schools as the focal point of local communities so they are available to everyone'.

Conclusion

Since the early 1990s childhood has become the catalyst of both pervasive anxieties about what is wrong with society and a key site for government intervention. What has become much clearer over the past 20 years is that, while there might be disagreement and ambivalence about what to do about the 'family', there is considerable consensus that the prime concern should be the 'welfare' of children, the overriding principle of the Children Act 1989.

However, New Labour has taken this to a higher level of commitment and in the process has moved away from seeing its prime focus as strengthening marriage and the family to one committed to improving the life chances for children. Increasingly, New Labour's main preoccupation has not been the centrality of marriage, the unity of the couple or even the permanence of parental relationships but the need to provide secure and stable arrangements for children (Lewis, 2001). The focus of policy has, therefore, subtly but significantly shifted from a focus on the family to one which is concerned directly with childhood vulnerability and well-being and upholding parental responsibility. Childhood has moved to the centre of policy priorities because it is at the fulcrum of attempts to tackle social exclusion and invest in a positive, creative and wealth-creating future. Policies in relation to childhood have become key to responding to many of the challenges posed by the social and economic changes related to globalisation (Wilkinson, 2001).

Children are seen as having a clear role in the reconstruction of society, both symbolically and practically. Symbolically, they represent a complex metaphor for the duties and responsibilities that all adults should fulfil within their 'families' and 'communities', together with the qualities that should be inculcated into children themselves. And it is in relation to the latter that parents take on their primary role. Whereas previously it was the family that was seen as the central building block of society and a key instrument of government, this is now changing. Because the family has been both deconstructed and disaggregated, children and parents (men and women) are seen to inhabit separate worlds and have separate interests. However, they are also seen as locked together both legally and emotionally, although the lines of accountability have been reframed. As I will argue in Chapter 6, under New Labour it has become quite explicit that parents have responsibilities to children which they must carry out on behalf of the wider community, and it is the child's development which is the overriding concern. In the process, childhood is

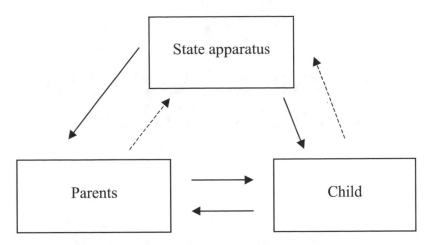

Figure 5.1   The triangular relationship of state–child–parents
Source: Dencik, 1989

taking on a significance which is qualitatively different to what has gone before. Thus, while 'partnering' is seen increasingly as primarily a private matter, subject to individual freedom of action and choice, 'parenting' is very much a public concern and therefore a legitimate site for state intervention.

Sixteen years ago Lars Dencik (1989), a Danish sociologist, argued that when sociologists of the family talked about the family's function in society, it was usually analysed as a two-sided relationship and children were seen as part of a family, with the parents acting as their spokesperson. However, he argued that this was gradually being superseded by a new development that he called an 'eternal triangle', which he represented in terms of a model (see Figure 5.1).

What I am suggesting is that, increasingly, this is the situation we have in England. More profoundly, as I will argue, the notion of 'the triangular relationship' can be seen to represent this emerging scenario in a range of powerful governmental and administrative technologies and mechanisms.

6

'Working Together to Safeguard Children'

From the outset, New Labour made it clear it had a much wider and more proactive approach to policies towards children than simply protecting children from abuse. We can see many of the key themes discussed in Chapter five of its White Paper *Modernising Social Services* published in the autumn of 1998:

> Social services for children cannot be seen in isolation from the wider range of children's services delivered by local authorities and other agencies. The Government is committed to taking action through a broad range of initiatives to strengthen family life, to reduce social exclusion and anti-social behaviour among children, and to give every child the opportunity of a healthy, happy, successful life. Examples of Government action on the wider front include the 'Sure Start' programme, the Crime Reduction Programme, Early Years Development and Child Care Partnerships, and the Green Paper 'Supporting Families'. Children's Social Services must be seen within this wider context. (DH, 1998a)

As the title of the White Paper implied, a major emphasis was placed upon introducing a range of new regulations, targets, monitoring and management systems for local authority social services departments. This was made quite explicit with the launch of the Quality Protects (QP) programme (DH, 1998b), a direct response to the Safeguards Review (Utting, 1997), which invested £885 million between 1999 and 2004 on the basis of detailed annual 'management action plans' (MAPs) from each local authority. At the core of the QP programme were eight broad objectives, together with numerous discrete performance indicators which local authorities had to meet. While a central feature was concerned with improving outcomes for 'looked after' children, particularly in terms of their educational achievements and support for those leaving care (Hayden et al., 1999), the programme was much wider.[1] It was explicitly conceptualised in terms of local authorities' overall responsibilities for 'children in need':

> Quality Protects is about improving the *well-being of children in need* for whom your local authority has taken on direct responsibilities those children who are *looked after*

by your local authority, children in the *child protection* system and *other children in need requiring active support from social services.* Children move in and out of the care system and getting decisions right about when they will benefit from public care and when services should be provided to them while living with their families is an essential part of the programme. (DH, 1998b, para. 5.2, emphases added)

The QP programme was a clear attempt to translate the individualistic, child development focus of the LAC project to the broader canvas of local authority management systems, monitoring and audit (Hayden et al., 1999), in a way which conceptualised local authority responsibilities broadly under the umbrella of 'children in need'. In effect children 'looked after' were a small – but significant and demanding – subset of 'children in need'. This was made quite explicit in *Caring for Children Away from Home: Messages from Research* (DH, 1998c), the summary of 13 Department of Health research studies funded in the light of the increased concerns about children accommodated in residential settings in the 1990s. While the report recognised that it had a 'scarcity of information' in relation to the 'early stages of children's services provision' (children 'in need'), it produced, for the first time, a map of the relationships between the different elements of children's services, and the relative numbers involved out of the total child population.

Figure 6.1 demonstrates that when the progress of a cohort of 'children in need' known to social services was tracked, it seemed that no more than one in twenty were ever 'looked after' away from home. Most continued to live with relatives and were helped by health, education or social services, while a substantial number, perhaps a quarter of a million, managed without any intervention at all. Similarly, about half the 30,000 children who were newly 'looked after' by the state each year were away from home for six weeks or less and, for the majority, whether short or long stay, the service provided was foster placements. It is in this context that the provision of 'family support' and out of home care were seen as part of a 'continuum' which encouraged local and health authorities to treat services as complementary rather than compartmentalised or even in opposition. In the process the focus of concern shifted from 'the protection of children from abuse' to the 'safeguarding and promotion of children's welfare'.

From 'The Protection of Children from Abuse' to the 'Safeguarding and Promotion of Children's Welfare'

This transformation is made clear via a comparison of Working Together (Home Office et al., 1991), published to coincide with the implementation of the 1989

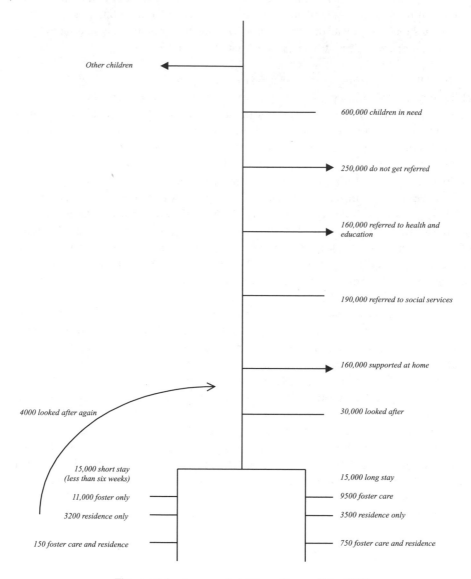

Figure 6.1   A map of children 'in need' in 1998
Source: DH, 1998c

Children Act, and the revised Working Together (DH et al., 1999), published at the end of the decade. The 1991 Working Together was very similar to that published at the time of the Cleveland report (DHSS, 1988), but revised to take into account the 1989 Children Act. As was evident from the subtitle – *A Guide* to *Arrangements for Inter-agency Co-operation for the Protection of Children from Abuse* (Home Office et al., 1991) – the focus of the document was the protection of children from abuse. Its rationale was made clear in the opening paragraph to the Preface:

> It is well established that good child protection work requires good inter-agency co-operation. It is important for all professionals to combine an open-minded attitude to alleged concerns about a child with decisive action when this is clearly indicated. Intervention in a family, particularly if court action is necessary, will have major implications for them even if the assessment eventually leads to a decision that no further action is required. *Public confidence in the child protection system can only be maintained if a proper balance is struck avoiding unnecessary intrusion in families while protecting children at risk of significant harm.* (Home Office et al., 1991, p. iii, emphasis added)

This emphasis on the importance of maintaining a balance between protecting children from abuse and protecting the privacy of the family from unnecessary intrusion – a central dilemma for the liberal state – in the context of the inter-agency *child protection system* permeated the whole document. The focus of the system was 'children *at risk* of significant harm' and thus carrying out a thorough and sensitive 'assessment of risk', drawing on a full range of information and engaging the parents and the child in *partnership*, was key to maintaining confidence. The assessment of 'risk' took on a strategic significance.[2]

While the essential principles at the core of the Children Act provided the legal framework, child protection work in relation to individual cases was clearly identified as a discreet activity proceeding through a number of stages[3] and that:

> The starting point of the process is that any person who has knowledge of, or suspicion that a child is *suffering significant harm*, or *is at risk of significant harm*, should refer their concern to one or more of the agencies with *statutory duties and/or powers to investigate or intervene* – the social services department, the police or the NSPCC. (Home Office et al., 1991, para. 5.11.1, emphases added)

It was clear that the *investigation* and *assessment* of 'significant harm' and the *risk* of 'significant harm' lay at the core of the inter-agency child protection system and that members of the public and other agencies had a responsibility to pass on their concerns to the statutory agencies, in practice social services departments.

However, even though the 1991 Working Together had been rewritten to be consistent with the 1989 Children Act, in the light of the developments and debates of the 1990s, discussed in Chapter 4, the focus and rationale of Working Together was to be transformed. This was most evident in the title of the revised guidance – *Working Together to Safeguard Children: A Guide to Inter-Agency Working to Safeguard and Promote the Welfare of Children* (DH et al., 1999).

As had been the case since 1973, the focus of the 1999 guidance was to clarify and underline the importance of inter-agency work, but whereas in 1991 the focus was 'the protection of children from abuse', in 1999 it was 'to safeguard and promote the welfare of children'. Part 1 underlined the importance of 'working together to support children and families' and began by stating:

> All children deserve the opportunity to achieve their full potential ... if they are denied the opportunity to achieve their potential in this way, children are *at risk not only of an impoverished childhood*, but they are also more likely to experience *disadvantage* and *social exclusion* in adulthood. (DH et al., 1999, para. 1.1, emphases added)

It was argued that while patterns of family life now varied and there was no perfect way to bring up children, good parenting involved caring for children's basic needs, showing them warmth and love and providing the stimulation needed for their development, within a stable environment and where they experienced consistent guidance and boundaries. Because 'parenting' could be challenging, parents required and deserved support. Both statutory and voluntary services should support families by helping all children to develop their full potential: through universal education and health services; by providing specialist help to those who needed it; and by providing support, or otherwise intervening, at times of adversity or crisis:

> In the great majority of cases, it should be the decision of parents when to ask for help and advice on their children's care and upbringing. Only in exceptional cases should there be compulsory interventions in family life: for example, where this is necessary to safeguard a child from significant harm. (DH et al., 1999, para. 1.5)

The guidance clearly framed the issues to be addressed in terms of 'an integrated approach' and the way to proceed was through 'competent professional judgements based on a sound assessment of the child's needs, the parents' capacity to respond to those needs including their capacity to keep the child safe from significant harm and the wider family circumstances' (para. 1.8).[4]

It also stressed that 'shared responsibility' for 'promoting children's well-being and safeguarding them from significant harm depends crucially upon effective information sharing, collaboration and understanding between agencies and professionals' (para. 1.10).[5]

The 1999 Working Together was explicitly revised in the light of *Child Protection: Messages from Research* (DH, 1995a), and the subsequent research on the implementation of the Children Act particularly in relation to family support (DH, 2001), and was framed in terms of the general duty placed on local authorities by the 1989 Children Act to *safeguard and promote the welfare of children*, which had been underlined by Sir William Utting's Safeguards Review (Utting, 1997). In locating the idea of safeguarding in these wider concepts, the guidance also underlined the broader responsibilities involved and this was reinforced by the wider agenda for children's services being implemented by the New Labour government. Social exclusion, domestic violence, the mental illness of a parent or carer and drug and alcohol misuse (Cleaver et al., 1999) were all identified as 'sources of stress for children and families which might have a negative impact on a child's health, either directly, or because they affect the capacity of parents to respond to their child's needs' (DH et al., 1999, para. 2.19).

While the guidance does have a brief discussion of physical abuse, emotional abuse, sexual abuse and neglect and their possible impact on the child, it does not attempt to itemise what might be the key 'signs' and 'symptoms' warranting interventions. It is the concept of 'significant harm', introduced by the 1989 Children Act, which is the 'threshold that justifies compulsory intervention in family life in the best interests of children' and 'the local authority is under a duty to make enquiries, or cause enquiries to be made, where it has reasonable cause to suspect that a child is suffering, or likely to suffer significant harm (s. 47)' (DH et al., 1999, para. 2.16). This directly reflected the arguments put forward by Wendy Rose at the Sieff conference in 1994, which I discussed in Chapter 4, and which lay at the core of the refocusing debate and *Messages from Research* (DH, 1995a). Essentially what might constitute 'significant harm' was *a question of degree*, and it was the impact on a child's development which should be the prime focus, because:

> There are no absolute criteria on which to rely when judging what constitutes significant harm ... sometimes, a single traumatic event may constitute significant harm eg a violent assault, suffocation or poisoning. More often, significant harm is a compilation of significant events, both acute and long-standing, which interrupt, change or damage the child's physical and psychological development. (DH et al., 1999, para. 2.17)

The concept of 'significant harm'[6] was clearly located within the more wide-ranging notion of a child's health and development and was very different to the ideas associated with the battered baby syndrome, which provided the underlying metaphor for concerns and responses to child abuse until the late 1980s. The 1999 guidance made it clear that 'if somebody believes that a child may be suffering, or may be at risk of suffering significant harm [they] should always refer his or her concerns to the local authority social services department' (para. 5.5), but that such concerns should be responded to by social services in the context of their much wider 'responsibilities towards all children whose health or development may be impaired without the provision of support and services, or who are disabled (described by the Children Act 1989 as children 'in need')' (para. 5.5).

For this to take place two developments were required. First, it was no longer adequate to respond to concerns about 'significant harm' in a linear and discreet

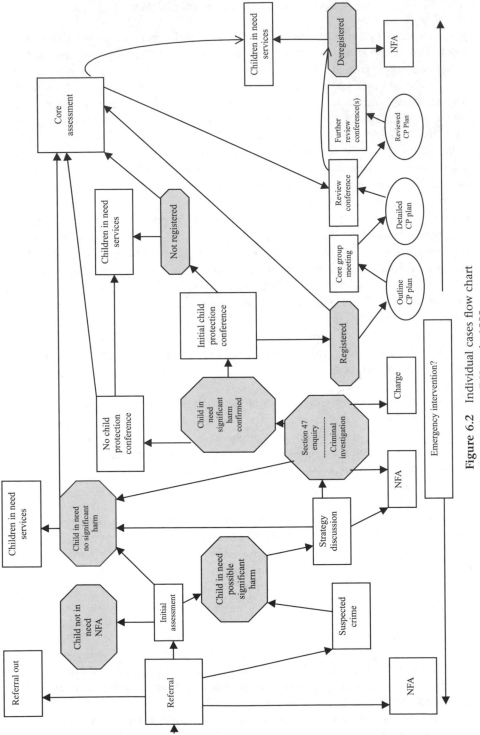

Figure 6.2 Individual cases flow chart
Source: DH et al, 1999

way, as outlined in the 1991 edition of Working Together 'stages of work in individual cases'. If the approach was to be 'integrated', the processes of the work were likely to be more complex, and the key elements and decision points needed to be made more explicit. As a result, and for the first time in England, the 1999 guidance included a flow chart for individual cases in Appendix 5. In many respects this was the first official representation of what an 'integrated' system might look like in relation to individual cases (Figure 6.2).

The second development was to have a more immediate impact. As we noted in Chapter 4, it was argued that if a more integrated system was to develop, in a way which was to seriously 'refocus' child protection and family support, a more rigorous, differentiated and overarching approach to assessment was required. The publication of the 1999 edition of Working Together was combined with the publication of the *Framework for the Assessment of Children in Need and their Families* (DH et al., 2000) and made continual cross-reference to the Assessment Framework to demonstrate how the new approach to Working Together could be conceptualised and operationalised. The two documents needed to be read and used together.

The section of Working Together which was revised the least was Part 8 concerning case reviews, which had been introduced for the first time in 1988. For when a child died, 'and abuse or neglect are known or suspected to be a factor in the death' (DH et al., 1999, para. 8.1), local agencies should consider immediately 'whether there are other children at risk of harm who need safeguarding'.[7] While case reviews were not designed to be 'enquiries into how a child died or who is culpable; that is a matter for coroners and criminal courts respectively to determine, as appropriate' (para. 8.3), the continued inclusion of Part 8 case reviews demonstrated that there were occasions when the more forensically focused concerns about 'learning lessons' when children died were not far away. The public inquiry mentality, which had infused the development of child protection procedures and systems and had been so implicated in the apparent overconcentration on forensic and investigatory approaches, had been far from dispelled. Clearly, agencies and practitioners would continue to need to account for what they did, why they did it and who they communicated with in the process of making decisions as the possibility of a Part 8 case review continued.

'The Framework for the Assessment of Children in Need and their Families'

The Assessment Framework, like Working Together, was issued as guidance under section 7 of the Local Authority Social Services Act 1970, which meant that it 'must be followed' by local authority social services unless there were exceptional circumstances that justified a variation. It thus had the same legal status as, and was incorporated into, Working Together. However, it was not only seen as relevant for those in social services, it was also intended to provide a valuable foundation for policy and practice for all professionals and agencies who managed and provided services to 'children in need' and their families. Taken together, the two documents consisted of 228 pages, compared to the 126 pages of the 1991 Working Together and the nine pages of the original DHSS circular in 1974 on 'non-accidental injury to children', which had first established the framework for the child protection system in England (DHSS, 1974). The Assessment Framework was also supported by the publication of a range of other material which included: practice guidance (DH, 2000a); assessment record forms (DH and Cleaver, 2000); a family assessment pack of questionnaires and scales (DH et al., 2000a); a summary of studies which informed the development of the framework (DH, 2000b); and a training pack which consisted of a video, guide and reader, which alone was 261 pages long (NSPCC/University of Sheffield, 2000). This was thus a very ambitious project which, as a whole, reflected the enormous growth in complexity in trying to provide detailed and codified guidance in this ever changing and high-profile area of work.

The Assessment Framework replaced the previous guidance on *Protecting Children: A Guide for Social Workers Undertaking a Comprehensive Assessment* (DH, 1988), which had only been concerned with comprehensive assessment for long-term planning in 'child protection cases'. The new Assessment Framework aimed to be far more all-inclusive and provided 'a conceptual map which can be used to understand what is happening to *all* children in whatever circumstances they may be growing up' (DH et al., 2000, para. 2.25, emphasis added). The Assessment Framework was

> predicated on the principle that children are children first, whatever may distinguish some children from others. This poses a challenge for staff – how to develop inclusive practice which recognises that *all children share the same developmental needs* to reach their optimal potential but that the rate or pattern of progress of individual children may vary because of factors associated with health and impairment. At the same time, due weight needs to be given to other important influences on children's development. Prominent amongst these are genetic factors, the quality of attachment to primary caregivers and the quality of everyday life experiences. (DH et al., 2000, para. 2.26, emphasis added)

The principles that underpinned the Assessment Framework were that all assessments should:

- be child-centred and therefore rooted in an understanding of child development

- ensure equality of opportunity and adopt an ecological approach
- be based on close inter-agency working, in terms of both approach and the provision of services
- be viewed as a continuing process, not a single event
- be carried out in parallel with other actions and the provision of services
- build on strengths rather than concentrate on difficulties.

The Assessment Framework was an explicit attempt to move the agenda for assessment from one that was almost exclusively concerned with the assessment of risk of significant harm to one which identified impairment in the context of children's development. Both the safeguarding and promotion of a child's welfare were seen as closely intertwined aims for intervention, so that it was important that access to services was via a common route. As Jenny Gray, who had the lead responsibility for developing the Assessment Framework at the Department of Health, argued, the framework:

> was developed on the understanding that assessing whether a child is in need and identifying the nature of this need requires a systematic approach which uses the same framework or conceptual map to gather and analyse information about all children and their families, but discriminates effectively between different types and levels of need. (Gray, 2002, p. 176)

It is clear, therefore, that the Assessment Framework took a much broader view of children's well-being than simply the prevention of abuse or the rescue of children from significant harm. It located the state's responsibility clearly in terms of achieving better outcomes for children in need on the same basis as all children, and required a much higher priority to be placed on achieving children's well-being by all community agencies concerned with children and families. It demanded a higher level of visible investment in children, with a continual monitoring of the impact of agencies, interventions and actions in accordance with the results, and had a focus on the assessment of need as opposed to the assessment of risk. The critical task was to ascertain whether a child was in need and how the child and the parents in the context of their family and community environment might be helped. The effectiveness with which a child's needs were assessed would be key to the effectiveness of subsequent actions and services and, ultimately, to the outcomes for the child. The guidance was a key element in the Department of Health's work to support local authorities implementing the Quality Protects programme for transforming the management and delivery of children's services, particularly objective 7 which aimed 'to ensure that referral and assessment processes discriminate effectively between different types and levels of need and produce a timely service response' (DH, 1988b, p. 16).

It was argued that effective collaborative work, between staff of different disciplines and agencies assessing children in need and their families, could only be achieved if there was a common language to understand the needs of children, shared values about what was in a child's best interests and a joint commitment to improving the outcomes for children. The Assessment Framework aimed to provide such a common language, shared values and commitment among agencies and professionals. It was also planned that the framework would assist the development of 'an integrated children's system', which would provide the basis for a unified approach to collecting and producing management information by the Department of Health.

The Assessment Framework explicitly built on the earlier work by the Department of Health to devise the Looking After Children system (LAC), which had delineated seven developmental dimensions for assessing outcomes for children 'looked after' and which I discussed in Chapter 4. It was claimed that subsequent research had established that these dimensions had been found to be universal for all children (Ward, 1995) and were therefore incorporated into the Assessment Framework (Cleaver et al., 2004).

The framework development team also considered the areas in which adults with parenting responsibilities should function well in order to help their children negotiate the various developmental stages as they grew up (Cleaver et al., 1999). Six dimensions of parenting capacity were identified: basic care; ensuring safety; emotional warmth; stimulation; guidance and boundaries; stability.

Finally, consideration was given to those areas in the wider family and community which were seen to have a direct impact on children's development and parents' abilities to carry out their roles effectively. It was argued that the care and upbringing of children does not take place in a vacuum and a wide range of environmental factors can either help or hinder parental functioning. The key family and environmental factors identified were: family history and functioning; wider family; housing; employment; income; family's social integration; and community resources.

It was argued that the most significant feature of the framework was that it focused on the complex *interrelationships* between the three dimensions, that is, children's developmental needs, parenting capacity (both mother and father) and environmental factors, and it was only by considering all three and the interrelationships between them that it would become possible to assess whether and in what way a child's welfare was being safeguarded and promoted. As the diagram representing the Assessment Framework made clear (see Figure 6.3), what constitutes the nature of safeguarding and promoting the welfare of the child is 'made up' from or derived from the information gathered and the judgements made about these three dimensions. The interactions between the dimensions require careful exploration during assessment, with the ultimate aim to understand and thereby identify the child's developmental

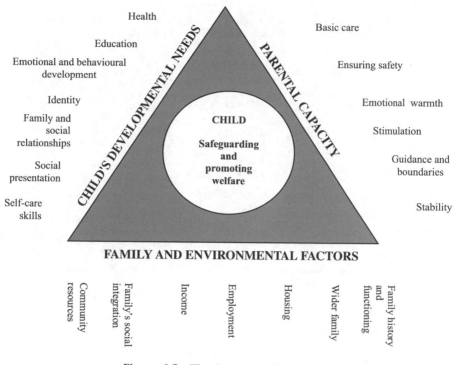

Figure 6.3 The Assessment Framework
Source: DH et al., 2000b

needs within their family context and provide, where appropriate, services which respond to those needs. This was a highly sophisticated model which was supported by a range of research, questionnaires, tools, a training pack and, perhaps most significantly, a powerful conceptual map.

In many respects the approach had the explicit intention of reformulating the way the relationship between the child, the parent and the state was to be thought about. In doing so, it attempted to blur the distinction between the 'public' authority and the 'private' family, which had come in for so much high-profile debate and political opprobrium over the previous 25 years, particularly in the context of a number of child abuse inquiries. As Harriet Ward (2002, p. 26) suggested:

> Once the focus broadens from a somewhat narrow concentration on risk to a more holistic, complementary assessment of the manner in which factors affecting the parents' capacity or the wider family and immediate environment are impacting on the child's developmental progress, then the inter-relationship between interventions becomes apparent. In particular, the emphasis on parenting capacity reinforces the argument that one way in which the state can safeguard the well-being of children is by

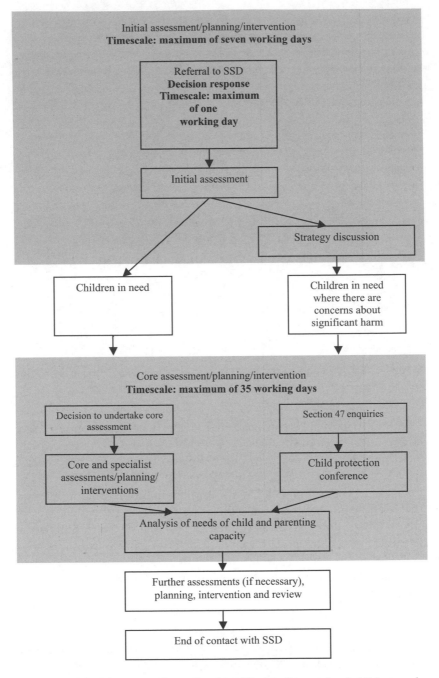

Figure 6.4   Maximum timescales for analysing the needs of children and
parenting capacity
Source: DH et al., 2000b

addressing the needs of parents. The Framework is not concerned with conflicting ideologies around parental responsibility and dependency, but rather with the need to promote and safeguard the well-being of children, regardless of the political context.

The Assessment Framework also had a number of different timescales built into it (Figure 6.4). It was expected that *within one working day* of a *referral* being received, there would be a decision about what response was required. A referral was defined as a request for services to be provided by the social services department, and the response might include 'no action' but that was seen as a decision and should be made promptly and recorded. The referrer should be informed of the decision and its rationale, as well as the parents or carers, and child if appropriate.

A decision to gather more information constituted an *initial assessment* which was defined as a 'brief assessment of each child referred to social services with a request for services to be provided' (para. 3.9). This should be undertaken *within a minimum of seven working days* but could be very brief, depending on the child's circumstances. It should address the dimensions of the Assessment Framework, determining whether the child was in need, the nature of any services required, from where and within what timescales and whether a further, more detailed *core assessment* should be undertaken. An initial assessment was deemed to have commenced at the point of referral to the social services department or when new information on an open case indicated an initial assessment should be repeated. All staff responding to referrals and undertaking initial assessments should address the dimensions of the Assessment Framework.

A *core assessment* was defined as an 'in-depth assessment which addressed the central or most important aspects of the needs of a child and the capacity of his or her parents or caregivers to respond appropriately to these needs within the wider family and community context' (para. 3.11). The timescale for the completion of the core assessment was a maximum of 35 working days from the point that the initial assessment was ended. The core assessment, while it had a broader remit, was seen as having some similarities with the original 'comprehensive assessment' (DH, 1988) which the Assessment Framework was replacing.

Conclusion

Taken together, the 1999 Working Together and the 2000 Assessment Framework can be seen to have considerably broadened the statutory responsibilities of social services departments and the requirements and expectations placed upon other voluntary and statutory health, welfare and criminal justice agencies. All were to be actively involved not just in 'promoting and safeguarding' children's welfare, but in the process of assessment from the initial point of contact. While the Assessment Framework had been developed from the earlier

LAC project, this was not simply for 'looked after' children but any child or family referred to social services. Because both sets of guidance were issued under section 7 of the Local Authority Social Services Act 1970 and thus should be followed unless there were exceptional circumstances that justify a variation, they could be seen to have the effect of considerably redrawing and blurring the boundaries and lines of accountability between the private family and public authorities and between public authorities themselves. The emphasis on gathering, sharing and recording information in a format to aid case assessment and planning went along with an ambitious longer term aim of improving management information and its collation by central government, with the overall aim of implementing an integrated children's system. Such a system would clearly be far more wide ranging, complex and inclusive than the earlier child protection system, which it would replace. In effect, the state, via Working Together and the Assessment Framework, was taking responsibility for promoting and safeguarding the welfare of, potentially, all children, for which the assessment of children's development was key.

These changing responsibilities are evident in Figure 6.5, which was produced as Figure One in the new Assessment Framework. It shows 'how the extent of need can be represented within the context of vulnerable children and all

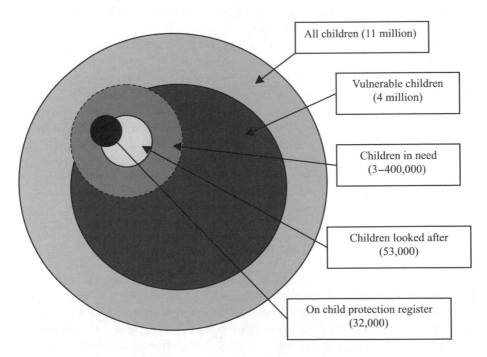

All children (11 million)

Vulnerable children (4 million)

Children in need (3–400,000)

Children looked after (53,000)

On child protection register (32,000)

Figure 6.5   Representation of extent of children in need in England at any one time
Source: DH et al., 2000b

children' (para. 1.6), where 'vulnerable children are those disadvantaged children who would benefit from extra help from public agencies in order to make the best of their life chances'. Four million children lived in families with less than half the average household income (DH et al., 2000b, p. 2, note 1). The figures for children looked after and those on child protection registers were taken from Department of Health statistics in 1999. The information on children in need was based on an estimate of children known to social services at the time. These estimates were subsequently shown to be very accurate. What is noticeable is that the circles are not mutually exclusive or concentric. Children in need includes both children looked after and children on child protection registers. However, it also includes a sizeable minority of vulnerable children and some outside the vulnerable children circle altogether. But the children in need circle is itself broken or porous, indicating that the boundary between 'children in need', 'vulnerable children' and 'all children' is far from clear cut and watertight. Thus, while social services now had statutory responsibilities for all 'children in need', clearly, following Figure 6.5, the boundaries of these responsibilities were not straightforward.

In many respects Figure 6.5 is as important a conceptual map of the thinking informing the Assessment Framework as the triangle in Figure 6.3, for it demonstrated how it was thought these various types and categories of children both related to each other and were 'made up'. It also demonstrated that the Assessment Framework itself would play a key operational role in 'making up' the aggregate statistics for management information systems in the future. Perhaps most crucially, the Assessment Framework and Working Together were designed to play key roles in the way day-to-day practice itself would be constituted for the purposes of making decisions, allocating resources and thereby representing the work in an integrated children's system. A major part of the rationale for both Working Together and the Assessment Framework was to make the work 'transparent', 'auditable' and 'accountable', in the context of the reconfigured and broadened responsibilities for social services departments and other agencies for children in need. In many respects a major purpose behind the changes was not simply to 'refocus' child protection and family support but to give the latter the same status and statutory significance as the former and make it accountable and auditable in an equivalent way.

If there were any doubts about the significance of these developments, they were to be dispelled by the public inquiry in the death of Victoria Climbié. The announcement of the public inquiry was made just as the new Working Together and Assessment Framework were being introduced. At the core of the inquiry was a major concern about how the case had been categorised for the purposes of assessment and intervention by the various agencies involved. Specifically, the inquiry report strongly argued that the case was defined as a 'child in need', as opposed to a 'child protection' case and was taken less seriously as a result. This was seen as a major factor contributing to her tragic death and the report argued explicitly that the prioritisation of work in this way was quite unacceptable. If a child in need was responded to inadequately, particularly if this was done in an unfocused, unsystematic and uncoordinated way, the implications for all the professionals concerned were no different than if the case had been treated as a section 47 investigation:

> It is not possible to separate the protection of children from wider support to families. Indeed, often the best protection for a child is achieved by the timely intervention of family support services. The wholly unsatisfactory practice, demonstrated so often in this Inquiry, of determining the needs of a child before an assessment has been completed, reinforces in me the belief that 'referrals' should not be labelled 'child protection' without good reason. The needs of the child and his or her family are often inseparable. (Laming Report, 2003, para. 1.30)

And perhaps more forcibly:

> the single most important change in the future must be the drawing of a clear line of accountability from the top to the bottom without doubt or ambiguity about who is responsible at every level for the *well-being of vulnerable children*. (para. 1.2, emphasis added)

Many of the 108 general and agency-specific recommendations in the inquiry report, together with the subsequent debate and formal responses to it, were concerned with how such accountability could be improved in the future. What was not in doubt was that it was *the well-being of vulnerable children* which was the overriding concern. I will return to these issues in Chapter 8. However, running in parallel with the changes discussed in this chapter were a number of significant developments in relation to the 'paedophile', and it is to these that I turn in the next chapter.

7
Policing the Paedophile

As I argued in Chapter 2, the 1990s witnessed a significant shift in official concern from intra- to extra-familial abuse. At the centre of these concerns was a growing sense of social anxiety about the nature and impact of 'paedophiles' and the need to develop new ways of containing and policing their behaviour. As I will argue, the media played an important and active role in this process and the 1990s to early 2000s was a key period for legislative change and policy development. In many respects, however, the changes introduced could be seen to run in parallel with those discussed in Chapter 6. While the primary focus there was to try and refocus child protection responses away from a narrow investigatory and forensic concern with risks to the child to one which was more broadly concerned with providing an integrated family support service for children in need and was thus inclusionary in intent, the changes I discuss in this chapter are rather different. Concerns about the assessment and management of risk are central and there is an explicit emphasis on developing practices which are focused on surveillance and monitoring, have the impact, often explicitly, of branding the paedophile as being different to the normal and thus subject to exceptional and, potentially, exclusionary official responses and where the police and probation services play the key roles.

The emergence and transformation of the paedophile into one of the most terrifying threats of contemporary times is itself an interesting reflection on the way social anxieties themselves have changed over the past 30 years (Pratt, 1997, 2000; Simon, 1998; Collier, 2001; Cowburn and Dominelli, 2001). The phrase 'abusive terrorist' used by Sir William Utting in his 1997 Safeguards Review clearly demonstrated that paedophiles had taken on a similar status/threat to any other terrorist. As Philip Jenkins[1] has argued:

> From the late 1970s on, the image of the rather pathetic child molester would be fundamentally altered into a new and far more threatening stereotype; the sophisticated and well-organised paedophile ... [and] was thus brought within the large ambit of sexual violence in general, and serial murder in particular. (Jenkins, 1992, p. 71)

The term 'paedophile' was not included in the *Shorter Oxford Dictionary* in 1973. It was included in *The Times* index for the first time only in 1977 and was used in scholarly works, at the time, to refer to a lone male sexually interested in children. However, by the 1990s, paedophiles were discussed in almost exclusively essentialist terms and were seen not simply as criminal but subject to an incurable and addictively dangerous pathology. As a consequence, they were perceived not simply as 'devious', but as 'evil' and 'monstrous', so that those who committed sexual offences against children should be cast out of the community. They were quite clearly 'other' and different to other criminals. However, because there were no clear identifiers which marked them out, it was crucial that society be ever vigilant about their presence. This posed particular problems for the criminal justice agencies who were charged with protecting the public. In this context and in the wake of a number of tragic and high-profile cases during the 1990s and early 2000s, a variety of increasingly sophisticated and wide-ranging assessment, management and surveillance systems have been introduced which are crucially dependent on the need for greater inter-agency cooperation and the sharing of information, with a view to trying to prevent children being harmed.

Constructing the Paedophile: The Role of the Media

I argued in Chapter 2 that the shift of official concern from intra- to extra-familial abuse during the 1990s was reflected in the changing focus of public inquiries which provided a key catalyst for policy change. As a consequence, public and political opprobrium about child deaths within the family received much less attention. Throughout the period there was a close association between *public* inquiries and whether and how such issues received attention in the media. The Glasgow Media Group's (2001) analysis of media reporting of child deaths within the family (usually involving a parent and/or step-parent) demonstrated that there had been a decline in media coverage of child deaths from a peak in the mid-1980s to 2000. This pattern was replicated in both the popular and broadsheet press, as well as the BBC and ITN news. It is interesting that while the figures for 1999–2000 indicated a slight increase in coverage, this was accounted for primarily by the space allotted to the case of Christopher and Harry Clark.[2]

As coverage of intra-familial child deaths declined from the late 1980s, media attention shifted to the sexual abuse of children, initially in the context of the 'Cleveland affair' and then in relation to the allegations of abuse in Orkney. This was then followed by coverage of abuse in children's homes.

News values played an important role in influencing not just which cases received attention but the way they were framed (Greer, 2003). The cases of child killings which received the most media attention in the 1990s were those where it was assumed that the child had been killed by a stranger,[3] because 'inside the newsroom, deaths at the hands of a stranger are regarded as much more newsworthy' (Glasgow Media Group, 2001, p. 12). This growing furore was to take on a new level of intensity with the death of Sarah Payne and the subsequent campaign by the *News of the World* in 2000, and the murders of Jessica Chapman and Holly Wells by Ian Huntley in 2002. However, media coverage and public concerns about the issue had been growing for a number of years prior to this.

Philip Jenkins (1992) identifies three stages in the emergence of the paedophile issue in the UK up until 1990, and argues that the emergence of the current image (and term) of the paedophile can be dated with some precision to debates that occurred in 1977 and 1978, the first stage, when he argues, three factors were important. First, the foundation of the Paedophile Information Exchange (PIE) in 1974, which explicitly used the term 'paedophile' to proclaim the rights of both men and children to decide on their sexual orientation and behaviour. The group took a libertarian approach and presented itself as part of a radical assault on traditional patriarchy (O'Carroll, 1980; Taylor, 1981). However, it was widely assumed that the group had clandestine motives to manufacture, import and distribute child pornography and create a database of likely victims. Media hostility reached a peak in late 1977/early 1978.

Secondly, this coincided with the establishment of the high-profile National Viewers and Listeners Association led by Mary Whitehouse who vociferously campaigned for controls on child pornography. The campaign received considerable support from all mainstream political parties and the media and secured the passage of the Protection of Children Act 1978 virtually unopposed, making it a criminal offence to produce, import or sell child pornography.

The third factor Jenkins identifies was a series of high-profile court cases where it was assumed homosexuality played a key part in forming elite networks, which often owed their origins to long-standing acquaintance at all-male public schools or Oxbridge colleges, and child pornography was linked not just to homosexuality but also to treason and political corruption. Media accounts of such cases invariably collapsed the categories and images of the homosexual into that of the paedophile and suggested that these activities were not only clandestine but also organised. These developments had the effect of confirming the concerns originally associated with the activities of PIE. While PIE never had a membership beyond 200 and had ceased altogether by 1985 (Plummer, 1995, p. 118), the mere existence of the group ensured that the term 'paedophile' had a meaning and significance with the media and the public which it had not had previously.

The second stage that Jenkins identifies is from 1983 to 1986 when there was an increased awareness of the existence of child sex rings. A range of stories emerged from different parts of the country that paedophiles were molesting and often abducting large numbers of children and, on occasions, murdering them with the intention of making 'snuff movies' and videos. For the first time, the police, often with social services, established specialist teams in some areas to identify and combat these activities.

Jenkins sees the third stage, covering the late 1980s and early 1990s, as the time when paedophilia was seen as a pervasive and major threat and when concerns about sexual abuse were also connected with fears about child murder by 'strangers'. In 1986 the police launched a national investigation, Operation Stranger, into 14 children murdered or missing between 1978 and 1986, reinforced by a police operation against child sex rings in London in 1987. As a result, by June 1987, a number of men had been arrested and in 1989 four, including Sydney Cook and Robert Oliver, were sentenced for the manslaughter of Jason Swift, a teenage male prostitute killed after a 'homosexual orgy with six men'. Paedophilia was now not only seen as clandestine and associated with child sexual abuse but also associated with violence and child murder by strangers. It could strike at any time, anywhere, and no child in the community could be thought safe. As we saw in Chapter 2, however, it was not only children in the community who were seen as vulnerable but also children in certain institutional settings, particularly children's homes. Such exceptional crimes required exceptional responses, one of which was contained in the 1991 Criminal Justice Act.

The 1991 Criminal Justice Act made explicit a sentencing scheme whereby courts could impose a prison sentence on only one of two specified grounds. The first was that the offence was so serious that only custody could be justified. The second was that the offender had committed a violent or sexual offence and a custodial sentence was necessary to *protect the public*. If the court decided that custody was required, the same two criteria would apply when the court moved to fix the length of the prison term. Thus if the crime was a sexual offence, it should be 'for such longer term ... as in the opinion of the court is necessary to protect the public from serious harm from the offender' (s. 2(2)(b)). Section 44 of the Act also extended the supervision of such offenders by the probation service after release from prison. Crucially, *public protection* was seen as an important role for the criminal justice system. While the general tenor of the legislation was based on 'just deserts', this was not applied to violent or sexual offenders.

Public, political and media concerns about paedophiles, however, were to reach a new level anxiety in the mid-1990s. Based on his analysis of paedophile stories in *The Times* from 1990 to 2001 and the *Daily Mail* from 1993 to 2001, Chas Critcher (2003) has argued that while the issue was relatively dormant from 1990 to 1993, recording barely one story a week, coverage was to increase from a total of 44 stories in *The Times/Sunday Times* and 29 in the *Daily Mail/Mail on Sunday* in 1993, to 88 in *The Times/Sunday Times* and 68 in the *Daily Mail/Mail on Sunday* in 1994, and up to 235 in *The Times/Sunday Times* and 175 in the *Daily Mail/Mail on Sunday* in 1996; this level of coverage continued to mid-1997.

The initial peak in 1994 was prompted primarily by the political crisis in Ireland arising from a series of allegations about child sexual abuse in the Catholic Church and, in particular, the persistent attempts by the Taoiseach Albert Reynolds to appoint Harry Whelehan as attorney general when the latter had failed to extradite a Catholic priest to Northern Ireland who was wanted for sexual offences against children. However, the surge in coverage by 1996 arose from events in Belgium when Marc Dutroux, a released paedophile, was arrested and charged with a series of brutal child murders. High-ranking politicians and civil servants were implicated in covering up the case and being part of paedophile networks. Critcher argues that the case became symbolic:

> In a *Times* editorial (22 August 1996), the Dutroux case, linked to sexual killers Rosemary and Fred West and the recent Dunblane massacre, becomes evidence of 'the unfolding horror' of 'behaviour lower than beasts'. Definition of the issue is not complex. 'Paedophilia is of a different order from most other crime, not just in its capacity to shock but in the pathology of its perpetrators'. Compared with other criminals, 'paedophiles follow a different pattern, closer to that of other addicts, and little moved by social pressure or moral restraint'. Paedophiles are 'obsessive and compulsive', psychological treatment is ineffective. A scheme of compulsory registration is justified but public attitudes must be reviewed. 'The nation's values insufficiently safeguard the nation's innocents'. (Critcher, 2003, p. 103)

By mid-1996 the unique threat posed by paedophiles was well established. Beyond this, however, many of the tensions and key elements of 'what to do' were also evident in public, political and media debates. As I noted in Chapter 5, the mid-1990s witnessed an increasing politicisation of issues related to crime and law and order (Nash, 1999). No one could afford to be seen as soft on crime and thus soft on paedophiles.

In March 1996, Michael Howard, the home secretary, proposed legislation to monitor sex offenders in the community, details of which were published in June for consultation (Home Office, 1996). The Sex Offenders Bill was published in December 1996, became law in March the following year, and came into force on 1 September 1997 shortly after the election of the New Labour government.[4] The Act established arrangements for a sex offender register and was designed to monitor and track such offenders (Cobley, 2000; Plotnikoff and Woolfson, 2000). Under Part I of the Act, people convicted and cautioned for most forms of sexual offence were obliged to register their address with the local police within 14 days of moving into a new home. The obligation was to continue for a period ranging from five years to life, depending on the offence and sentence length. Subsequently the 1997 Crime (Sentences) Act introduced a mandatory sentence for a second conviction for a serious violent or sexual crime.

The media were dominated by discussions about the legal changes. There was considerable political consensus about the issue and the two pieces of legislation went through Parliament virtually unchallenged. Only the former Conservative MP Matthew Parris signalled opposition, commenting about the Sex Offenders Bill 'that there is no reason for this Bill. No reason at all. It is simply a piece of electioneering' (*The Times*, 24 January 1997, 'All-party witch-hunt').

However, as Jenny Kitzinger (1999, 2004) has demonstrated, during 1997 both media coverage and public debate shifted rapidly as communities and sections of the media began to agitate for public access to the register and demand that communities be notified when dangerous individuals moved into their neighbourhood. Journalists and pressure groups began actively to campaign for the introduction of the British equivalent of Megan's Law in the USA (Lovell, 2001; Pawson, 2002). This legislation was introduced in 1996 and was named after Megan Kanka, a seven-year-old New Jersey girl, who was raped and murdered by a twice-convicted sex offender who lived across the road (Hebenton and Thomas, 1997). It seemed that public fear and anger, fuelled by an active media, were not satisfied by government attempts to monitor paedophiles in the community. As Kitzinger (1999) has demonstrated:

> Protest rapidly spread from one area to another, and concern quickly escalated: the role of the local press in voicing these concerns was crucial ... the theme of 'paedophiles within-the-community' received extensive regional media coverage across the UK from Aberdeen to Brighton, from Leicester to Belfast, from Teesside to Lancashire. (p. 209)

Articles often included quotations from local residents' groups, which had formed in response to the paedophile threat. However, many newspapers adopted a more proactive role and assumed the role of guardians of public safety. For example, Robert Oliver, convicted of the brutal sexual assault of Jason Swift, was repeatedly pursued by journalists on his release from prison in October 1997. The *Sun* asked readers to phone an emergency number if he was spotted and as a consequence he was driven out of Swindon, but when he moved to Brighton, the local paper published his picture on its front page, with the headline 'Beware this evil pervert' (*Evening Argus*, 14 October 1997, cited in Kitzinger, 1999). In other cases newspapers alerted people to the presence of paedophiles either by knocking on the doors of neighbours and asking how they felt living next door to a convicted sex offender or printing photographs and details of offenders with their last known address. The Scottish *Daily Record*, for example, published a double-page spread of 38 photographs in February 1997, together with the names of the convicted offenders and details of their offences (Kitzinger, 2004). While we can see such developments as contributing to a strong 'authoritarian populism' (Bottoms, 1995) in relation to the issue, it is also important to recognise that there were a number of tensions which lay at the core of the government response. While the government was keen to demonstrate that it was taking the threat posed by paedophiles seriously, it was also trying to ensure that law and order did not break down in the communities where paedophiles lived. While it wanted communities to be vigilant, it did not want to encourage vigilantism.

Protecting the Public

By the time New Labour came into power in 1997, the issue of protecting the public had become a central preoccupation and aim of criminal justice policy. It was driven by two overlapping imperatives. First, the protection of the public from the risk of serious harm, both physical and psychological, posed by violent offenders; and, second, the desire to respond more effectively to the growing perceived risk presented by paedophiles, associated with the increase in child sexual abuse in a range of settings outside the family (Grubin, 1998). Both concerns gave rise to legislative and policy changes that aimed to extend the use of custody for dangerous offenders via the use of preventive sentencing and selective incapacitation on the grounds of risk (Feeley and Simon, 1994; O'Malley, 1998; Kemshall and McIver, 2004), and extended the monitoring and surveillance of sexual offenders in the community and on release from prison, including the use of registers and tracking systems (Hebenton and Thomas, 1996, 1997; Thomas, 2004b). The Crime (Sentences) Act 1997 and the Sex Offenders Act 1997 were key elements of the approach.

However, because the Sex Offenders Act was not retrospective, it was estimated that approximately 100,000 sex offenders cautioned or convicted prior to the implementation of the Act on 1 September 1997 were not covered by the registration arrangements, thus leaving them outside the remit of the registration procedures (Home Office, 1997b; Marshall, 1997). Partly in response to these concerns and in an attempt to reassure the media and the public, the government introduced the sex offender order in the 1998 Crime and Disorder Act. The order was designed for all convicted sex offenders in the community who were not required to keep their details up to date under the register. The sex offender would not automatically be required to start registering, but if a 'trigger event' came to the attention of the police, for example someone acting suspiciously near a playground or school, and the police knew they had previous convictions for sex offences against children, an application could be made to a court for a sex offender order. The order would require the person to register, and would also lay down areas of the community they could not enter and/or lay down activities to be desisted from because of the risk they posed to children.

While sex offender orders were juridically constituted, in that they required an application to and the presentation of evidence to court in relation to those who had previous convictions or cautions for sexual offences, they departed from a juridical conception of the individual as they were explicitly risk-oriented and had public safety as their overall aim. While they referred to previous infringements of the law in making a distinction between those who could be classed as sex offenders and those who could not, their main purpose was protection from _future_ harm through _prevention_ by the assessment of risk (Ashenden, 2002). Sex offender orders could be applied for where a sex offender's

> behaviour in the community gives the police reasonable cause for concern that an order is necessary to protect the public from serious harm from him. There is no test of serious in respect of the actual behaviour, which has to be considered only in terms of its relevance for _future_ offending. (Home Office, 1998a, s. 2, para. 2.4.2, emphasis added)

The notion of preventing future harm to the public, through the assessment and management of risk in relation to offenders who are seen as posing an exceptional threat, lies at the core of recent attempts to protect the public and the introduction of sex offender orders exemplifies this. Thus 'while there is a difficult balance to be struck between the rights of the defendant and the need to protect the community, the need for such orders is dictated by the importance of protecting the public, in particular children and vulnerable adults (Home Office, 1998a, para. 2.4.3).[5]

This increased emphasis on public protection during the 1990s was crucially dependent on the development of new ways of thinking, organising and operating in the criminal justice agencies themselves. Two key elements were the introduction of new arrangements for sharing and managing information in the context of an increased emphasis on multi-agency cooperation, together with the rise and institutionalisation of new forms of risk assessment (Kemshall, 1996, 2001).

Much of the early impetus for this came from the probation service, in response to sustained government attack from the late 1980s about its overly welfarist ideology and its alleged lack of effectiveness in reducing reoffending (Worrall, 1997; Raynor and Vanstone, 2002). In their search for new ways of demonstrating the value and effectiveness of the service, local probation managers began to seek improvements in ways to identify and supervise offenders who might pose a serious threat of harm to the public. Formal risk assessment increasingly became standard practice during the 1990s, both in the preparation of pre-sentence reports and in advance of the supervision of prisoners released on licence. Probation services also began to engage in much closer liaison and information sharing, initially with prisons, but increasingly with police, social services and other agencies (Maguire et al., 2001).

A small number of probation services began to place this cooperation on a formal basis by brokering formally constituted public protection panels (PPPs), which met regularly to exchange information, assess the level of risk and formulate plans in relation to those identified as potentially dangerous offenders

(PDOs). The number of such panels grew from the mid-1990s as other areas followed their lead (Kemshall and Maguire, 2001). They also expanded in size and scope, with most including senior representatives from the probation service, the police, social services, housing departments and health authorities as well as voluntary organisations. While initially the main focus was on offenders leaving prison under a statutory probation licence, many panels also began to consider cases of individuals who were thought to be dangerous but who were under no statutory control, with cases being brought to the panel by any of the partner agencies. It seems that while convicted violent and sexual offenders remained the most frequent objects of their attention, the panels also discussed potentially dangerous offenders of many kinds, including suspected offenders who had never been convicted (Kemshall and Maguire, 2001).

However, following the introduction of the sex offender register in 1997 and the furore in the media about community access to the register, it became clear that the legislation gave no clear guidance to the police on what they should do with the information collected, nor did it deal directly with the controversial issue of disclosure. The issue of 'community notification' had been debated in Parliament at the committee stage of the Bill but it had been decided to leave this to the discretion of the police (Thomas, 2000, pp. 111–12).

The Home Office published guidance on the new law for the police in England, Wales and Northern Ireland (Home Office, 1997b), with similar guidance published by the Scottish Office for Scotland (Scottish Office, 1997a). Further guidance was sent to local authority social services and social work departments (NHS Executive 1997; Scottish Office, 1997b). The stated intention was that the guidance should be considered as 'interim' whilst further work continued on drawing in other agencies, such as housing departments and schools.[6] The Home Office interim guidance (Home Office, 1997b) limited itself to taking practitioners through the Act and its implications but had little to say on the resource implications for the police or how, in relation to the register, they should verify that correct addresses were being notified or how they would be given advance notice that a new name was to be added. While the courts and prisons were willing to routinely advise the police each time a new name was added, doctors and healthcare professionals were more reluctant. They interpreted the Act as putting duties and responsibilities on the offender only, and it followed, therefore, that the offender should consent to them notifying the police, and that they would override a withholding of consent only if they judged it to be in the public interest (Thomas, 2000, p. 116).

In this complex situation and in the light of the Home Office guidance, Kemshall and Maguire (2001) argue that the way practice developed by the late 1990s was that: in consultation with the local probation service, police forces would undertake a risk assessment of every offender who registered; where the level of risk was considered high enough to require it, a plan would be drawn up to 'manage' the risk and appropriate information and tasks would be shared with other agencies; and decisions on whether to notify other organisations, private individuals or a whole community would be made by the police on a case-by-case basis, taking into account their duty to prevent crime, as well as the law on data protection and the relevant Articles of the European Convention on Human Rights.[7] While the new procedures applied only to sex offenders rather than potentially dangerous offenders as a whole, and the prime responsibility for their implementation fell to the police rather than the probation service, most areas responded to the Sex Offender Act by either wholly or partially integrating the two sets of arrangements into a general multi-agency system of risk assessment and management. Many areas systematically 'risk assessed' whoever came to their attention as potentially dangerous offenders and maintained shared databases of PDOs akin to those held on officially registered sex offenders (Kemshall and Maguire, 2001, p. 242). However, practice varied widely. At one extreme, multi-agency panels took on all new cases on the sex offender register, in addition to potentially dangerous offenders, while at the other extreme they dealt only with the highest risk cases of any kind and thus left the bulk of sex offender cases to the police (see Maguire et al., 2001). The register itself was held on the police national computer which was available to all forces in the UK. It came on line on 1 September 1997 and by the end of the year 88 per cent of offenders had notified the police of their whereabouts – 3365 out of a possible 4524 (Thomas, 2000, p. 117).

The follow-up to the interim guidance was published in draft form in August 1999 and aimed to 'draw upon the good practices' established since the 1997 Act came into force (Home Office PSTU, 1999). The guidance reaffirmed the idea that information exchange between agencies was to be integrated into risk assessment and management systems and was not to be seen as an end in itself. It also emphasised the principle that information sharing should be rooted in the powers and duties of any agency and not be exchanged simply because another agency requested it. The police and other agencies were encouraged to draw up inter-agency protocols outlining how information would be shared. However, the murder of Sarah Payne the following summer and the high-profile campaign carried by the *News of the World* demonstrated that the issues were far from resolved.

The death of Sarah Payne and the *News of the World* campaign

Just as Parliament was going into its summer recess and children were breaking up from school for their long summer holiday, the naked body of Sarah Payne was found dead in a Sussex field on 17 July 2000. The *News of the World* Sunday newspaper immediately began a major campaign to name and shame paedophiles by printing 49 photographs, together with names, towns and districts where they were living, along with brief details of their offences and convictions, promising to publish details on all 110,000 child sex offenders they believed to be in the community.[8] The newspaper asserted that 'the murder of Sarah Payne has proved police monitoring of these perverts has failed', demanded that paedophiles sentenced to life should never be released and outlined Megan's Law in the USA. The story was to dominate the media throughout the summer.[9]

Other newspapers and sections of the media were more equivocal or openly hostile to the *News of the World* campaign; however, the 30 July edition of the paper continued in a similar vein. Another set of sex offenders was 'named and shamed' and the paper continued to demand 'real' life sentences, as well as explicitly demanding that 'every parent had a right to know if there is a convicted paedophile living in their neighbourhood' through open access to the sex offenders register, which the newspaper termed 'Sarah's Law' following Megan's Law (Thomas, 2003). A *News of the World* editorial rebutted criticisms of its campaign and gave much emphasis to a scheduled meeting between the paper, the Association of Chief Police Officers (ACPO), the Association of Chief Officers of Probation (ACOP), the National Society for the Prevention of Cruelty to Children (NSPCC), and the National Association for the Care and Resettlement of Offenders (NACRO). The paper described the meeting as a 'summit on Sarah', called to determine 'ways in which we can better protect our children'. As Critcher (2002a) has demonstrated, other newspapers began to shift their position and admitted that the campaign had considerable public support and could no longer be dismissed. An *Observer* feature argued that 'today the *News of the World*'s latest perverts' gallery will be condemned by the chattering classes and its editor will go on insisting that she, not they, are in tune with the public mood. She is probably right' (cited in Critcher, 2002a, p. 523). Perhaps even more significantly, the *Mirror*, the main competitor of the Rupert Murdoch-owned, popular daily paper the *Sun*, the sister paper of the *News of the World*, came out in support in a special edition on 3 August.

On 6 August the *News of the World* extensively reported the outcome of the 'summit'. The newspaper agreed to suspend its 'naming and shaming' campaign on the basis that the other organisations had signed up to Sarah's Charter. While the newspaper claimed that the charter included its two main demands for indeterminate sentences and public access to the sex offenders register, disclosure was to be controlled to 'responsible members of the public', with stiff penalties for misuse, and indeterminate sentences would only follow after a 'risk assessment process'. However, when, where and how often offenders registered would be more closely specified.

Efforts to find a compromise had been intensified because, following the 'naming and shaming' of Victor Burnett who admitted to the abuse of 140 children and claimed to be 'on the verge of reoffending' in the *News of the World* of 30 July, the situation on the Paulsgrove estate in Portsmouth where he lived had posed a major threat to public order. There had been a march of angry residents to his home and a week of angry protests ensued. A list of around twenty alleged paedophiles had circulated among a group calling themselves Residents against Paedophiles and protestors had demonstrated outside the homes of suspected paedophiles, daubing slogans on their walls, issuing threats, overturning and burning cars. The protestors had included children carrying banners such as 'Don't house them hang them' (photograph in *The Independent on Sunday*, 13 August 2000). The protests received massive coverage in all sections of the media and were subject to considerable critical debate. Several families fled, one convicted paedophile went to ground and two alleged paedophiles committed suicide (Ashenden, 2002). Other protests took place in other parts of the country.

While it defended its actions, the *News of the World* campaign was seen to have unleashed an outbreak of vigilantism and mob rule which was roundly condemned. At the same time, the revelations that paedophiles had been rehoused on the Paulsgrove estate without residents' knowledge made their actions understandable. The *Guardian* talked of the chasm that divided the 300 or so estates like Paulsgrove from the more affluent, sheltered parts of Britain where calmer discussion prevailed, and the *Daily Mail* commented that 'lynch law only flourishes when public policy and public opinion are out of balance' (cited in Critcher, 2002a, p. 524). While the nature of vigilantism was deplored, its vehemence seemed to sharpen the debate. What the protests demonstrated was that while parents, particularly mothers, were expected to take responsibility for their children's safety, making judgements about what was an appropriate risk and communicating to their children what was safe and what was not safe, they were not being given the information to do so. In effect 'the community' was given major responsibilities for their children but in a context where they were not in receipt of the information whereby this could be done. As a consequence, it seemed that trust between a significant number of parents and the authorities had all but broken down. The authorities were placing paedophiles in their midst unbeknown to the parents who lived there (Bell, 2002).

The gap between public policy and public opinion was further underlined in an opinion poll published in the *News of the World* at the end of August, showing a large majority for the introduction of indeterminate sentences and Sarah's Law, and the collection of 700,000 names on a petition supporting the changes was presented to the home secretary.[10] In mid-September the home secretary met with the parents of Sarah Payne whose death, he said, 'had touched everyone's lives' and, via a press release, outlined the government's new proposals, but at no point made any reference to the *News of the World* campaign (Home Office, 2000).[11]

However, the Home Office did not give way on the central parts of the *News of the World* campaign for indeterminate prison sentences for all sex offenders and unlimited access to information on the register. The existing arrangements for 'controlled disclosure' were to continue. What was to be introduced was a new mandatory duty placed on the police and probation service to establish formal arrangements for assessing and managing the risks posed by sex offenders. No longer was this to be left to local discretion. These were to be called multi-agency public protection arrangements (MAPPAs). All the new proposals were included in the Criminal Justice and Court Services Bill, which had been published in March 2000 but which had not completed its parliamentary process.

These various changes and extensions in the sex offender legislation can be seen as an attempt to provide an accommodation between the overtly moral, populist and political demands of sections of the press and the associated vigilante action within certain communities and attempts to develop a managerialist, rational and risk-based response to the threats posed by paedophiles (Evans, 2003). The naming and shaming of paedophiles within the popular press and among specific communities had aimed to eliminate danger by exposing and/or hounding out the 'evil' and 'monstrous' from within the community, and 'its imagined ideal is that of safety through exorcism of the dangers posed by paedophiles and the achievement of a pure community' (Ashenden, 2002, p. 215).

In contrast, the measures introduced by the government from the early 1990s onwards, and epitomised by the requirement to establish MAPPAs in 2001, attempted to manage risk through knowledge and the containment of individuals considered to be a threat (Kemshall and Maguire, 2003; Maguire and Kemshall, 2004); they aimed to govern risk through predictive knowledge of individual behaviour. The response was

> a technical and administrative response to a problem of social order; it operates under the image of a disciplined society and its imagined ideal is that of a secure society to be achieved through the prevention of harm, where this is premised on the management and regulation of risk by professionals. Within this strategy, therefore, there is an attempt to turn the danger posed by paedophiles into governable risk. (Ashenden, 2002, p. 215)

However, both responses assert that protecting the vulnerable is of greater importance than individual liberties and, in response to paedophilia, override the premises of a liberal order in significant ways. As Critcher has argued, the *News of the World* campaign not only had a significant effect on the position taken by the pressure groups who signed up to Sarah's Charter but also the government itself. While remaining opposed to Sarah's Law, it conceded on many of the procedural reforms and was clearly considering wider ones. These became apparent during reports on the trial of Roy Whiting who was convicted of the kidnap and murder of Sarah Payne on 12 December 2001. Indeterminate sentences, detention of those with a 'severe personality disorder' and disclosure to juries of previous related offences were all being actively considered.[12]

By 2001 political and media debate was almost completely dominated by the need to develop measures to deal with the exceptional threat posed by paedophiles either in the community or in a variety of institutional settings. Very rarely was there any recognition that the majority of murders and sexual assaults on children were usually perpetrated by fathers, uncles, stepfathers and grandfathers and other men known to the child (La Fontaine, 1990, 1994; Grubin, 1998; West, 2000; Pritchard and Bagley, 2001).

The role of the media was central in helping to frame public debate and influence the political and legislative agenda. From 1973 media stories about child abuse were prompted by particular 'scandals'. While this was initially focused on physical abuse within the family, by the late 1980s the focus was also concern about sexual abuse. However, prompted by the Cleveland and Orkney affairs, this was initially more concerned with the state overinterven-ing in the 'privacy' of the family (Gough, 1996; Franklin and Parton, 2001). Subsequently, the 1990s were dominated by stories about sexual abuse, but sexual abuse outside the family (Kitzinger and Skidmore, 1995; Skidmore, 1995, 1998; Kitzinger, 1996, 2004), initially in children's homes and schools but by the end of the decade almost exclusively by 'strangers' (Gallagher et al., 2002) in the community. Those who perpetrated such 'perversions' were characterised as 'paedophiles' who posed a significant violent as well as sexual threat.

Throughout the period we can note a close, almost incestuous, relationship between 'public' inquiries and the media, for both have impacted significantly on the way both public perceptions and public policy have developed. However, the media campaigns about paedophiles were not prompted by public inquiries. While the death of Sarah Payne and the subsequent trial of Roy Whiting were crucial to the campaign launched by the *News of the World*, the template for the campaign and the demands it was making for policy change were more independently generated and were informed by changes in America concerned with Megan's Law. The media, rather than simply reflecting and shaping public debate via their reporting of public inquiries, could be seen to be actively trying to change public policy in a more independent way, and in the process could be seen to voice a range of concerns of parents in the community rather than the views of various experts and researchers. While the government tried to establish a compromise, in the process, it put increasing responsibilities on the police and probation services to assess and manage risk. In effect, child abuse, through its close association with the paedophile threat, had become increasingly construed as a public protection as opposed to a child welfare issue as far as public policy was concerned.

In summary, concerns and knowledge about child sexual abuse had become more prevalent by the late 1990s and the media had played a key role in bringing this about.[13] However, anxieties about keeping children safe had become almost exclusively projected onto fears about paedophiles in the community (Evans, 2003). In transforming concerns about child sexual abuse into a public protection issue, the prime responsibility for doing something about it increasingly became the responsibility of the police and the probation service.

Multi-Agency Public Protection Arrangements

The Criminal Justice and Court Services Act 2000 came into operation on 1 April 2001. For the first time it imposed a statutory duty on the police and the probation service to work together to protect the public from sexual and violent offenders and other offenders who might cause serious harm to the public. No simple definition of either of the first two categories was provided and the third category was deliberately wide to ensure that no offender who might pose a risk of serious harm to the public was excluded. The initial guidance (Home Office, 2001) which the home secretary issued on the new multi-agency public protection arrangements (MAPPAs) required the police and the probation services, as the 'responsible authorities', to establish, in each of the 42 areas of England and Wales, systems and procedures:

- for sharing information and for inter-agency working on all the relevant offenders

- to ensure that those offenders assessed as potentially posing the highest risk were referred to a multi-agency public protection panel (MAPPP)

- for the operation of the MAPPP

- to monitor, review and, if necessary, revise the arrangements

- to consider resource allocation, multi-agency training and community media communication

- to produce an annual report on the public protection arrangements and how this was being discharged.

The sharing of information, together with the assessment and management of risk, lay at the heart of the arrangements in order to prevent future harm to the public. The guidance required the police and probation service to negotiate the involvement of social services, health and local authority housing and perhaps leisure services as well as working closely with the prison service. Essentially, the assessment and management of risk was seen to start with the collation and sharing of information, because:

> The timely exchange of clear, accurate, reliable and relevant information is essential to the speedy identification of offenders who may pose serious risks to the public. The

new arrangements strengthen those already in existence: when an agency becomes aware of an individual who might present a serious risk of harm, that agency will share details of that person with other partner agencies within existing public protection protocols. Simultaneously, it will also gather any information held within its own agency from the area where the offender previously lived or was held. With a clear understanding of an offender's history and current circumstances, a thorough risk assessment is then undertaken. (National Probation Service, 2003, p. 11)

Risk assessments would result in offenders being placed in one of four categories: low, medium, high or very high, and would identify the factors that placed an offender in a particular risk category. This should enable the police, probation and other agencies to target those factors and thereby effectively and safely manage the risk. Typically, where the risk was assessed as low or medium, offenders would be managed through the 'normal' mechanisms and might include probation supervision and registration as a sex offender. In cases in which the risk was assessed as being high but not the highest, inter-agency work should enable effective risk management. Only in a very few cases, in which the risk was assessed as being very high, was it envisaged that an agency would refer a case to a MAPPP. In such situations, the MAPPP would aim to ensure that joint agency discussion, planning and management would take place. Effective management of risk was seen to depend on good supervision which comprised imposing the right conditions and enforcing them. A failure to keep to the conditions would lead to probation taking enforcement action which might result in custody.[14]

In late 2002 the Home Office produced a White Paper *Protecting the Public: Strengthening Protection against Sex Offenders and Reforming the Law on Sexual Offences*, which formed the basis of the Sexual Offences Act 2003. The primary purpose was to update the law on consent to ensure that the criminal law protected everyone equally from non-consensual sexual activity, but did not criminalise sexual activity that took place between consenting adults in private.[15] The government also announced its intention to develop a new database to be known as ViSOR (violent and sex offender register), which would give the police and probation services better access to the full range of information held on dangerous offenders nationally, including all sex offenders. Following the review of the Sex Offenders Act 1997, announced in the summer of 2000, the new legislation also tightened up the notification requirements of the register. If a registered sex offender changed his name or address, he must tell the police within three days, rather than fourteen days as previously, and he was required to tell the police if he spent seven days or more in a calendar month at any other address, rather than fourteen days as before.

We can thus see the various legislative changes and the introduction of MAPPAs[16] in particular as taking further the trend which had been evident over the previous ten years in fundamentally shifting the balance between respecting an individual's rights to privacy and freedom, on the one hand, and the need to protect the public on the other, in favour of the latter (Matravers, 2003). Even so, while the exchange of information between agencies had become central to the risk assessment and management process, it still needed to comply with the Data Protection Act 1998 and the Human Rights Act 1998. This was a particularly sensitive issue in the light of events in Paulsgrave and the calls for Sarah's Law (Power, 2003). A decision to disclose information to a 'third party' would thus only be taken as part of a carefully managed process, which would require the proposed disclosure to be authorised by a senior police officer, who must assess each case on its merits and deem it necessary for the protection of the public. Such disclosure also had to be part of a risk management plan.

Soham and Intelligence Systems' Failures

The question of when and to whom it was appropriate to disclose information in order to ensure public protection was to become a huge issue in late 2003, following the conviction of Ian Huntley for the murder of Jessica Chapman and Holly Wells in Soham in the summer of 2002. While the nature of the circumstances and the specifics of the case were somewhat different to the murder of Sarah Payne by Roy Whiting, the furore it unleashed and the questions it raised about the competency of the police and the social services departments involved were to have wide-ranging reverberations.

Ten-year-olds Holly Wells and Jessica Chapman disappeared from the Cambridgeshire village of Soham on 4 August 2002. Their disappearance prompted one of the biggest police 'manhunts' ever carried out. The story received huge media attention, with the *Sun* and the *News of the World* offering a £150,000 reward a week after their disappearance and Express Newspapers offering £1 million for information leading to the conviction of the person who abducted them. The two girls' bodies were eventually found on 17 August and Ian Huntley, the senior caretaker at a local school, and Maxine Carr, Ian Huntley's girlfriend and a teaching assistant at the school which the girls attended, were arrested for their murder.[17] On 17 December 2004, Ian Huntley was convicted of their murder and sentenced to two life sentences. Maxine Carr was found guilty of conspiring to pervert the course of justice by giving Hartley a false alibi but she was cleared of the more serious charges of assisting an offender.

However, it had emerged that Huntley had previously been suspected of nine sex crimes, many involving underage girls, but none had ever led to a conviction, when he had lived in the Grimsby area, covered by the Humberside police and northeast Lincolnshire social services. Within hours of Huntley's conviction, David Blunkett, the home secretary, announced an inquiry into what he described at the 'shocking and horrendous' failures which had not stopped Huntley from taking up his job as a caretaker. The inquiry, chaired by Sir Michael Bichard, was to inquire into child protection procedures in the Humberside police and Cambridgeshire constabulary and in particular 'to access the effectiveness of the relevant intelligence-based record keeping, the vetting practices in those forces since 1995 and information sharing with other agencies, and to report to the Home Secretary on matters of local and national relevance and make recommendations as appropriate'. The inquiry took evidence between 13 January and 30 April 2004 and the report was published on 22 June 2004. At the core of the inquiry was the sharing of 'soft' non-conviction information by the police and also social services, particularly in relation to pre-employment screening arrangements for jobs with children. Such arrangements had been introduced in 1986 and refined on numerous occasions since (Smith, 1999; Thomas, 2004a). The primary focus of the inquiry was on how information or intelligence was recorded, retained, used, stored and deleted within the framework established by the data protection legislation.

The statement at the beginning of the Bichard Inquiry Report (2004, para. 6) that:

> The Inquiry did find errors, omissions, failures and shortcomings which are deeply shocking. Taken together, these were so extensive that one cannot be confident that it was Huntley alone who 'slipped through the net'

was reflected in the way the inquiry was reported in all sections of the media and captured in the national press the following day (23 June 2004): 'There May Be More Huntleys Out There' (*Daily Mirror*); 'How many more Huntleys?' (*Daily Mail*); 'A catalogue of failure that led to murder' (*Guardian*). One of the key failings was the inability of the Humberside police and northeast Lincolnshire social services to identify Huntley's behaviour pattern soon enough because both viewed each other in isolation and social services failed to share information effectively with the police. There were also 'systematic and corporate' failures in the way in which Humberside police managed their intelligence systems (Bichard Inquiry Report, 2004, para. 8). The inquiry concluded that the problems arose, at least in part, from a widespread failure to appreciate the value of intelligence, particularly within Humberside police.

The inquiry made a series of recommendations. First, that there should be a new system for registering those wanting to work with children and vulnerable adults, perhaps evidenced by a licence or card, which would be constantly updated to indicate when police forces held intelligence on an individual.[18] The register would be easily accessed, subject to security protection, by any employees, including parents employing tutors and sports coaches. Second, the introduction of a national police IT intelligence system, with the Home Office taking the lead. Third, clear guidance on record creation, retention, review, deletion and the sharing of information, particularly in relation to non-conviction-related information. Fourth, that more training should be made available, particularly to school governors and head teachers, to ensure that interviews to appoint staff reflected the importance of 'safeguarding children'. The report also made some specific proposals with regard to the referral by social services to the police of sexual offences against children:

- The government should reaffirm the expectation that social services should, other than in exceptional circumstances, notify the police about sexual offences committed or suspected against children.

- National guidance should be provided to assist social services departments in making the decision about when to notify the police or not.

- Social services records, in particular the Integrated Children's System (ICS), should record those cases where a decision is **not** to notify the police.

- The decision making in these cases should be inspected by the Commission for Social Care Inspection (Bichard, 2004, p. 11).

The major way to combat 'the devious person [who] is determined to seek out opportunities to work their evil' (para. 79) and try and ensure that 'someone like Huntley' did not slip through 'the net' was seen primarily in terms of making sure that 'intelligence records are accessed effectively ... [which] it is quite clear did not happen because of serious failings over a period of several years' (para. 80).

The following month, July 2004, a further report was published after the decision to establish a 'serious case review' (under the chairmanship of Sir Richard Kelly) by the northeast Lincolnshire Area Child Protection Committee to examine the way in which statutory agencies had discharged their functions in respect of Ian Huntley and the young women from northeast Lincolnshire with whom he had had a relationship or sexual involvement between January 1995 and November 2001 (Kelly, 2004).[19] The review had been set up:

Primarily to consider how well the statutory agencies in North East Lincolnshire responded to the individual needs of the young people known to them who had contact with Ian Huntley during the period before he moved to Soham. (Kelly, 2004, para. 2)

Staff shortages, lack of training, and poor structures and communication between agencies were among the failures identified in the report. However, as in the Bichard report, while *Working Together to Safeguard Children* (DH et al., 1999) was thought to be sound, it was also thought that it could be strengthened in certain areas.

Of the seven girls under the age of consent discussed in the report, the handling of a case involving girl MN, who was indecently assaulted by Huntley when she was 11, was described as the 'most worrying'. MN alleged that Huntley, then aged 22 and the boyfriend of her 17-year-old friend, had assaulted her. The case was passed to the police as one of 'stranger abuse', believed to require no further involvement from social services. Huntley denied her claim and the police decided not to prosecute as there was insufficient evidence and a conviction was thought unlikely. The review report notes no attempt seemed to be made to consider MN as a 'child in need' under the Children Act 1989 and recommended that the DfES should look at Working Together to make it clear that victims may require a service as 'children in need' (Kelly, 2004, pp. 29–30).

Two of the young people involved in allegations of rape made against Ian Huntley were aged 17 at the time. While above the age of consent for sexual intercourse, they were still both children under section 105 of the Children Act 1989. If it had been thought that either was suffering or likely to suffer significant harm, the review report felt that a referral to social services should have been made in accordance with section 47 of the Act. Yet no liaison took place between the police or social services, nor was there any evidence that it was considered. As a result, the report recommended that the review by the DfES of guidance on extra-familial abuse should also include circumstances where the victim was aged 16 or 17. The report also supported the recommendation of the Bichard inquiry that the government should reaffirm the expectation that social services should, other than in exceptional circumstances, notify the police about sexual offences committed or suspected against children (Kelly, 2004).

The Kelly report was centrally concerned with examining the actions of the police and social services, as individual agencies and jointly, in making connections between each of the girls' cases and the same alleged perpetrator. While the Bichard inquiry focused in detail on the failures of the intelligence systems in Humberside police, the Kelly report commented that:

> There was no equivalent system failure in the social services department because there were no equivalent systems. As in other social services departments, the child protection files in North East Lincolnshire were and are organised by name of child concerned. There is no facility to interrogate the electronic record in any other way. (Kelly, 2004, para. 211)

Although the report made no specific recommendation about this, it was clear that these cases underlined the importance of making good links between the work of ACPCs (to be replaced by local safeguarding children boards under the Children Act 2004, which I discuss in the next chapter) and the recently instituted MAPPAs involving the police and probation services. As the report argued, 'the importance of these links to the protection of vulnerable children from potentially harmful adults is obvious' (Kelly, 2004, para. 218).

Conclusion

The period since 1991 has seen dramatic changes in attempts to 'protect the public'. Not only has the paedophile become one of the most reviled figures in society, subject to public outrage and media outing, the sex offender, particularly the violent sex offender, has been subject to increasingly exceptional attempts at surveillance and monitoring. These developments, combined with the virtual disappearance of public inquiries into intra-familial abuse, meant that by 2001 child protection had become as much if not more of a public protection issue than a child welfare issue, where the police and the probation service were seen to play key roles. In effect, by 2001, two systems were running in parallel. The one symbolised and institutionalised through MAPPAs and the other through the ACPCs, where social services departments were the lead agency. While both systems emphasised a multi- or inter-agency approach and the sharing of information was key, their focus was somewhat different. While the former was focused primarily on the offender, together with the assessment and management of risk, the latter had increasingly moved to emphasise the importance of providing family support services for children in need. While the former approach tended to be exclusionary, the latter was more inclusionary in intent. Crucially, however, the two systems had developed independently of each other and while the same agencies were involved and aimed at an extensive coverage of both children and adults in their ever-widening and overlapping 'nets', the rationales, philosophies and overall intentions of the two systems were very different. Similarly, while the focus of the former was almost exclusively men who posed a serious threat to children in the community, the focus of the latter was parents (predominantly women) trying to bring up children in often difficult and stressful situations. While both aimed to improve the sharing of information, the potential for misunderstanding and misinformation seemed considerable.

These issues were glaringly illustrated in the Bichard (2004) and Kelly (2004) inquiry reports in relation to Ian Huntley, the convicted murderer of Holly Wells and Jessica Chapman. The two systems established to *safeguard children* and *protect the public* seemed incapable of talking to each other and, crucially, drawing on and exchanging information and intelligence to which each had access. This was clearly illustrated in the Kelly report, when it asked whether any new databases established by social service departments should be designed so as to be searchable by the name of alleged offender as well as by the name of the child concerned or the family. The report recognised that this was a difficult issue which stretched well beyond its terms of reference:

> On the one hand, without the collective sharing of information child protection will fail, as has been regularly demonstrated in the past. If there is information on social services databases which might be relevant to other agencies it would be perverse not to

make it available to them; and it may be unwise to rely on any information on social services systems also being on police systems. On the other hand there are real issues of both confidentiality and practicability involved. (Kelly, 2004, para. 219)

The Kelly report agreed with the Bichard report that these were important issues and should not be something that should be left to northeast Lincolnshire to work out for itself:

> There is in our view a strong case for the DfES to establish with all the stakeholders concerned a consensus on whether or not electronic records held by child care services should be constructed so as to be searchable for names of alleged offenders, and to issue appropriate guidance. (Kelly, 2004, p. 54)

These are issues to which I will return in the final chapter after I have discussed the important developments related to the Laming Report, the Joint Inspectors Report, and the major reconfiguration of children's services arising in the Green Paper *Every Child Matters* and the Children Act 2004 in Chapter 8. What is evident, however, is that by 2004, it was no longer only a question of trying to improve and refine the internal mechanisms of systems to safeguard children, it was also important to ensure that different systems were consistent with each other, so that information and intelligence could be more readily exchanged across their somewhat unstable boundaries.

8

'Every Child Matters'

The publication of the Green Paper *Every Child Matters* (Chief Secretary to the Treasury, 2003) marked a significant development in government policy in relation to children and childhood. While it was presented as a direct response to the public inquiry into the death of Victoria Climbié (Laming Report, 2003), it was much more than this. It aimed to take forward many ideas about intervening at a much earlier stage in order to prevent a range of problems in later life, namely those related to educational attainment, unemployment and crime, particularly for children seen as 'in need' or 'at risk'. In this respect it aimed to build on much of the research and thinking I discussed in Chapter 4 and the policies introduced by New Labour in relation to childhood, where child development was seen as key and children were conceptualised primarily as future citizens. As I will argue, the three years prior to the publication of the Green Paper saw a number of important developments in this respect and while many of the key recommendations of the Laming Report were consistent with these and helped to promote their legitimacy, they were only tangentially concerned with child abuse. As a result, issues around child abuse sit uneasily with the central aims of these policy developments. However, because of the high media, public and political opprobrium arising from the death of Victoria Climbié and the need for the government to be seen to be actively responding to the Laming Report, the government was provided with an ideal opportunity for introducing wide-ranging and radical changes, which would not only bring about major organisational change but would also fundamentally reconfigure the relationship between the state, professionals, parents and children. The combination of wanting to introduce changes which would broaden the scope of prevention while trying to reduce the chances of a child dying in the tragic circumstances experienced by Victoria Climbié meant that the role of the state would become broader, more interventionist and regulatory, all at the same time.

The Laming and Joint Chief Inspectors' Reports

In Chapter 3, I compared the public inquiries into the deaths of Maria Colwell and Victoria Climbié in order to demonstrate some of the major social changes that had taken place during the intervening 30 years. However, as far as the media were concerned, it was the similarities in the findings of the inquiries which were the central issue. The fact that public inquiries had kept coming up with similar findings only made this most recent tragedy even more indefensible (Munro, 2004a; Reder and Duncan, 2004a, 2004b). One of the striking features of Victoria's case was the apparent number of occasions when the most basic intervention on the part of the staff concerned could have made a material difference to the eventual outcome (Garnham, 2001). The report, the media and all politicians, when commenting on the case, expressed outrage that there had been more than twelve opportunities to save Victoria but they all had been missed.

The report argued that much of the responsibility for Victoria's death lay with senior managers in their respective agencies, and that clear lines of accountability from frontline practitioners to government ministers needed to be established for 'the well-being of all vulnerable children'. It concluded that while the legislative framework was 'fundamentally sound', there was a 'yawning gap' in its implementation, and its 108 recommendations laid out a blueprint for achieving greater levels of accountability and closing this gap. It was felt that 46 of the recommendations should be implemented within three months and a further 38 within six months. The remainder should be implemented within two years. The report concluded that it was not appro-priate to try and separate out child protection from other state child welfare activities and thus rejected the idea of a national child protection agency, which had been recommended by the Institute of Public Policy Research (Kendall and Harker, 2002), a New Labour think tank. Instead, the report favoured the creation of a 'national agency for children and families' to ensure better cooperation and communication between different organisations nation-ally, regionally and locally.

The report was very clear that improvements to the way information was exchanged within and between agencies were imperative if children were to be adequately safeguarded, and that staff must be held accountable for the quality of the information they provided (para. 1.43). Lord Laming reported that he

> was told that the free exchange of information about *children and families about whom there are concerns* is inhibited by the legislation on data protection and human rights. It appears that, unless a child is deemed to be in need of protection, informa-tion cannot be shared between agencies without staff running the risk of con-travening this legislation. This has two consequences: either it deters information sharing, or it artificially increases concerns in order that they can be expressed as the need for protection. This is a matter that the Government must address. It is not a matter that can be tackled satisfactorily at local level. (Laming Report, 2003, para. 1.46, emphasis added)

The report argued that doubts about the exchange of information between services, combined with inadequate client information systems, in the context of 'a highly mobile society' where over ninety million people passed through the ports of entry each year, meant that children were left unnecessarily vulnerable. The report was thus in favour of establishing a national database covering all children:

> the benefit of such a database would be that every new contact with a child by a member of staff from any of the key services would initiate an entry that would build up a picture of the child's health, development and educational needs. (para. 1.47)

The report received wide political support, particularly in terms of its analysis of what had gone wrong in this case and the broad principles about how to move forward. Alan Milburn, the minister of health, immediately ordered that an audit should take place in relation to social services and health[1] to see how local services measured up to the recommendations in the Laming Report. He also promised that, within six months, clear and much shorter guidance would be produced for professionals working with children and families in relation to what to do if there were 'concerns about a child's welfare'. On the more fundamental proposals for radical change, however, he said that the government would respond more fully in the spring when it would publish a Green Paper on 'children at risk'.

The Laming Report was published on 28 January 2003. Three months previously, on 14 October 2002, a much less publicised, but equally signifi- cant report had been published, *Safeguarding Children: A Joint Chief Inspectors' Report on Arrangements to Safeguard Children* (DH, 2002a). It was jointly pro- duced by: the chief inspector of social services; the director for health improve- ment, Commission for Health Improvement; Her Majesty's chief inspector of constabulary; Her Majesty's chief inspector of the Crown Prosecution Service; Her Majesty's chief inspector of the Magistrates' Courts Service; Her Majesty's chief inspector of schools; Her Majesty's chief inspector of prisons; and Her Majesty's chief inspector of probation. This was a complex task which involved inspectors developing joint inspection arrangements and inspecting each other's services. It clearly demonstrated that *safeguarding children* was seen as a central responsibility of government and fell under the auspices of numerous government departments. No longer was it solely or even primarily a social services' responsibility.

Beyond this, however, the report claimed that, up until this point, the notion of *safeguarding children* had not been defined. While it argued that the safety and welfare of children had become an issue of increasing public concern over the previous 50 years and that it was crucial to the future well-being of society (para. 1.1):

The term safeguarding has not been defined in law or Government guidance. It is a concept that has evolved from the initial concern about children and young people in public care, to include the protection from harm of all children and young people, and to cover all agencies working with children and families. We have taken the term to mean:

- all agencies working with children, young people and their families take all reasonable measures to ensure that the *risks of harm to children's welfare* are minimised; and

- where there are *concerns about children and young people's welfare*, all agencies take all appropriate actions to address those concerns, working to agreed local policies and procedures in full partnership with other local agencies. (DH, 2002a, para. 1.5, emphases added)

This definition demonstrated that not only was safeguarding the responsibility of a wide range of health, welfare and criminal justice agencies, who needed to work closely together and share information, but also that safeguarding was about *concerns about children and young people's welfare* as well as *risks of harm to children's welfare*. We thus have far more agencies identified as being responsible and a broad focus of what those responsibilities should be.

The Joint Chief Inspectors' Report identified similar findings to the Laming Report. Many services were found to be under pressure and experiencing major difficulties in recruiting and retaining skilled and experienced staff, which was having a major impact on safeguarding arrangements for children and young people. In a minority of areas, there were long-standing tensions and poor cooperation between agencies and it was difficult to achieve the necessary level of inter-agency commitment to ensure that arrangements to safeguard children were effective. Perhaps most crucially, and very much reflecting what the Laming Report would argue, many staff from all agencies were confused about their responsibilities and duties to share information about child welfare concerns with other agencies and were not confident about whether other agencies shared information with them. The Joint Chief Inspectors' Report argued that there were few formal agreements between agencies about how and when information should be shared.

Unlike the Laming Report, however, the Joint Chief Inspectors' Report (DH, 2002a) also commented on the development and functioning of systems and services in relation to 'potentially dangerous persons' and their relationship with the much longer established arrangements for protecting children in health and social care.[2] While it found that multi-agency public protection panels (MAPPPs) were in place in all areas, in the absence of detailed national guidance, they had been developed in different ways. While there were good working relationships between the police and probation services, there was no consistency in how they addressed their tasks. Significantly,

MAPPPs and area child protection committees (ACPCs) did not have any formal links with which to address their common concerns in safeguarding children and all were struggling to respond to unconvicted people who presented 'a high risk of harm to the public, including children'. It seemed that the development of MAPPPs had taken place in parallel with and independently of ACPC arrangements. One of the 30 recommendations of the Joint Chief Inspectors' Report was, therefore, to 'ensure that the relationship between MAPPPs and ACPCs is clarified' (para. 2.11). However, the overarching and central recommendation of the report was to 'ensure the safeguarding of children is firmly and consistently reflected in national and local service planning' (para. 2.1) and this was addressed to the Department of Health, the Home Office, the Department for Education and Skills, and the Lord Chancellor's Department. The issue of trying to safeguard children was not only one which affected a wide range of professionals and agencies but went to the heart of government. Clearly, however, the systems set in place had become increasingly complex.

An attempt to reduce this complexity was made in May 2003 when further 'practice guidance' was published: *What to Do if You're Worried a Child is Being Abused* (DH et al., 2003). This was the shorter guidance produced in response to Alan Milburn's statement on the day of the publication of the Laming Report. However, as the guidance said, while it aimed to summarise the key processes, it did not replace Working Together (DH et al., 1999) or the *Framework for the Assessment of Children in Need and their Families* (DH et al., 2000). It was just 50 pages long and was also produced in a summary format which was less than half that size.

While the title of the guidance suggested that its focus was child abuse, its remit was much broader. Rather, the guidance was about 'what should be done if you have *concerns about children*, in order to safeguard and promote the welfare of children, including those who are suffering, or at risk of suffering, significant harm' (DH et al., 2003, p.13, emphasis added). 'Child abuse' was defined in terms of 'concerns about children' and sharing 'concerns' with statutory agencies was seen as a key element in enhancing the safeguarding and welfare of children more generally. While the document was entitled *What to Do if You're Worried a Child is Being Abused*, it clearly reflected *Working Together to Safeguard Children* and the Assessment Framework concerns about a child's 'welfare', which were seen as central and formed the focus for the various processes involved in deciding what to do in individual cases and deciding what the nature and significance of the concerns were.

The document tried to make explicit the processes and stages involved when any practitioner had concerns about a child and underlined the importance of sharing information for the purposes of safeguarding and promoting the welfare of children. In the light of the Laming Report, the comment in the guidance on the significance of information is particularly pertinent:

Sharing of information amongst practitioners working with children and their families is essential. In many cases it is only when information from a range of sources is put together that a child can be seen to be in need or at risk of harm. You may be anxious about the legal or ethical restrictions on sharing information, particularly with other agencies. You should be aware of the law and should comply with the code of conduct or other guidance applicable to your profession. These rarely provide an absolute barrier to disclosure. You should be prepared to exercise your judgement. *A failure to pass on information that might prevent a tragedy could expose you to criticism in the same way as an unjustified disclosure.* (DH et al., 2003, p. 43, emphasis added)

Thus, failing to share concerns about a child's welfare could lead to major criticisms of the practitioner if, at a later date, a child was found to have suffered significant harm.

'Children at Risk'

The years 2001–3 were not only the years when the reports by Lord Laming and the chief inspectors were being prepared. The period also witnessed considerable activity in other parts of government, which were trying to bring about major changes to policy and practice in relation to children and young people. However, the focus here was not on child abuse or overhauling the child protection system. Here the focus was more concerned with trying to forestall a range of problems related to crime, educational attainment and social exclusion more broadly. Much of the thinking and research which informed the establishment of the Sure Start programme in 1998 was being taken forward in ways which had implications for a range of new initiatives as well as mainstream services and across government itself.

In July 2000 the Children and Young People's Unit (CYPU) was launched by Gordon Brown (the chancellor of the exchequer), David Blunkett (the secretary of state for education and skills) and Paul Boateng (minister for young people and the family at the Home Office). While it was responsible for overseeing and administering the new £450 million Children's Fund for community-based partnership projects for 5–13-year-olds, its brief was much broader. Building on the work already developed in the first term of the New Labour government and following the report of the Social Exclusion Unit (2000) on young people, it was asked to help join up policy making across departments by removing barriers to effective working and encouraging local coordination through developing new, as well as rationalising existing, plans and partnerships. At the same time, the prime minister set up a dedicated Cabinet committee for children and young people, chaired by the chancellor of the exchequer.

In its first report, the CYPU stated that the

Early identification of problems, and the effective marshalling of a range of support services in a coordinated way is critical and must feature centrally in our long-term strategy to improve the effectiveness of services to individual children and young people. We will be looking at the variety of arrangements in place to support children, as well as those designed to support parents and families directly. It is especially in this area of *positive prevention* that the voluntary and community sectors, with their freedom to innovate, ability to gain trust and their support for solutions that come from families and children themselves, can play such a vital and enhancing role. (CYPU, 2001a, p. 29, emphases added)

These overarching aims were even more evident in the two key objectives set for the Children's Fund. The first was 'to ensure that in each area there is an agreed programme of effective interventions that pick up on early signs of difficulty, identify needs and introduce children and young people and their families to appropriate services'; while the second was 'to ensure that children and young people who have experienced early signs of difficulties receive appropriate services in order to gain maximum life-chance benefits from educational opportunities, health care and to ensure good outcomes' (CYPU, 2001a, p. 6). It was hoped that services that were described as 'universal' would have mechanisms to identify 'children at risk of social exclusion'. Access to services was to be through self-referral, peer suggestion or family advice, as well as professional referral, and while it was possible to pick up children and young people who were already receiving statutory services, the primary purpose was to support children and young people before their difficulties required statutory services.

The Children's Fund had a number of sub-objectives which give a clear insight into what it was hoped such an approach would achieve:

- to promote school attendance and improve the educational performance among 5–13-year-olds in the area
- to ensure that fewer young people aged 10–13 commit crime and fewer children aged 5–13 become victims of crime
- to reduce child health inequalities among those aged 5–13 living in the area
- to ensure that children, young people and families feel that the preventive services developed are accessible
- to involve families in building the community's capacity to sustain the programme and thereby create pathways out of poverty.

The Children's Fund was another element in the New Labour assault on social exclusion and also a strategic intervention, along with the cross-departmental work of the CYPU, to bring about a shift in mainstream funding away from crisis and to prevention: 'in the best interests of children and young people, the creation of effective and successful preventive services should underpin the reconfiguration of local provision in the longer term' (CYPU, 2001b, p. 17). This strategy became an even more explicit part of government thinking and planning from mid-2001, following the re-election of the New Labour government in June.

On 25 June 2001, the Chief Secretary to the Treasury Andrew Smith announced seven initial cross-cutting reviews that would contribute to the *2002 Spending Review*, including a review into services for 'children at risk', and Chapter 28 of the *2002 Spending Review*, entitled 'Children at risk', set out a central plank of government activity for its second term (HM Treasury, 2002). The review argued that despite extensive investment in services for children, most were not having the desired positive impact on the most disadvantaged children. The recommendations sought to ensure that support for children at risk was better focused on both preventive services and the preventive elements of mainstream services that 'address the known risk factors':

> Children at risk do not form a self-contained, easily defined group. Many children and young people can be vulnerable to risk factors such as poor parenting, disability and poverty at some point in their development. Without the support of preventive and appropriately targeted services, these risk factors can lead to crisis and in some cases lasting effects which perpetuate the cycle of deprivation, social exclusion and poverty. (HM Treasury, 2002, para. 28.3)

The *2002 Spending Review* took a three-pronged approach to strengthening preventive services: improving strategic coordination at a local level; delivering sustainable services; and filling gaps and improving services. It stated that achieving integration required strong leadership at both a national and local level, underpinned by 'effective performance management, driving forward reform'. While this reform had already begun, the government believed that it was crucial to bring about further change. In particular:

> local partners must agree to carry out new functions including: better strategic planning; systematic identification, referral and tracking regimes to ensure children don't fall through the services safety net; and allocating responsibilities for individualised packages of support for those at greatest risk. The Government believes there is a case for structural change to effect the better coordination of children's services, and will pilot Children's Trusts which will unify at the local level the various agencies involved in providing services to children. (HM Treasury, 2002, para. 28.5)

It was argued that mainstream services failed a significant minority of children and young people, either because they focused on the majority and ignored specific needs, or because they focused on crisis and acute intervention rather than prevention and the early identification of need. To address this, the government had introduced targeted programmes such as Sure Start and the Children's Fund, with discrete delivery arrangements outside mainstream public services. However, the review recommended the adoption of a common framework for integrating the lessons learned from these developments, so that mainstream services could better respond to the full range of children and young people's needs.

Following the publication of the *2002 Spending Review*, a variety of government statements were made with great rapidity. On 17 July 2002, the Home Secretary David Blunkett, in his statement 'Justice for All', referred to a joint paper on long-term prevention for 'children at risk'. On 16 August, John Denham, the new minister for children and young people at the Home Office, announced that local systems to identify, refer and track (IRT) children at risk of, for example, offending, drug taking and teenage pregnancy would be put in place across the country in the course of the following year and this would be a key focus for the Children's Fund in the future.

On 6 September 2002, John Denham made a further statement that from April 2003 all local agencies responsible for delivering services to children and young people would be asked to agree a coordinated strategy for preventive services for children and young people aged 0–19. The letter to local authority chief executives also included interim guidance on the key elements of a local preventive strategy:

> The aim of the preventative strategy is to promote positive outcomes and to prevent children and young people experiencing negative outcomes, both as children and young people, and later in their lives as adults. By addressing the risk factors that make children and young people vulnerable to negative outcomes, such as being excluded from school, running away from home or becoming involved in crime, the local preventative strategy will set the direction for services to reduce social exclusion. (CYPU, 2002, para. 1.2)

Following Sinclair et al. (1997), prevention was described as 'the promotion of child well-being by enabling children and young people to develop their full potential, and the promotion of family well-being by enabling parents/carers to meet the overall needs of their children and themselves' (para. 2.1) and:

> The local preventative strategy should set a framework for services, through which effective support can be provided at the most appropriate level and point in time. At all levels of service (universal, targeted, specialist or rehabilitative) the *aim should be early intervention, in response to assessment of risk and protective factors*, to improve the outcomes of the children they serve. (CYPU, 2002, emphasis added)

The identification, referral and tracking (IRT) of children at risk was seen as a key mechanism to help to deliver the local preventive strategy, and the Children's Fund preventive strategy for services to children aged 5–13 was seen as a key support for developing this wider preventive strategy. Then, speaking to the National Social Services Conference in Cardiff on 16 October 2002, Alan Milburn, the secretary of state for health, declared his intention 'to tear down the traditional service boundaries which too often impede the delivery of a seamless service to the most vulnerable' (DH, 2002b). Profound changes in family structures, the way people were employed and the expectations of public services meant that the monolithic 'one size fits all' structure of social services must be broken up. A key element of the changes was that specialised services for children and older people would be created. Instead of crossing a whole series of disciplines such as education, health and social services where, he argued, there was unnecessary confusion, mixed messages and fragmented decision making, children's services would come together in children's trusts, while the NHS and social services for older people would be brought together in care trusts.

While the organisation of social service departments had increasingly been based on structures based on particular client groups, this announcement was set to reshape dramatically how social services were organised and delivered. In effect, it marked the official death of the central principle of the Seebohm reforms of the early 1970s, which established social service departments as providing a generic family service and where social work represented its distinctive professional hallmark.

It was clear that major reforms were being planned by the government and the period immediately prior to the National Social Services Conference in 2002 saw the publication of two other documents which reflected authoritative views outside government, one from the influential think tank closely associated with New Labour, the Institute of Public Policy Research (IPPR) (Kendall and Harker, 2002), and the other from the Local Government Association (LGA), the NHS Confederation and the Association of Directors of Social Services (Local Government Association et al., 2002). On one significant issue the two reports took quite different positions and this not only received publicity but was to be the focus of wide debate over the ensuing months. The LGA report emphasised the importance of developing holistic services for all children, while the IPPR report called on the government to consider setting up a separate dedicated national child protection service, which would emphasise specialist skills and aim to improve multi-agency working. Crucially, it would try and clarify staff roles:

> It could help remove families' uncertainties about whether social services are investigating them or supporting them, which can be a barrier to both effective working with families and to building wider public support for social care as a whole ... separating

the 'control' element of children's services may be a crucial step in enabling the rest of social care to deliver the empowering and enabling agenda. (Kendall and Harker, 2002, p. 17)

However, on many issues the two reports had much in common and were generally supportive of the direction in which government policy was heading, particularly in terms of the emphasis on prevention and early intervention, trying to make policy and practice more joined up and accountable and trying to enhance community involvement. Apart from the issue of whether there should be a separate child protection agency, any differences were relatively minor and generally reflected a difference of emphasis.

At the end of October, the Prime Minister Tony Blair promised that a Green Paper on 'children at risk' would be published in the following spring on identifying ways of improving services for vulnerable children and young people. It would consider measures to reduce levels of educational underachievement, offending, antisocial behaviour, teenage pregnancy and ill-health. Child abuse was not mentioned. The Green Paper was to be drafted by a new subcommittee in the Cabinet Office, chaired by the Chief Secretary to the Treasury Paul Boateng, with John Denham, minister for children and young people, having day-to-day control of the Cabinet Office team. The prime minister said that 'prevention has been at the heart of the government's approach to tackling social exclusion. Sure Start, the Children's Fund, targeted services to children in deprived areas, and Connexions are widening opportunities to all children and families. But we have to go further' (quoted in Jerrom, 2002, p. 12).

The Green Paper would focus on the identification, referral and tracking of children and the provision of mainstream and specialist services to them. It would look at the whole scope of children at risk to ensure that problems would be tackled as early as possible. The announcement of the Green Paper was clearly an attempt to take forward the various developments previously signalled in the *2002 Spending Review* and subsequently highlighted in a variety of new initiatives and statements by ministers. However, ministers were also conscious that the Laming Report was due to be published in January 2003 and that it would be helpful to be able to say that the government had established a process whereby the report's recommendations could be seriously considered alongside its main thrust of policy for children and young people. Clearly, however, the latter had not been seriously concerned about policy and practice in relation to child abuse and child protection. The focus was not on children at risk of abuse but on those at risk of exhibiting a range of problem behaviours, including offending, drug taking, teenage pregnancy, educational underachievement and school exclusion, where it was felt there needed to be a much greater emphasis upon early intervention, for which IRT was seen as central.

John Denham, the minister for children and young people, dismissed concerns that the impact of labelling and stigmatising young children by an IRT system might outweigh the benefits of any intervention, and said the proposals had not met any significant resistance from the agencies or professionals involved:

> The dangers are far greater when services don't work together effectively. It is not the system that prejudices the child, or the fact that they are on a database of shared information. It is the fact that the child is showing through their behaviour, their educational development, self-harm, whatever it may be, real signs of risk. That is what you are identifying so that you are able to respond properly. (quoted in Rickford, 2002, pp. 20–1)

He believed that it was important that professionals used the kind of information that would be on a tracking system positively, as a way of meeting the needs of children and young people.[3] However, one of the first questions for the Green Paper team was going to be how wide to cast the net:

> If you cast it too broad you can't respond to all the young people you are picking up. If you cast it too narrowly you will miss some young people who are at significant risk. (John Denham, quoted in Rickford, 2002, p. 21)

The Green Paper

In June 2003 the government appointed the first Minister for Children, Margaret Hodge, to be based in the Department for Education and Skills. While the post was not of Cabinet rank, it signalled a major reorganisation and coordination of children's services at central government level.[4] The new ministerial post demonstrated the government's commitment to 'join up' children's services and would be reflected locally by the creation of 'children's trusts', which were expected to be led by local authorities or contracted out to public interest companies. The trusts, which would be piloted later in the year and bring together education, health and social services into new organisations, would be responsible for commissioning most children's services. Further details of the changes were expected the following month when it was anticipated that Margaret Hodge would launch the Green Paper.

 In the event, and embarrassingly for the government, the launch was delayed, when, soon after taking up her new post, Margaret Hodge came under considerable pressure from the opposition and much of the media to resign over the re-emergence of major criticisms over the way she had handled allegations of abuse in children's homes when she was leader of Islington council in London in the 1980s and 90s. The allegations in the *London Evening Standard* said that young people in Islington children's homes had 'descended into a life of degradation and exploitation', with suspicions that pimps were having sex with children and young people in care were being seduced into drugs, homosexuality and prostitution. Abuse by residential staff was said to be common, with evidence of a 'paedophile ring'. However, the situation had not been tackled by the council because it was claimed that councillors, including Margaret Hodge, had not wanted to be seen as homophobic. At the time, it had been branded by the right-wing press as one of London's 'looney left' councils. It was one of the many cases of allegations of sexual abuse in children's homes in the 1990s and was the subject of an inquiry (White and Hart, 1995), which confirmed a number of the allegations but did not lay the blame at the door of the leader of the council. However, the allegations were resurrected in July 2003 as evidence of her unfitness for this new and ground-breaking ministerial appointment.

The Green Paper was eventually launched on 8 September 2003 by Tony Blair. He said that he wanted it to serve as a permanent memorial to Victoria Climbié. In his Foreword, the prime minister stated:

> For most parents, our children are everything to us: our hopes, our ambitions, our future. Our children are cherished and loved. But sadly, some children are not so fortunate. Some children's lives are different. Dreadfully different. Instead of the joy, warmth and security of normal family life, these children's lives are filled with risk, fear, and danger and from what most of us would regard as the worst possible source – from the people closest to them. Victoria Climbié was one of those children. At the hands of those entrusted with her eventual care she suffered appallingly and eventually died. Her case was a shocking example from a list of children terribly mistreated and abused. The names of the children involved, echoing down the years, are a standing shame to us all ... responding to the inquiry headed by Lord Laming into Victoria's death, we are proposing here a range of measures to reform and improve children's care. (Chief Secretary to the Treasury, 2003, p. 1)

The Green Paper was explicitly presented as a response to the Laming Report and to be centrally concerned with child abuse and was represented as such in the media. The leader in the *Daily Mirror* the day after the launch was typical:

> Two years ago, after the horrific details of the killing of Victoria Climbié were revealed, the *Daily Mirror* demanded that real action should be taken ... of course, there is still no guarantee that there will not be another scandal involving another poor child. But the moves announced yesterday by Tony Blair are a real effort to prevent one. (p. 6)

It was only towards the end of his Foreword that Tony Blair stated that the Green Paper was also putting forward ideas on a number of related issues, including parenting, fostering, young people's activities and youth justice. In fact, while informed by the Laming Report, the Green Paper was primarily concerned with taking forward the government's proposals for reforming children's services which it had been developing for some years, but with a broader remit than previously. Rather than being entitled 'Children at Risk' the

Green Paper was entitled *Every Child Matters*. This is not to say that the Green Paper was not centrally concerned with risk, it was, but in such a way that any child at some point in their life could be seen as vulnerable to some form of risk. The government, therefore, needed to ensure that all children were potentially covered by its proposals. Risk was a pervasive threat to all children. Rather than only being concerned with child protection in a narrow sense or even children in need, it was the *safeguarding of all children and childhood itself* which was the central concern. The Green Paper argued that society needed to do more to protect children and ensure that each child fulfilled his or her potential. Security and opportunity must go hand in hand: 'Child protection must be a fundamental element across all public, private and voluntary organisations. Equally we must be ambitious for all children, whoever they are and wherever they live' (p. 3).

The central argument for the need for radical change was 'past failings', of which the deaths of children from Maria Colwell to Victoria Climbié were the most scandalous examples, and these failures stemmed from a *failure to intervene early enough*. The common threads were well established: poor coordination; a failure to share information; the absence of anyone with a strong sense of accountability; frontline workers trying to cope with staff shortages and poor management; and a lack of effective training. However, these failures were not only seen to characterise child abuse tragedies but were endemic across all children's services:

> The most tragic manifestation of these problems is when we fail to protect children at risk of harm or neglect. But the problem of children falling through the cracks of different services goes much further. Too often children experience difficulties at home or at school, but receive too little help too late, once problems have reached crisis point. (p. 5)

And it was on this terrain that the broader aims of the government reforms were explicitly connected to the findings and recommendations of the Laming Report,[5] because, as the Green Paper asserted, 'as Lord Laming's recommendations made clear, child protection could not be separated from policies to improve children's lives as a whole' (p. 5). It was thus important to focus on the universal services which every child used, and on the more targeted services for those with additional needs. The policies set out in the Green Paper were thus designed to both protect children and maximise their potential and set out a framework for services that covered children and young people from 0–19 living in England. It aimed:

> To reduce the numbers of children who experience educational failure, engage in offending or anti-social behaviour, suffer from ill health, or become teenage parents we need to ensure we properly protect children at risk within a framework of universal

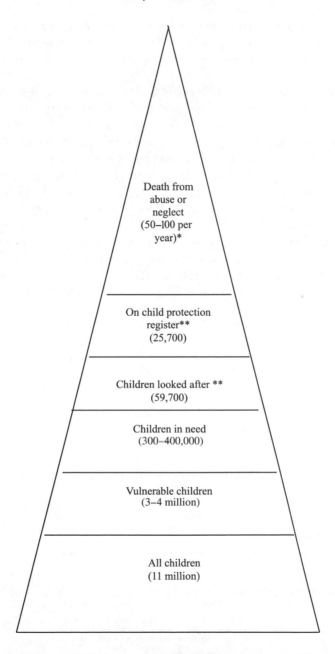

Key: * These children may or may not be on the child protection register, or looked after, or vulnerable.
   ** These children are included in the children in need figure, and not all children on the child protection register are children looked after.

Figure 8.1 *Every Child Matters*: categorising children
Source: Chief Secretary to the Treasury, 2003, p. 15

services which supports every child to develop their full potential and which aims to prevent negative outcomes. That is why this Green Paper addresses the needs of children at risk in the context of the services we provide for all children. (pp. 5–6)

Thus, in response to the question posed by John Denham in the quotation at the end of the previous section, the 'net' had been cast very wide to include all children and young people. The framework which informed the Green Paper was represented in terms of two triangles: the first of which (Figure 8.1) was adapted from one of the conceptual maps included in the Assessment Framework (see Figure 6.5). This tried to represent both the numbers of and relationships between different categories of children. The second (Figure 8.2) represented the types of services associated with 'specialist', 'targeted' and 'universal' and the relationships between them.

Underpinning the proposals were two basic assumptions concerning the nature of recent social change and the state of current knowledge and these informed the whole document. First, it was stated that over the last generation, children's lives had undergone 'profound change'. While children had more

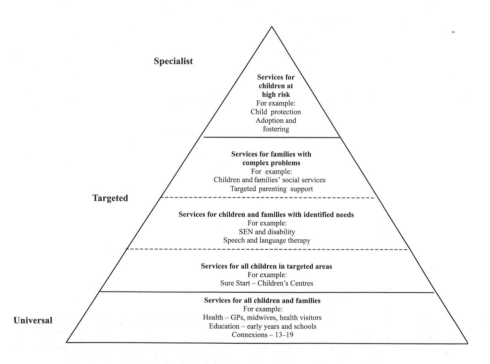

Figure 8.2 *Every Child Matters*: targeted services within a universal context
Source: Chief Secretary to the Treasury, 2003, p. 21

opportunities than ever before and had benefited from rising prosperity and better health, they also faced more uncertainties and risks. They faced earlier exposure to sexual activity, drugs and alcohol, and family patterns were changing. There were more lone parents, more divorces and more women in paid employment, all of which had made family life more complex and which I discussed in Chapter 3 as being important characteristics of the move to a late modern society. Secondly, the Green Paper asserted that these changes had come about at a time when 'we better understand the importance of early influences on the development of values and behaviour' (p. 15). It was thus important to ensure that this knowledge was drawn upon to inform the changes being introduced to respond to the new and more complex situations facing contemporary children and childhood: 'we have a good idea what factors shape children's life chances. Research tells us that the risk of experiencing negative outcomes is concentrated in children with certain characteristics and experiences' (p. 17). While research had not built up a detailed picture of the causal links, certain factors were said to be associated with poor outcomes, which included:

- low income and parental unemployment

- homelessness

- poor parenting

- poor schooling

- postnatal depression among mothers

- low birth weight

- substance misuse

- individual characteristics such as intelligence

- community factors, such as living in a disadvantaged neighbourhood.

The more risk factors that a child experienced, such as being excluded from school and family breakdown, the more likely it was that he or she would experience negative outcomes.[6] The Green Paper argued that:

> research suggests that parenting appears to be the most important factor associated with educational attainment at age ten, which in turn is strongly associated with achievement later in life. Parental involvement in education seems to be a more important influence than poverty, school environment and the influence of peers. (p. 18)

A range of protective factors were also said to help children overcome disadvantage, including:

- strong relationships with parents, family members and other significant adults

- parental interest and involvement in education, with clear and high expectations

- positive role models

- individual characteristics such as an outgoing nature, self-motivation and intelligence

- active involvement in family, school and community life

- praise, recognition and feeling valued.

'Children are particularly affected by their experience during the early years before they reach school age' (p. 18). The Green Paper, therefore, built on the government's existing plans to strengthen preventive services by focusing on four key themes: supporting parents and carers; emphasising early intervention and effective protection; overcoming weak accountability and poor integration; and workforce reform.

Supporting Parents and Carers

The Green Paper stated that it intended to put the support of parents and carers at the heart of improving children's lives. To build additional capacity in this area, the government announced the creation of a parenting fund of £25 million over the next three years, and said it was consulting on a long-term vision to improve parenting and family support through:

- *universal services*, such as schools, health and social services and childcare, providing information and advice and engaging parents to support their child's development

- *targeted and specialist support* to parents of children requiring additional support

- *compulsory action* through parenting orders as a last resort, where parents were seen as condoning a child's truancy, antisocial behaviour or offending.

Clearly parents had 'responsibilities' as well as 'rights' and these would be enforced where it was felt to be warranted. Because all children deserved the chance 'to grow up in a loving, secure family', where this could not be provided by parents, local authorities would be encouraged to use adoption, and it was recognised that a major effort was required to recruit more foster carers and ensure that they had the skills and support needed to care for 'vulnerable children'.

Early Intervention and Effective Protection

However, it was the emphasis on *early intervention and effective protection* that most clearly demonstrated how the new approach built on developments previously promulgated by the CYPU and how the approach aimed to be distinctive from the essential principles of child welfare policy established in the post-war period. And it was here that a clear link was established between the Green Paper and Lord Laming's recommendations. Because some children required extra help because of the disadvantages they faced, the key was said to be to ensure that children received services at the first onset of problems, 'to prevent any children slipping through the net':

> The Victoria Climbié inquiry highlighted the failure to collect basic information and share it between agencies or across local authority boundaries. For instance, nobody checked whether Victoria was in school. Despite her case coming to the attention of various agencies on twelve occasions professionals made decisions based on little information about Victoria's previous contact with a series of services. Judgements were made based on separate snapshots rather than a picture built up over time. (p. 52)

Similarly, services often came too late for children with problems such as special educational needs or behavioural disorders or those suffering from neglect. The Green Paper's vision was to intervene earlier by: improving information sharing; establishing a common assessment framework; introducing a lead professional; integrating professionals and co-locating services.

The proposals for *improving information collection and sharing* were central and while these built on the development of the IRT, in order to ensure that no child was overlooked, all children were to be included. The long-term aim was to integrate information across services and ensure that professionals shared 'concerns' at an early stage.[7] It was planned that information would be stored and accessed electronically by a range of agencies. Ideally, the information systems would be based on national data standards to enable the exchange of information between local authorities and partner agencies and be capable of interaction with other data sets.

In order to capture fully the concerns of a range of professionals over time, it was felt that there was a strong case for giving practitioners the ability to flag 'early warnings' on the system when they had a 'concern' about a child, which, in itself, may not meet the usual thresholds for intervention. The decision to place such a 'flag of concern' on a child's record, which could then be picked up by another agency making a similar judgement, would lie with the practitioners and 'it would be a matter of professional judgement whether the combination of two or more flags of minor concern warranted some form of action' (p. 53).

The proposals would alter fundamentally the relationship between the state and the family or, in practice, the relationships between government, professionals, parents and children, and the control and construction of information was key:

> There is a balance to strike between sharing enough information to help safeguard children effectively and preserving individuals' privacy. The Government wants to prevent situations where a child does not receive the help they need because of too rigid an interpretation of the privacy of the child and their family. In order to get the balance right, we are consulting on the circumstances (in addition to child protection and youth offending) under which information about a child could or must be shared, for preventive purposes, without the consent of the child or their carers. (pp. 53–4)

To take such a strategy forward, the government planned to 'sweep away the legal, technical, cultural and organisational barriers to information sharing so that, for the first time, there can be effective communication between everyone with a responsibility for children' (CYPU, 2003).

So that core information could follow the child between different services, it was also planned to *establish a common assessment framework*, which would further develop the Assessment Framework (DH et al., 2000), informed by assessment protocols used in other services such as Connexions, youth offending teams, health visiting and special education. This would be informed by the considerable work that had been carried out since the launch of the Assessment Framework to develop and implement an 'integrated children's system', which was concerned with planning, intervention and review, as well as assessment. While originally directed primarily at social services departments and therefore with a narrower focus, it was informed by a broader way of thinking which was consistent with the Green Paper. In particular, the 'integrated children's system', which would only be operable if the recording systems were implemented in an electronic format, was crucially concerned with overcoming the conceptual, professional and technical barriers between the way children 'looked after', 'protected', 'in need' and 'vulnerable' were approached.[8] As well as reducing unnecessary assessment, the process of developing and using a common assessment framework would play a critical role in 'improving inter-professional relationships ... [and would] underpin and be reinforced by the structural and workforce reforms' (p. 59).

Children known to more than one specialist agency would have *a single, named lead professional* who would be responsible for ensuring a coherent package of services to meet the individual child's needs. The lead professional could also act as the 'gatekeeper' for the information sharing systems: 'Other professionals could have partial access but only the lead professional would be aware of the detail. It could be the lead professional who would make a judgement about whether, taken together, the early warnings logged by different practitioners merited intervention' (p. 60).

However, the Green Paper argued that while common assessments and information sharing would constitute a major step forward, further integration was needed. Professionals would be encouraged to work in *multidisciplinary teams* co-located in and around schools, Sure Start children's centres and primary healthcare settings.

Accountability and Integration

In order to 'put children at the heart of our policies, and to organise services around their needs' (p. 9), the Green Paper argued that radical reform was needed not just to 'break down organisational boundaries' but also to overcome local and national 'fragmentation'. The government's aim was that there should be one person in charge locally and nationally and that key services for children should be integrated within a common organisational focus at both levels. The changes at central government level had begun with the appointment of the new Minister for Children Margaret Hodge. At the local level, it was intended to legislate to create a new post of 'director of children's services', who would be accountable for local authority education and children's social services, and create a 'lead council member responsible for children'.

In the longer term it was planned to integrate services for children and young people under a director of children's services as part of children's trusts. These would bring together local authority education and children's social services, some children's health services, and could include other services such as youth offending teams. Children's trusts would normally be part of the local authority and would report to local elected members. It was hoped that most areas would have such trusts by 2006.

It was also proposed that 'local safeguarding children boards' would be created as the *statutory* successors to area child protection committees. While they would take on the previous responsibilities of ACPCs, it was anticipated that they 'could commission independent serious case reviews and manage a service to look at unexpected child deaths to decide which need serious case reviews, and draw out any public health lessons' (p. 74).

Finally, the government stated that it intended to legislate to establish a statutory 'children's commissioner' who

> would act as a children's champion independent of Government, and would speak for all children but especially the disadvantaged whose voices are too often drowned out. The Commissioner would advise Government and also engage with others, such as business and the media, whose decisions and actions affect children's lives. (p. 79)

However, the commissioner would only investigate individual cases where the issues had a wider relevance to other children, as directed by the secretary of state.

Workforce Reform

It was clear, however, that the reforms were unlikely to achieve their goals unless the major problems with staff recruitment and retention were addressed. The Green Paper planned to review rewards, incentives and relativities across children's services to try and improve skills and effectiveness and make working with children an attractive career option. The aims were to be achieved by:

- a high-profile recruitment campaign

- more flexible training routes into social work

- common occupational standards across children's practice linked to modular qualifications, which would allow workers to move more easily between jobs

- a common core of training for those who worked solely with children and families and those with wider roles such as GPs and the police.

A 'children's workforce unit' in the Department for Education and Skills would develop the pay and workforce strategy and, working with the relevant employers, staff and government departments, would look to establish a 'sector skills council for children and young people's services'. In addition, it was planned to develop a programme to foster high-calibre leadership and for the chief nursing officer to undertake a review of the contribution that health visitors, nurses and midwives could make to work with children at risk. This last proposal was particularly pertinent because health visitors, nurses and midwives provided a universal service and could have particularly strong views about the change to their roles, in light of the requirements to identify 'warning signs' and share information about children, including entering this on a database. These professions placed a particular priority on gaining the confidence of and working in close partnership with parents, particularly mothers.

Effective Protection

Clearly, therefore, the aim was to introduce an integrated, early intervention, multidisciplinary service where there were clear lines of accountability. Child protection was not to be separated from support for families but was meant to be 'part of a spectrum of services provided to help and support children and families' (p. 64). The Green Paper was published on the same day as the government's official response to the Laming and the Joint Chief Inspectors'

Reports, *Keeping Children Safe* (DfES et al., 2003). This went through the 108 recommendations in the Laming Report and the 30 recommendations of the Joint Chief Inspectors' Report and stated what the government had done to meet them. Only two of the 138 recommendations were rejected, the rest were accepted or accepted in principal.[9] Of the 107 recommendations accepted from the Laming Report, the government said that it had discharged its responsibilities to 29 of them by issuing *What to Do if You're Worried a Child is Being Abused* (DH et al., 2003) and for a further 60 of the recommendations, by the 'checklist of good practice' audit ordered by ministers immediately after the publication of the report at the end of January.[10] In relation to the remainder of the recommendations, which Lord Laming said would take two years to implement, the government pointed to the reforms it was introducing in the Green Paper.

The clear message, however, was that not only would child protection be seen as embedded in the new systems but it would be reflected in the criteria for inspections and the practice standards that all agencies with responsibilities for children would need to measure up to. There would be a shared responsibility across all agencies for protecting children through new statutory duties. Already the government had modified the framework for clinical governance through the new National Service Framework for hospital standards and child protection was now included in the National Policing Plan. The relationship between child protection and preventive responsibilities was seen as interrelated and interdependent, and the concept of safeguarding was central to this. This was neatly summarised in the final paragraph of *Keeping Children Safe*; in the process it also identified a key tension and possible fundamental problem in the new approach:

> In the longer term, increased investment in prevention and early intervention should reduce the number of children being harmed. But some serious cases, like Victoria Climbié's, are deliberately concealed, and systematically planned. In the short term, therefore, increased investment in prevention and early intervention may uncover unmet needs relating to these more serious cases. But by raising the priority given to *safeguarding children* with all organisations, by giving a wider range of organisations and professionals greater responsibilities to provide support, and by helping practitioners and their managers to work together better, children should be better *safeguarded*, and the lessons learnt from Victoria's death. (DfES et al., 2003, p. 26, para. 123, emphases added).

Conclusion

On 4 March 2004 the government published the Children Bill and its response to the Green Paper consultation entitled *Every Child Matters: Next Steps* (DfES,

2004a). While the consultation had prompted the government to allow greater flexibility in the proposed organisational arrangements[11] and indicated that it now expected that children's trusts would be established by 2008 rather than 2006, the central proposals and principles of the Green Paper were little changed. As Margaret Hodge said in the Foreword to *Next Steps*, the vision was of 'a shift to prevention while strengthening protection' (p. 3). To do so required certain legislative change and the key theme of the Children Bill was to encourage partnership and sharpen accountability by:

- placing a new duty on agencies to cooperate among themselves and with other local partners to improve the well-being of children and young people so that all work to common outcomes

- a tighter focus on child protection through a duty on key agencies to safeguard children and promote their welfare through new local safeguarding children boards and the power to set up a new database containing basic information about children

- ensuring clear overall accountability through a director of children's services who would be accountable for local education and children's social services and lead local change, and a lead council member for children's services

- enabling and encouraging local authorities, primary care trusts and others to pool budgets into a children's trust, and share information better to support more joining up on the ground, with health, education and social care professionals working together based in the same location such as schools and children's centres

- creating an integrated inspection framework to assess how well services work together to improve outcomes for children

- taking on new powers to intervene in children's social services where an area was falling below minimum standards and intervention was seen as necessary

- the creation of a children's commissioner.[12]

In many respects we can see the changes as trying to bring together many of the main themes and developments evident since the mid-1990s. There was a clear and serious attempt to try and address the tensions which had become evident in the relationship between child protection and family support but where family support had taken on a much wider brief after New Labour came to power in 1997. The emphases on early intervention, multi-agency working, integration and the sharing of information were key. Practitioners in a wide range of health, welfare, education and criminal justice agencies would be expected to raise and share their concerns at an early stage so that all efforts were made to safeguard and promote the welfare and development of children so that harm could be avoided and opportunities maximised. Under s. 8(5)(b) of the Bill, professionals would be required to share information if they had 'any cause for concern'. This was a lower threshold than 'significant harm or the likelihood of significant harm' or 'a child in need'. To all intents and purposes, England was introducing a mandatory reporting system, akin to that in the USA, but on the all-inclusive basis of any 'cause for concern' (Munro, 2004b, 2004c; Payne, 2004). The changes were ambitious and the government was not exaggerating when it claimed that the Children Bill was 'the most far-reaching reform of children's services for 30 years'. Rather than simply being a response to the Laming Report into the tragic death of Victoria Climbié, it had a much longer and more complex genealogy. Clearly, however, Lord Laming's report provided the key political momentum whereby these major changes could be introduced. The Children Bill received royal assent on 15 November 2004.

9

Towards 'the Preventive State'

I have argued in this book that the major social changes we have lived through over the last 30 years, which I have characterised as the move to a late modern society, have opened up considerable social anxieties in relation to childhood and children's safety. Our emotions in relation to children have become increasingly 'volatile and contradictory' (O'Malley, 1999), so that the responses developed under the auspices of the social state no longer seem adequate. On the one hand, we have attempted to normalise our approaches to child protection by seeing those who might harm children in the context of the family, primarily mothers, as doing so because of stress and poor environments (Ghate and Hazel, 2002). What is required, therefore, is a series of differentiated interventions which offer support and encourage *social inclusion*. On the other hand, however, we have constructed policies, primarily in relation to paedophiles, who are almost exclusively men, which are essentialist, punitive and primarily *exclusionary*. Perpetrators are seen as 'other' and outside the norms of a civilised society (Garland, 1996).

While this demarcation is helpful, it does not tell the whole story. It is clear that outbursts of public emotion, particularly in the media, have been influential in informing developments in both areas. Both systems have been faced with trying to develop rational, coherent responses to what are seen as new dangers, in a climate which is highly emotive and politicised, and increasingly there is an expectation that the two systems will share information so that the problems associated with the tragedy in Soham can be avoided. What underpins both is an understanding of childhood as a stage of innocence and vulnerability, and that a few adults are potentially dangerous. However, the central principle which lies at the core of all recent policy developments to improve the safeguarding of children is the importance of prevention and early intervention, where the collation and sharing of information becomes key.

In recent years we have seen the emergence of what Steiker (1998) has called 'the preventive state'. While the preventive state can be seen in many guises, Steiker argues that it can be characterised in terms of two sets of 'prophylactic measures': those which aim to intervene earlier rather than simply detect, investigate and respond to crises; and those which involve direct restraints on the liberty of certain individuals because they are believed to be particularly dangerous. It is to the nature and characteristics of 'the preventive state' and its implications for the relationships between children, parents and professionals that I turn in this chapter.

I argued in Chapters 1 and 2 that the liberal compromise established in the late nineteenth century, whereby the family was essentially privatised, given the prime responsibility for rearing children and only subject to intervention in exceptional circumstances, was the key principle which informed policy and practice for much of the twentieth century. In many respects, informed by the development of a range of new professions and forms of social and psychological knowledge, a central focus of the social state was to support the family and reinforce the position of children within it. The family was thoroughly functional to both the welfare state and organised modernity, and social work provided a key element in maintaining the fine balance between upholding the privacy of the family while ensuring that children were protected. However, I have suggested that from the early 1970s, this balance was found increasingly wanting and was no longer able to cope with the strains placed upon it by the range of major social changes characteristic of a late modern society.

While various efforts were made to repair the systems which had been put in place, including the passing of the 1989 Children Act, I have argued that these issues came to a head in the 1990s. Two developments were key. First, following the publication of *Child Protection: Messages from Research* (DH, 1995a), attempts were made to *refocus* children's services in terms of the relationship between a forensically driven conception of child protection and services to provide family support and, second, in the wake of the death of James Bulger, a range of new approaches to tackle antisocial and criminal behaviour among children and young people were established. A common theme in both was the assertion, in terms of the longer term outcomes for children, of the importance of the circumstances where children were being brought up in context of *emotional neglect* and where the primary concern should be the *style of parenting.*

What was required was the establishment of a more wide-ranging, integrated approach, which emphasised early intervention and where assessment was not simply concerned with a narrow emphasis on the identification of risk of 'significant harm', which thereby failed to pay attention to the wider needs of the child. The focus should be, following the overriding principle of the 1989 Children Act, to 'safeguard and promote the welfare of the child', where the child's health and development were key. This conceptualisation achieved a fusion of concerns related to children as 'victims' and children as actual or potential 'villains'.

To take such a project forward, however, required a more proactive and wider role for the state, which took place after the election of the New Labour government in 1997. New Labour introduced a range of new initiatives which were underpinned by a number of assumptions:

- the earliest years of life were seen as the most important for child development

- a significant minority of children were vulnerable to multiple and mutually reinforcing disadvantages which considerably increased their chances of social exclusion and maladaptive development

- service provision was uncoordinated, crisis-oriented and failed to intervene early enough to have a positive longer term benefit.

Crucially, while there were major social changes which were having wide-ranging impacts on family/household relationships and communities, it was assumed that we now had a level of knowledge which allowed interventions to have a positive impact, but that these were being held back by failures of implementation and a traditional division of responsibilities between professionals and services which failed to put the child at the centre. Research and knowledge about child development and advances in the way information could be used and shared were key. However, it is important to remember that the primary drivers for these initiatives, until the Laming Report into the death of Victoria Climbié, were concerns about social exclusion and attempts to tackle the causes of crime, not child abuse. It was concerns about children as actual or potential 'villains' and not as 'victims' which were central, and it was in this context that the emphasis on early intervention, family support and a focus on vulnerable children was being developed. Concerns about children not fulfilling their potential and becoming social problems in the future were the driving force for change as much as children being at risk of parental abuse. It was the Treasury and the Home Office which were often the key departments developing the new initiatives, along with the Department for Education and Skills.

However, in terms of some of the key conceptual maps and new technologies being introduced to bring about change, many of these were developed by the Department of Health and were informed by key pieces of research and practice development directly related to attempts to refocus child protection and improve the quality of services for looked after children, particularly in the wake of growing concerns about institutional abuse. In the process, initiatives originally designed for a small number of children who were the direct responsibility of the state were refined and increasingly applied to a much wider child population.

The Dispersal of State Care/Control

In this sense we can see that policies which were originally designed for the few have been seen as having relevance for the many and have thus radiated out beyond their original confines. Let me give four significant examples to illustrate how the role of the state and its relationship with children and parents began to change in significant ways and how these were informed by the development of ideas and technologies originally designed for children for whom the state had a more direct responsibility.

First, the notion of 'safeguarding' was a key concept in the Children Act 1989. However, it was the report by Sir William Utting (1997), *People Like Us*, often referred to as the Safeguards Review, which underlined the importance of the concept of safeguarding. While the report was concerned with policies and practices in relation to children living in public care, the notion of safeguarding was also seen as a minimum necessary requirement for ensuring every child's physical and emotional health, education and sound social development. It quickly came to have a much wider relevance than only for children in public care.

Second, the development of the Assessment Framework and, more recently, the integrated children's system (ICS) and the Common Assessment Framework explicitly drew on the Looking After Children (LAC) project and assessment and action records (AARs), which were originally developed for children looked after in public care. While it has been refined, the LAC system has provided the core conceptual framework and technology for assessing and monitoring children who come to the notice of health and welfare agencies everywhere. Such a development reflects the attempt to conceptualise 'looked after' children as a small subset of the much broader categories of children living at home and vulnerable children more generally (see Figure 6.1 and Figure 6.5).

Third, as I argued in Chapter 4, the study by Gibbons et al. (1995) was crucial in demonstrating that only 4 per cent of children referred to a social services department for a child protection investigation were ever removed from home on a statutory order and only 15 per cent were ever entered on a child protection register. The vast majority were filtered out at a much earlier stage. However, the researchers found that many of the cases filtered out were children in need. Among those filtered out there was considerable evidence of lone parenthood, unemployment, domestic violence and mental illness, with the majority of families dependent on income support. Similarly, many of the children had been referred to social services, sometimes for a child protection investigation, on numerous occasions previously. But, because the system was forensically driven and thus had a narrow view of what constituted child protection, few of the cases filtered out received any sort of service. The result was that the system of filters produced what could be represented as a funnel which was wide at the top and narrow at the bottom (see Figure 4.1). The picture was one of children not reaching the threshold for child protection interventions but not getting any preventive help either. It was in this context that a central debate opened up about the need to refocus children's services and develop an integrated childcare system where services would be provided along a continuum (Figure 4.4).

This emphasis on developing an integrated childcare system, where health and education services were as important as social services and where interventions should take place at a much earlier stage, was taken much further after New Labour came to power, culminating in the Green Paper *Every Child Matters*. As a result, the funnel of Gibbons et al. (Figure 4.1) has been inverted to become a wide-based pyramid in the Green Paper (Figure 8.2) to ensure that no child is missed (Figure 8.1). The concerns of *Messages from Research* have thus broadened to include all children. Attention has shifted from trying to refocus the relationship between child protection and family support for children in need – ostensibly a social service department responsibility – to one which is concerned with all children and where all professionals who come into contact with children are to be held responsible.

Fourth, this broadening of concerns radiating from the centre is evident in the way official statistics have been collated. This is an important reflection of the way the state attempts to measure and monitor what it sees as its key responsibilities. Until 1988 the only statistics that were required were those on the number of children in local authority care and the nature of that care (see Parton, 1985b). After 1988, national statistics were also generated in relation to those on child protection registers (see Corby, 1990). It is only since 2001 that statistics have been required and made available nationally in relation to children in need, which includes figures for children looked after and those on a child protection register. Based on a sample week in September/October 2001, it was calculated that a total of 376,000 children in need were in receipt of such services, of which 59,700 were looked after (www.doh.gov.uk/cin/index.htm). The generation of such statistics reflects the change in how these issues are thought about and the priority they are being given. Clearly, children in need have become a statutory responsibility and this should therefore be reflected in the numerical 'facts' and categories which the state sees as relevant to its operations. The way statistics are now collected and represented reflects the broadening role which the state has taken on.

In many respects these changes reflect the analysis of Stan Cohen 20 years ago, when he tried to capture some of the major changes, during the 1960s and 70s, in the nature of state social control. He likened state social control to a gigantic fishing net (Cohen, 1979, 1983, 1985), where society was the ocean and the fish were 'deviants'. If we replace deviants with children, the trajectories of change identified by Cohen seem somewhat prophetic:

> a gradual expansion and intensification of the system; a dispersal of its mechanisms from more closed to more open sites and a consequent increase in the invisibility of social control and the degree of its penetration into the social body. (Cohen, 1985, pp. 83–4)

There is dispersal, proliferation, elaboration and diversification. While the old system remains, overall it expands, so that while intervention intensifies on the original population of children looked after, new categories of children are drawn in. In the process there is blurring of the boundaries between different categories of children, institutions and professionals, such that the division between the public and the private becomes increasingly porous and fluid. The state increasingly broadens its responsibilities and thereby 'penetrates' and 'absorbs' institutions which were seen as beyond its purview, particularly the family and the community, so that the boundaries and lines of accountability of civil society are redrawn.

In trying to ensure that children do not fall through the nets of child protection and family support, various attempts have been made to broaden the nets and ensure that the mesh which holds them together is tightened. At the same time, new nets have been laid so that a much greater part of the sea/ society is covered. In the process, the priority is not only that children are protected from significant harm but that the welfare of as many children as possible is safeguarded and promoted. It is in this context that the conceptual maps represented in Figures 6.1, 6.5, 8.1 and 8.2 are best understood. The boundaries between the 'abused' child, the child 'in need', the 'vulnerable' child and the child 'at risk' increasingly overlap and are blurred in our attempts to safeguard and promote the welfare of the child. In the process, the child as victim and the child as villain are both seen as in need of attention, because, for both, it is their health and development which should be the focus.

At the core of these changes is a view of dispersal as a set of flows from the state to other agents and agencies that have become engaged in the tasks of governing childhood and which generates potentially new tensions and instabilities. It involves an extensive remaking of both vertical and horizontal relations of power, authority and control to engage these diverse agents and agencies, where the state acquires expanded capacities of direction, regulation and surveillance over them (Clarke, 2004).

In Chapter 4, I argued that by the early 1990s the child protection system could be characterised in terms of the need to identify 'high risk', in a context where notions of working together were set out in increasingly complex yet detailed procedural guidelines and where professionals were required to identify forensic evidence. The question now arises as to whether the broader, dispersed and more integrated approach currently being introduced is qualitatively different from what went before, or whether the effect will be to broaden the child protection system in such a way as to include a much wider proportion of the child population and the adults, both parents and professionals, who have responsibilities for them.

Comparing Child Protection Systems

Recent years have witnessed a growing interest in comparing the child protection systems of different countries (see, for example, Cooper et al., 1995;

Hetherington et al., 1997; Gilbert, 1997; Harder and Pringle, 1997; Pringle, 1998; Parton and Matthews, 2001; Khoo et al., 2002; May-Chahal and Herczog, 2003) and different approaches to family support (see, for example, Hellinckx et al., 1997; Canavan et al., 2000; Katz and Pinkerton, 2003). These studies allow us to assess the way child protection cases are defined and handled by official agencies in different jurisdictions. One of the important variations identified is the extent to which reporting systems emphasise a legalistic and narrowly defined child protection response or a more family service orientation. In some systems, it is the act or threatened act of abuse which is primarily perceived as the problem that demands the protection of children from harm, in the form of a 'child-saving' approach. Until the mid-1990s this was the dominant approach in England, as well as in the other nations in the UK, North America and Australia. The preliminary intervention takes the form of an investigation and assessment of risk and is backed by the full legal powers of the state which stands, ever ready, to sanction the removal of a child if necessary.

In contrast, other approaches see the nature of problems as arising more from family conflict or dysfunction, which, in turn, is seen to stem from social and psychological difficulties which are much more responsive to public aid. Child maltreatment is seen as being enmeshed in a web of problems that include parents' psychological and relationship difficulties, a child's behavioural problems, communication problems within the family and socioeconomic stresses. Depending on the nature of the problem, cases are referred to a variety of agencies that provide support, counselling, advice and therapy to the whole family and/or to individuals. The approach is generally benign, aimed at helping and providing a more reciprocal and mutually supportive relationship between the state and the family. This approach is more characteristic of child protection systems in northern Europe and the Nordic countries. It has been argued that the major problem with the family service orientation, however, has been its difficulty in engaging with issues associated with sexual abuse, both within and outside the family (Pringle, 1998).

The way I have described the two approaches is very much as ideal types and it is clear that they are not mutually exclusive. Thus, for example, a number of states in both the US and Australia have, in recent years, been looking to reform their child protection systems in order to take on board some of the key characteristics and values evident in the family service approach. Perhaps the most radical approach, however, has been that adopted in England, with its attempt to integrate child protection and family support in the way I have described. In doing so, any tensions, contradictions and anomalies are in danger of being glossed over under the integrative umbrella, which asserts a consensus on what constitutes the welfare of the child.

Clearly, integration is not simply concerned with broadening conceptions and integrating services. What the ideal types outlined above demonstrate is that the approaches have different philosophies and underlying assumptions about the nature of the family and, most crucially, the most appropriate relationship between parents, children and the state (Parton, 1997, pp. 10–18). To designate a case as family support locates the power primarily with the parents, whereas to designate a case as child protection shifts the power and responsibility to the state and state agents. With the former, the core assumption is that the provision of services is voluntary and agreed, while in the latter, compulsion and formal mandates on the adults, both professionals and parents and carers, are dominant.

While difficult to define (Featherstone, 2004), family support principles emphasise strengths-based, non-deficit partnerships between participants, provide flexible and culturally sensitive services, and participant empowerment through involvement in planning and governance (Weiss, 2003). These are some of the principles which have informed much of the work of Sure Start, the Children's Fund projects and many of the other community-based initiatives launched by New Labour (Hodgson, 2004). However, it is not straightforward to integrate such an approach with one which is explicitly suspicious of parents and carers, emphasises centralisation, accountability and the sharing of information between professionals, particularly where professionals are encouraged/required to flag up any 'causes for concerns' they might have about a child to a database. Increasingly, it seems, the surveillance of children and parents, particularly mothers, is becoming the dominating characteristic of the attempts in England to integrate children's services, because 'every child matters'.

Prevention and Surveillance Systems

In Chapter 1, I argued that from the mid-nineteenth century onwards a variety of new forms of knowledge and intervention developed which had as their focus the 'normal' development of the child and the crucial role of the 'natural' family in this. It was assumed that children could be shaped and moulded through the production and application of knowledge and will. Such a belief was derived from a confidence in the power of rational understanding and the possibility of human control over nature and society (Prout, 2003). Children were seen as important because they represented society's future. Because the *modern* project attempted to take control of both society and nature through rational knowledge and planning, the investment in and control of children and childhood were seen as important means of shaping the future.

However, the major changes I summarised in Chapter 3 demonstrated that many of the assumptions that lay at the core of this project no longer seem to hold. Increasingly, it seems that modernity's project of rational control had limits and unintended consequences (Bauman, 1989, 1992). There was a growing mood of uncertainty and ontological insecurity, which replaced the more rigid notions of identity, authority and morality which were so dominant in the earlier part of the twentieth century. What I have called late modernity has seen the emergence of new patterns of family life and significant changes in the labour market, work and the global economy. The complexities and fluidities of day-to-day life have become increasingly evident, such that we have become less sure of a variety of social institutions and social experts. It seems that in a world which is increasingly shifting and uncertain, children – precisely because they are seen as unfinished – become a prime site for trying to control the future (James and James, 2001, 2004).

At a time when the intensification of global competition, the speeding up of economic processes, the demand for more compliant and flexible labour and an increased networking of national economies erode the state's capacity to control its own economic activity, the shaping of children as the future labour force is seen as an increasingly important option (Prout, 2000). As a result, in England, we have witnessed considerable policy change and increased central control on the content and focus of education (Tomlinson, 2003) and early years services.

At the same time, more and more children are seen to be at risk of a variety of new threats and dangers which the late modern world is throwing up and these are amplified and projected via an increasingly pervasive media, which provide the crucial mechanisms whereby our knowledge and understanding of the world are framed. These increased fears about risk to children and childhood are characterised by the decline of many traditional forms of solidarity, particularly the family, religion and community life, which were seen as playing a vital role in mediating between the isolated individual and the wider society. The net result seems to be to give rise to an increasingly instrumental range of attempts to extend control *over* children and the environments in which they live. A growing emphasis has thus been placed on the need for preventive policies, which aim to intervene at a much earlier stage in order to avoid risks to children (France and Utting, 2005). It is as if the more complex society becomes, the more we have attempted to control and intervene at an earlier stage to prevent harm to children. Being for prevention is like being against sin, because ensuring that something undesirable does not happen is self-evidently better than dealing with the consequences once it has; it appeals to a universal value base (Hardiker et al., 1991).

However, as Richard Freeman has argued, prevention's intellectual architecture is quintessentially modernist, because 'preventive interventions are essentially acts of social engineering predicated on the capacity of states and the integrity of scientific and professional expertise' (Freeman, 1999, p. 234). The idea of prevention is built on scientific understandings of cause and effect and the possibility of prediction,[1] together with the capacity for controlled intervention by government in social life (Scott, 1998). This is most evident in the standard conceptualisation of primary, secondary and tertiary forms of prevention, which is borrowed from the public health branch of medical science

(Freeman, 1992). At the same time, policies in relation to prevention are used to (re)define the respective responsibilities and lines of accountability between different agencies for the management of different social risks (Garland, 2001). What is being prevented is not so much the problem itself but the collapse of the various systems which have been in place to manage it. The fact that coordination is seen as so important to the success of prevention testifies to the complexity of the organisational environment in which it takes place and its role in managing relations between agencies.

Thus, as society becomes more complex, preventive interventions themselves become more complex to engineer, but the failures simply summon up renewed attempts to improve prevention: 'The effect of failure seems to be to intensify attempts at prevention. Just as it seems less possible, so it becomes more necessary' (Freeman, 1999, p. 237). This is exactly the process in the area of child protection over the past 30 years, where a proliferation of new systems and procedures have been promulgated while the object of intervention has broadened and professionals and their agencies are required to intervene earlier and earlier. In the late 1960s the object of intervention was 'the battered baby syndrome', in the 1970s 'non-accidental injury', in the 1980s 'child abuse' and by the late 1990s the child's 'safety and welfare'.

Policies and practices which emphasise prevention and early intervention are intimately connected to systems of surveillance. In the late modern world, where concerns about safety and risk have become central, there is a quantitative increase in surveillance (Dandecker, 1990; Lyon, 1994, 2001; Staples, 1997), such that surveillance has become one of the key institutional components of late modern society. Partly because of the growing reliance on new information and communication technologies (ICTs), we are now witnessing a convergence of what were once discreet surveillance systems to the point where we can now speak of an emerging 'surveillant assemblage' (Haggerty and Ericson, 2000). Surveillance is driven by the desire to bring systems together to combine practices and technologies and integrate them into a large whole (Marx, 2002). It is this tendency which allows us to speak of surveillance as an 'assemblage', with such combinations providing an exponential increase in the degree of surveillance capacity.

Today we are not just concerned with the surveillance of convicted paedophiles and children who have been or might be abused, but also with children who are in need, at risk or vulnerable, in fact every child, and anyone who is or might be responsible for children is implicated where there might be a 'cause for concern'. However, we should not see this growth in surveillance as an instrument of oppression, because it is centrally involved in the production and distribution of knowledge about diverse populations, for the purpose of managing their behaviour and development at a distance. In the context of prevention, surveillance is promoted as a vital component of positive population strategies.

These developments both reflect and feed into some potentially fundamental shifts in what are seen as the core elements of child welfare policy and practice. Crucially, the gathering, inputting, sharing and manipulation of information becomes a key activity and the relationship between the user/client/parent/ child and the professional becomes very different (Harlow and Webb, 2003; Garrett, 2004). It is not simply that the former needs to provide the latter with information in order to receive a service but that the professional requires information to feed into the computerised surveillance systems to demonstrate that they are doing their job and making themselves accountable in the process. While citizenship and social order has always depended to a large degree on relations of mutual visibility between the citizen and the state, increasingly citizens are subject to new forms of informational, mediated power, which are complex in their operations and consequences.

However, and as was evident in the Laming, Bichard and Kelly inquiries, these systems are not only complex but can become unstable and develop a life and (il)logic of their own, almost beyond human control or comprehension. As more and more complex models of representation and data sets are called for, the likely effect will be increased volatility, change and disorder requiring more and more demand in efforts at systems management (Van Loon, 2002). Instead of an increased sense of security, the very technological systems geared towards securing and regulating seem to engender an increased sense of insecurity.

In particular, because surveillance systems transcend traditional institutional boundaries, systems developed to serve one purpose can be used for other purposes in ways which were not anticipated at the time of their invention. In his analysis of paper-based records, Stanton Wheeler (1969) pointed out that they could be combined to serve new purposes and the computerisation of record keeping has greatly expanded this potential. An explicit aim of the current changes to safeguard and promote the welfare of children is to bring various health and welfare professionals together (either face to face, or through electronic media) to monitor and intervene with at risk individuals, thereby combining the cumulative knowledge derived from the various surveillance systems particular to each. Increasingly, surveillance is an explicit part of the practice changes being introduced in relation to both children and dangerous adults, and, particularly in the light of the Bichard (2004), Kelly (2004) and Joint Chief Inspectors (DH, 2002a) reports, it is being recommended that the information available to child welfare systems and public protection systems should, in some way, be made available to each other.

It is important to recognise, however, particularly with the introduction of ICT and other forms of electronic media, that surveillance is not simply a hierarchical, top-down process of observation. It flows through a network of open circuits whereby everyone is potentially visible so that 'disappearance' thereby disappears (Graham and Wood, 2003) and the nature of 'appearance' itself is subject to continual construction and reconstruction. Mathieson (1997) has argued that there is now a bottom-up form of observation now at work, 'synopticism', which parallels Foucault's (1997) panopticism.[2] Synopticism essentially means that a large number of individuals are now able to focus on the activities of the 'powerful' so that the gaze can be reversed. In particular, the wide range of print and electronic media allows the general public to scrutinise their leaders and others in quite new ways, particularly via public inquiries. Television, video cameras, tape recorders and photographs play an important role. But beyond this, the infinite retrieval of emails, telephone conversations and electronic records of all sorts means that a whole variety of information, decisions and communication can be called upon to hold professionals, senior managers, politicians and others to account. While not a democratic levelling of the hierarchy of surveillance, these developments cumulatively highlight an increasingly fractured criss-crossing of the gaze so that no one is irrefutably above or outside the surveillance systems.

Gilles Deleuze (1990) suggests that in these surveillance systems, we are not simply dealing with 'individuals' but with 'dividuals', that is, not with subjects with a unique personality that is the expression of some inner fixed quality, but with elements, capacities, potentialities and so on, which are entered into multiple codes and identification numbers according to certain criteria and characteristics which can then be analysed, quantified, reassembled and subject to calculation. Surveillance is thereby increasingly 'designed in' to the flows of everyday existence. These new strategies dissolve the subject and put in its place a concern with a combination of risk factors. As a result, the essential focus of policy and practice no longer simply takes the form of a direct face-to-face relationship between the professional and the client but resides in managing and monitoring a range of abstract factors deemed liable to produce risk for children.[3] Where previously knowledge was seen as embedded in the practices of professionals, increasingly it is embedded in the systems which they operate and of which they are a part.

Intervention increasingly becomes probabilistic and anticipatory and is not just based on the diagnosis of pathology in an individual subject or set of relationships but on an actuarial analysis of risk factors which are continuously monitored and managed (Green, 1997). What the new preventive policies primarily address, both in relation to the dangerous in the context of public protection and the safeguarding of children in the context of children's services, is not so much individuals but factors and statistical correlations of heterogeneous elements. They deconstruct the concrete subject of intervention and reconstruct a combination of factors liable to produce risk. Their primary aim is not to confront a concrete danger, but to *anticipate* any forms of eruption of danger.

We seem to have arrived at a situation in which a general system of risk prediction and risk management of child abnormalities is being put in place (Castel, 1991), where professionals are being required to identify a range of factors whose connection with abnormalities or vulnerability is primarily abstract and statistical, for example age of mother, previous history, household composition, labour market status, and a combination of factors may lead to the allocation of a service or some other form of intervention. In effect, information gathered from a variety of sources is brought together to consider the nature and significance of risk for the child:

> 'Prevention' in effect promotes suspicion to the dignified scientific rank of a calculus of probabilities ... A conception of prevention which restricted itself to predicting the occurrence of a particular act appears archaic and artisanal in comparison with one which claims to *construct* the objective conditions of emergence of danger, so as then to *deduce* from them the new modalities of intervention. (Castel, 1991, pp. 288–9)

Thus while the concept of prevention has been construed as a positive and benign approach to children's welfare, because of its close association to surveil-lance and risk, in practice this may be rather different. The new mentalities of risk not only reconstitute the nature and focus of the work and the nature of the relationships between professionals and their clients, they are also significant in the way workers think about and organise themselves and are organised, their obligations and the way they are made accountable (Parton, 1998). As Mary Douglas (1992) has argued, the concept of risk has become increasingly central to politics and public policy in recent years, precisely because of its use as a forensic resource, and the more individualised a society becomes, the more significant becomes the forensic potential of the idea of risk. Its forensic uses are particularly important in the development of different types of blaming systems, and 'the one we are in now is almost ready to treat every death as chargeable to someone's account, every accident as caused by someone's criminal negligence, every sickness a threatened prosecution' (Douglas, 1992, p. 15). Risk assessment and risk management – the identification, assessment, elimination or reduction of the possibility or consequence of loss or misfortune – become key for all the professionals involved (Garland, 2003).

Within these new government strategies for both children's services and public protection, audit becomes one of the key mechanisms for responding to failure. As Michael Power (1994, 1997) has argued, audit and inspection have come to replace the trust once accorded to professionals. Audit responds to failure and insecurity by the managerialisation of risk. Risk is rendered man-ageable by new relations of regulation between the political centres of decision making and the frontline professionals, via the introduction of a variety of new procedures, forms, devices and systems for making and noting decisions and thereby making them visible. In the process, the professionals who are to be audited are themselves transformed in order to make them auditable. Where the key concern is risk, the priority is liable to be making a *defensible* decision where the required processes and procedures have been followed, rather than making the *right* decision (Howe, 1992; Dingwall et al., 1995). This has been made quite explicit in Home Office guidance (2003) where, following Kemshall (2003), the first feature of good practice is that decisions are 'defensible'. In the context where the most diligent efforts of practitioners cannot always prevent serious harm, 'in place of infallibility we must put defensibility – making the most reasonable decisions and carrying them out professionally in a way which can be seen to be reasonable and professional' (Home Office, 2003, p. 5).

The danger is that, in an area of work which is highly sensitive and where the media are always looking for 'mistakes' and so any case is potentially high profile, trust is difficult to maintain. Concerns about risk to the professional and risks to the organisation (Townley, 2002; Farrell and Morris, 2003) are liable to dominate. Once concerns about risk become pervasive, the requirement to develop and follow increasingly complex organisational procedures becomes essential and the room for professional manoeuvre and creativity becomes severely limited (Parton, 1996b).

The current situation is full of paradox, for while most agree that certainty in child welfare is not possible, the political and organisational climate demands it. Professionals, not just social workers as previously, have been found wanting and are no longer trusted. The result seems to be that the various changes introduced act to sidestep the paradox and substitute *confidence in systems* for *trust in individual professionals* (Smith, 2001), so that the introduction of the most up-to-date technology becomes a major priority and the processing and manipulation of information becomes the key element for judging and managing change.

The continual refinement and reform of 'systems' demonstrate that services for children are conceived as instrumental machines which need to be updated to take account of new challenges and the new knowledges and technologies that are available. The fact that they may have failed points only to the need for their robust repair and new manuals, diagrams and flow charts are required to make the increased complexity of the systems comprehensible. This approach is bound up with a particular understanding of public provisions for children:

A very instrumental and atomising notion, in which provisions are technologies for acting upon children, or parts of children, to produce specific, predetermined and adult-defined outcomes. (Moss and Petrie, 2002, p. 9)

Perhaps the most profound implications of these changes are the way they are reframing the relationships between the public and the private and, in particular, the relationships between the child, parents, professionals and the state and society more generally. It is not simply that the relationship between the public and the private has become more blurred but that it is becoming more mobile and hybrid (Sheller and Urry, 2003). More specifically, the development and use of a range of new electronic, digital technologies transforms the way information can be gathered and communicated and thereby the way state agents and others can monitor and manage the world and are themselves monitored and managed.

Individualisation and Self-realisation

Recent changes to both broaden and intensify attempts to safeguard and promote the welfare of children have thus had the effect of increasing the attempts at the regulation and surveillance of children themselves, and the adults who have responsibilities for them, whether these be professionals or parents. However, as I argued in Chapter 1, it is inappropriate to conceive of the modern project as only being concerned with the control of society and nature. It was also aimed to enhance self-realisation and emancipation; the belief that a world subject to rational control would also create the conditions in which people could shape their own lives through the formation and exercise of self-consciousness, creativity and agency. Tensions between individual self-realisation and social control and between the aspirations for individual self-creation and regulation lay at the heart of the modern project from its inception, and these tensions have become more sharply focused in the context of late modernity. In trying to resolve these tensions, primarily by increasing our attempts to control, discipline and regulate, we are in great danger of failing to maximise the possibilities for responsible adults and more particularly children and young people themselves to play a central part in realising and creating their own lives.

As I argued in Chapter 3, the process of *individualisation* (Giddens, 1990, 1992; Beck, 1992a, 1992b; Beck and Beck-Gernsheim, 2002) points to the processes whereby people increasingly see themselves as unique, with chosen rather than prescribed or standard identities, and hence act accordingly. This is not simply a psychological shift but is the product of a variety of social processes, including:

- the pluralisation of family form

- the more wide-ranging and relativised norms about the standards whereby life can be lived

- the growing significance of consumption and lifestyle in influencing identity

- more open, personalised and globalised forms of communication prompted by electronic media, the internet and mobile phones.

The concept of individualisation makes it possible for children to be seen as persons in their own right and have new-found rights and responsibilities, so that children not only have a right to a 'life of their own' but they also 'individualise' themselves and are active agents who design their own lives (James and Prout, 1997). It is in this context that we can see the wider significance of the growing emphasis on seeing children as having a voice and having access to decision making, including rights of participation as enshrined in Article 12 of the UN Convention on the Rights of the Child. There is little doubt that, while uneven and highly contested (Foley et al., 2003), the idea of children's rights is now seen as an important part of public policy and practice in ways which were unthinkable 30 years ago (Franklin, 2002). The views of children and young people were prioritised in the Quality Protects programme and the early work of the Children and Young People's Unit and are expected to play an active role in decisions which affect them while being looked after. Similarly, the Green Paper *Every Child Matters* (Chief Secretary to the Treasury, 2003) claimed that its overall goals were based on consultations with children, young people and families and that similar consultations informed its *Next Steps* document (DfES, 2004). Rhetorically at least, children and young people are now included in policy and practice in quite new ways.

More significantly, while it is clear that children and young people are active agents in their own lives, when we look at evidence about what troubles them, as opposed to what worries adults, and what they do about it, we often find that children and young people develop strategies which bypass adult-centric children's services. For example, research conducted for the National Commission of Inquiry into the Prevention of Child Abuse (Wattam and Woodward, 1996) and also by ChildLine (the national confidential telephone helpline for children and young people) (MacLeod, 1996) clearly demonstrated that while children and young people were becoming more able to tell others about sexual abuse (in the 1986 ChildLine report, the figure was only 20 per cent, while in 1996 it was 53 per cent), relatively few reported it to a statutory social services agency. The 1996 ChildLine figures showed that just 3 per cent told someone in a social services department. Half told friends and about a quarter told mothers. It seems that telling others rarely leads to official reporting. Similarly, in the NSPCC prevalence study of child maltreatment (Cawson et al., 2000; Cawson, 2002), which interviewed a representative sample of over 3000 young people aged 18–24 years old, only a quarter of the people who had experienced sexual abuse as a child told anyone it had occurred. A quarter told someone later, but 31 per cent never told anyone by their early adulthood. Of those who had talked to someone, 55 per cent had told a friend, 29 per cent their mother or step-mother, 11 per cent their father, 13 per cent a sibling, 2 per cent a social worker, 7 per cent the police, 5 per cent a teacher, and 1 per cent a helpline.

Corinne Wattam (2002) has demonstrated, from her analysis of recent studies of child protection referrals to social services departments, that less than 5 per cent of referrals come directly from children and young people themselves. Referrals come from adults, and while a small number come from relatives and neighbours, by far the biggest proportions come from schools, the police, health professionals and other social workers.

Research which seeks the views of children and young people themselves gives an important insight not only into how children and young people experience formal services but also how they negotiate and address problems. Featherstone and Evans' review of research (2004) indicates that while the majority of children seem satisfied with their lives, a small but significant proportion report serious unhappiness revolving around problems with friends, tensions with and between parents, the illness or death of someone close to them and problems with school and personal appearance. Bullying between children emerges as a significant issue for many children. There are important differences between children in terms of their worries and willingness to express these; girls tend to report more worries than boys (Ghate and Daniels, 1997), while older children tend to report more worries than younger children (Balding et al., 1998).

What becomes apparent is that children and young people's help-seeking behaviour is determined by the *subjective meaning* which they give to events and this is often at variance with what adults might expect. It is not always the originating problem which causes the 'worst experience' but the secrets and difficulties associated with it (Butler and Williamson, 1994, 1996). A lack of information or explanation and a sense of helplessness can create as much, if not more, distress than the original problem itself. Only by listening to the *meaning* imputed to such experiences by the young people concerned can those seeking to support and help them secure a measure of understanding of how these experiences are affecting them and what they want done about it. A major problem with the current attempts to collate and share a wide range of information about concerns that professionals have about children is that they grossly underestimate the background and contexts for those concerns and, crucially, the meanings imputed to them by the key actors, particularly the children and young people themselves.

While the opportunity to share difficulties on their own terms is critical in helping children to cope, it was clear in the study by Ian Butler and Howard Williamson (1994, p. 65) that a significant minority were 'cautious, reluctant and even fearful about discussing such issues with anyone let alone adults, who might potentially be able to help'. The study demonstrated that many young people had lost faith in adults' capacity to help them to deal with their problems, to the point that many had entirely given up on them. The reasons for this were commonly shared: adults were incapable of understanding; they imposed their own views; they either trivialised problems or overreacted – sometimes over the same issues – and thus were inconsistent.

These insights have been further developed by Christine Hallett and her colleagues (Hallett et al., 2003) who interviewed 86 young people aged 13–14, living in Scotland, about who they were most likely to turn to for different problems. When aggregated, the most common people were best friends, both parents, mothers, and siblings. What was striking were the issues raised by the young people about the problems of accessibility to formal agencies. The first involved simply locating the person who might be able to help them. Most of those living at home were unclear how to access social workers and counsellors, their usual solutions being to look in the telephone book or magazines. Another source of information was the school and the posters or leaflets provided there. A few said they would ask parents or use the internet. In contrast, those who lived in residential homes were more confident about how to access formal agencies and many of them had contact telephone numbers for social workers. It may be, therefore, that the current plans in England to locate services in schools and early years services may improve accessibility, while the growth in the use of mobile phones and the internet, particularly by young people, could be given more thought in relation to how these resources could be developed, but only if children and young people play a central role in determining how these services operate.

The second issue identified by Hallett et al. (2003) involved accessibility once someone was located. For example, doctors were often perceived as being too busy, while guidance teachers and school nurses were noted for their lack of availability. The third issue was identified particularly by girls. They expressed a preference for the person providing help and support to be female. Fourthly, it was clear that age was an important influence on who young people talked to. Friends, siblings and, to a lesser extent, cousins were seen as more likely to understand problems than adults, largely because of their current or recent childhood experiences. Mutual sharing of problems was an important feature in the best friend or sibling relationship, as young people felt it was important that they could help each other with their worries, in contrast to the one-sided problem solving which typified their relationships with adults. Most thought adults would often act inappropriately because of their older age and were more likely to be moralistic rather than understanding.

The most important factor which influenced whether young people were prepared to discuss their problems was whether they felt they could trust the person they were telling to keep their problems confidential and this was a major reason why they did not talk to adults, particularly in formal agencies:

> Confidentiality and trust were of utmost importance for the young people when deciding whether or not to tell someone about a problem. They considered that informal networks (particularly friends) could usually be relied upon more than formal agencies to provide confidentiality. In particular if individuals were known to them, a better judgement could be made as to how trustworthy they were. One of the major concerns to the young people was that personal knowledge about them would be spread around. Some felt that if they really did not want a certain problem to be known it would be better not to tell anybody at all. (Hallett et al., 2003, p. 132)

This clearly poses a serious challenge to a policy direction in children's services which aims at integration and increasing the sharing of information between a range of health, welfare, educational, and criminal justice professionals. The anticipation of adults' reactions is a major inhibitor upon children and young people sharing their problems. Many clearly feel that adults will take control of their problems and insist something is done about them against their will. Issues around trust and confidentiality are absolutely key to ensuring that the way children's services develop do not have the impact of disempowering and alienating children and young people. These are complex issues (Wattam, 1999; Alderson and Morrow, 2004; Williamson et al., forthcoming) but get to the heart of the ways in which adult/child relations might be reconfigured, ensuring that children and young people can realise and individualise themselves according to criteria and outcomes which they determine rather than those which are generated by adults or, more to the point, by the various systems and procedures which are designed to promote and safeguard their welfare.

What these research studies also demonstrate is that many children and young people, far from being weak, immature and incomplete, are very able to make sense of the world and have many strengths (Dahlberg et al., 1999; Moss et al., 2000; Moss and Petrie, 2002). The image that comes across is that the child 'is rich in potential, strong, powerful, competent and, most of all, connected to adults and other children' (Malaguzzi, 1993, p. 10). They have agency and actively construct their lives in response to a whole range of worries and problems that they might have (Thomson and Holland, 2002). However, their responses and self-realisation are clearly constrained by a number of contextual factors including their age, gender and living circumstances. The overriding constraining contextual factor is simply their status as 'children', which structures the nature and impact of their powerlessness, lack of privacy and the lack of legitimacy accorded to their worries (Qvortrup, 1994).

It is clear from the thousands of children who access helplines, such as ChildLine, that the fact that the service is anonymous, enabling children to maintain a degree of control over what happens to them, is a major positive for children. It suggests that not only do children need to be empowered, they need, literally, to be given more control over what they use, when and with whom. It is clear that children and young people do not simply want to be asked about their worries and concerns but also want to be involved in the formulation of any 'action' as a result (Sinclair, 2004). This involves refusing or negotiating compliance and having the right to say 'no' to what might be on offer. An approach which wants to take the views of children and young people seriously suggests that there are a number of issues which have to be addressed each and every time they come to the attention of a professional. These include:

- children's definitions of the problem

- their own options for action

- their choice of safe and trusted persons

- the need to maximise their autonomy within relationships
- the open sharing of information with the young person
- the scope and limits of confidentiality.

If these issues cannot be addressed adequately, it is difficult to see how the relationship can in any way be reciprocal.

Perhaps the central question is whether and how far the adult world is able to assist children to feel safe and have their problems addressed according to how children define safety or whether they *appear* safe according to adult definitions. Clearly, the issue of children's rights and participation (Hill et al., 2004) in the context of individualisation is now a serious one. It also seems that the growing use of ICT, including the internet and mobile phones, means that children can now participate in and create new networks of communication for themselves, which provide considerable potential for them to move beyond the traditional public/private divide, thereby creating new ways of articulating and addressing their problems. These developments not only provide new mechanisms for the control and exploitation of children, but also provide opportunities for their self-realisation (Hutchby and Moran-Ellis, 2001; Calder, 2004).

More fundamentally, however, the recognition that children have agency and competences demonstrates that they can and do make a positive contribution not only to their own welfare but that of others (Brannen and Moss, 2003). The division of the world into children who are dependent, immature and incompetent and adults who are independent, mature and competent fails to appreciate the increasing fluidities and complexities of contemporary life. Children, as well as adults, have resources and strengths, including a whole range of informal relationships and networks both between each other and with a range of different adults (Armstrong et al., 1998).

Moss and Petrie (2002) argue that we need to move beyond an instrumental view of children's services which is primarily concerned with producing specific, predetermined and adult-defined outcomes. They recommend the concept of 'children's spaces', which understands provisions as environments for many possibilities where children can live their childhoods, as a way forward:

> Children's spaces foreground the present, rather than the future: they are part of life, not just preparation for it. They are spaces for children's own agendas although not precluding adult agendas, where children are understood as fellow citizens with rights, participating members of social groups in which they find themselves agents of their own lives but also interdependent with others, co-constructors of knowledge, identity and culture, children who co-exist with others in society on the basis of who they are, rather than who they will become. (Moss and Petrie, 2002, p. 106)

This approach connects with arguments and proposals put forward by Cooper et al. (2003) which draws on their work comparing the child protection system in England with other countries in Europe (Cooper et al., 1995; Hetherington et al., 1997; Cooper and Hetherington, 1999, 2001). They argue that the way the child protection system has developed in England is overly proceduralised, defensive and conflict ridden. Conflict rather than consensus characterises the way things operate in practice. There is a lack of trust and problems over confidentiality are central. In such a context the views and experiences of all involved – particularly the child, the parent(s) and relevant professionals – need to be respected and opportunities for dialogue and negotiation need to be opened up (Cooper and Hetherington, 1999). This includes the recognition that peoples' timescales may be very different and imposing requirements which give little opportunity for discretion may well be counterproductive.

Time is a major issue. Proper discussion, proper reflection, proper representation and participation all take time. A concern with risk, however, invariably has the opposite effect. By being so concerned with anticipating the future in the present, we put particular pressures on the present to act, or not to act. Saving time by speeding up is a primary motive behind most technological and organisational innovations. However, the emphasis on urgency inhibits reflection and (re)consideration and ultimately contributes to the proliferation of uncertainties, latent contingencies and, thus, further risks. In doing so, decision making is dominated by a form of technological culture in which risk aversion becomes the predominant ethical imperative (Van Loon, 2002).

Most of the changes introduced in recent years to promote the safeguarding and welfare of children have been premised on assumptions which are primarily rationalist and thoroughly modernist in approach. In so doing, they grossly underestimate that much of the work – as is demonstrated by the emotive responses in the media when cases are seen as being mishandled – is influenced by feelings of shock, overwhelmedness, fear, loathing and relief. They grossly underestimate the intensity of emotions and that moving on may require mourning for lost attachments and versions of the self which the various parties involved may be deeply invested in. Destructiveness, hostility and coercion can be involved. The art and emotions of practice, by their very nature, can be uncertain. As Froggett (2002) and Ferguson (2004) have argued, there is a fundamental dimension to the work that is irrational, emotional and expressive. The issues are complex and cannot be reduced to the imposition of rational criteria and processes.

In this context, Cooper et al. (2003) argue that 'spaces' and forums where children, parent(s) and professionals can engage in dialogue and negotiation are key, particularly in those situations where at least one of the parties is 'worried'. They argue for the establishment of 'confidential spaces' where the different parties can explore their complex dilemmas within defined and mutually understood boundaries of confidentiality. The structure they propose for such confidential spaces would involve multidisciplinary teams of competent, trained professionals who are able to act authoritatively and are all provided with supervision. The limits of confidentiality would be stated clearly, but the process of negotiation would be central.

My purpose here is not to detail how these ideas might be operationalised but to indicate that there are a number of different ways of developing services which can be considered if children, and the adults who have responsibilities for them – parents, wider family networks and professionals – are to be engaged. Information and who controls it is crucial; however, it is the *meaning* attached to the information rather than the information per se which has to be struggled with and this is a complex process. Perhaps one way of reframing the approach would be to start from an assessment of children's rights, rather than their needs. To do so would require children's participation in the process.

Conclusion

A major problem with the changes currently being introduced in England is that because the systems are so extensive, the definitions of concern so broad and the fact that the professionals who have responsibilities for children are held so (publicly) accountable (if things go wrong), there is a huge potential that worries about children's vulnerabilities will lead to a huge explosion of activity which only tangentially relates to the concerns of children and young people themselves. One suspects that in the context of Figures 8.1 and 8.2, and when there are insufficient resources available, an increasing amount of energy and time will be taken up by professionals, working in the reconfigured children's services, developing and applying a variety of different 'threshold criteria', which aim to identify what sort of 'cause for concern' is being dealt with, what services (if any) should be allocated and who is responsible. Similarly, depending on how the case is categorised – which in some instances will be subject to considerable negotiation – the level of confidentiality with which information is handled will also be the subject of considerable negotiation. For example, whether a concern about a child is seen as indicative of their actual abuse, or their vulnerability to not fulfilling their potential, will have important implications for what information is seen as relevant and who has access to that information. These are complex issues.

While children are being placed at the centre of the new services, there is a great danger that the services will not be child-centred. Children are not simply to be the objects of concern, but the objects of sophisticated systems of assessment, monitoring and surveillance. However, what comes across from listening to the accounts of children and practitioners is that many of the issues are complex and not subject to easy resolution. Conflict and the need for negotiation often characterise the work. In being so concerned about early intervention and the assessment, monitoring and management of risk, there is a danger that we lose sight of the need to alleviate suffering in the here and now.

What is evident, however, is that in the context of the social changes I have characterised as late modernity, children and the idea of childhood itself have become objects of concern in their own right. In the process, the way we address these concerns is itself subject to a major tension. Rather than the tension being framed almost exclusively by the relationship between the privacy of the family and the interventions of the public authority to protect the child as previously, this is now also concerned with the balance that needs to be struck between encouraging and supporting children in their agency and self-realisation, as opposed to subjecting them to wider and more complex forms of regulation. The way different late modern societies address this issue, and thereby strike the balance, varies. However, in England, the balance seems to have been struck more in favour of increased control and regulation. In the context of major changes in the family and increased individualisation, the response in England has primarily been concerned with setting up a range of new systems so that every child will have their place, and a range of responsible adults, both professional and parental, will be held accountable for their monitoring and the identification of problems at an early stage. While superficially appealing, the history of the past 40 years suggests there will be a whole range of unintended consequences and that the future will be littered with new and even more complex examples of systems failure, such that even more vigorous attempts at system repair will be demanded.

If we are serious about wanting to ensure that children feel safe, it seems that it is not simply that the voices of children and young people have to be heard but that they have to be given more control about what happens to them once they have raised their voice. This is a major challenge. In a period of increased anxiety about childhood, it is understandable that there is an emphasis on adults wanting to regulate the lives of children more and more. It takes considerable maturity to give the primary control to children and young people themselves so that they can report what they want, where and when, and how 'their concerns' should be addressed, so that they feel they have a large degree of control about what happens to them. The challenges are even more pronounced with young children. However, what we do and how we respond have considerable implications not only for children and young people themselves but also for the way adults see the world and want to develop it in the future.

Some years ago Nikolas Rose (1999) argued that:

Childhood is the most intensively governed sector of personal existence. In different ways, at different times, and by many different routes varying from one section of society to another, the health, welfare, and rearing of children have been linked to the destiny of the nation and the responsibilities of the state. The modern child has become the focus of innumerable projects that purport to safeguard it from physical, sexual or moral danger, to ensure its 'normal development', to actively promote certain capacities of attributes such as intelligence, educability, and emotional stability.

Throughout the nineteenth century and our own [twentieth century], anxieties concerning children have occasioned a panoply of programmes that have tried to conserve
and shape children by moulding the petty details of the domestic, conjugal and sexual
lives of their parents. (1999, p. 123)

If my analysis is correct, it seems likely that in England the intensity of the
government of childhood is being considerably increased at the beginning of
the twenty-first century. The challenge is to ensure that the systems being
introduced do not become inherently complex and unstable, and are subject to
human control, so that they become the vehicles for the increased safety and
emancipation of children and young people, rather than their opposite.

Notes

Chapter 1 Child Welfare and Modern Society

1 For a more detailed analysis, see Henrick (1994, 2003), Heywood (1978), Parton (1985a, Chapter 2), and more specifically in the context of child sexual abuse, Ashenden (2004).

2 See Behlmer, 1982; Hendrick, 1994, 2003; Heywood, 1978; and Parton, 1985a, Chapter two, for more detailed discussion of these developments.

3 For example, Bowlby's work (1951) on the importance of 'attachment', which was to prove so significant in informing the philosophy and approach to the new children's departments, was developed at this time.

4 See Perkin (1989) and Polsky (1991) on the growing significance of the new professions in the twentieth century.

5 In terms of need, there were important demographic changes, particularly with regard to the increased proportion of the population not just over retirement age but aged over 75. Because of the increased incidence of illness, infirmity, disability and social isolation associated with old age, there was greater demand placed upon the social security, health and social care services. It also seemed that the 'rediscovery of poverty' in the mid-1960s indicated that the assumption that the severe and widespread social deprivations of the inter-war period had been overcome by the welfare reforms was somewhat exaggerated (Abel-Smith and Townsend, 1965). Not only had improvements in technology and expertise, in effect, created new needs, particularly in terms of demands for health services, it also seemed that the proportionate increase in welfare expenditure was caused by the labour-intensive nature of the services, which could not easily be sub-stituted by new technology as in the manufacturing industry. The relative costs of providing welfare services rose faster than the national rate of inflation (Gough, 1979).

6 This was most explicitly evident if and when a case went to court for a supervision or care order where the parents and children (or anyone else) were not recognised as separate parties to the proceedings and thus officially could not have separate legal representation.

Chapter 2   Child Abuse and the Growing Crisis in Child Protection

1   See Dingwall (1986) for a critique of the way the 'rule of optimism' was interpreted and used in the report.

2   Whenever a case involves an incident leading to the death of a child where child abuse is confirmed or suspected, or a child protection issue likely to be of major public concern arises, there should be an individual review by each agency and a composite review by the ACPC. [area child protection committee] (Home Office et al., 1991, para. 8.1, p. 57)

3   Reder and Duncan (1999) reported an annual average of 53 Part 8 reviews between 1990 and 1995, while the SSI reported that about 60 such cases were taking place per year (SSI, 1995). A report by Geoffrey James (1994) indicated that in the early 1990s the Department of Health received about 120 notifications per year of child deaths or incidents of serious harm to children which might be of public concern, but not all were subject to a Part 8 review.

4   See Jenkins (1992) Chapters 7 and 8 for a critical discussion of the way cases of ritual abuse were constructed and the role of the media; and Bibby, 1996, for a wide-ranging analysis of the nature and extent of 'organised abuse'.

5   The Home Office issued an updated version of the memorandum in 2000. The new version emphasised the wider needs of the child and brings the memorandum into line with the most recent legislation.
    It is important to note that the publication of the memorandum in 1992 was not a direct response to events in Orkney, or Cleveland for that matter. Throughout the 1980s there had been considerable concern expressed in several quarters as to how children were treated in criminal courts, particularly in cases of alleged sexual abuse and where the success or failure of the case was likely to hinge on their evidence. In 1987 a working group issued a report, generally referred to as the Pigot Report (Home Office, 1989), which made a number of recommendations for extending the provisions for child witnesses in order to make the process easier for children and reduce the need for children to have to give their testimony in open court. Many of these were included in the Criminal Justice Act 1991, which abolished the competency requirement, allowed for committal proceedings to be bypassed under certain circumstances, and permitted video recorded evidence to be admitted but only for evidence in chief. Justice Pigot also recommended a code of practice for practitioners to ensure that evidence would not be prejudiced during the initial assessment of cases. It was this function which the memorandum aimed to fulfil. The document provides advice on the use of video recorded interviews with child witnesses for criminal proceedings and aimed to build on the Working Together approach, whereby the police and social services would jointly investigate cases of child abuse to combine 'the interests of the child and justice' (see SSI, 1994; Davies and Westcott, 1999; and Williams, 2002, for a more detailed discussion of these issues and the related research).

6   The terms of reference for the review were:

  - to review the safeguards introduced for England and Wales by the Children Act 1989 and its implementation in 1991, and the further measures since taken to protect children living away from home, with particular reference to children's residential homes, foster care and boarding schools;

  - to assess whether these safeguards are the most effective that can realistically be designed to protect such children from abuse and other harm and whether they are being satisfactorily enforced;

  - to make recommendations accordingly to the Secretary of State for Health and the Secretary for Wales (Utting, 1997, p. vii).

7   In fact, Lord Laming was appointed by the secretary of state for health and the home secretary to conduct three parallel statutory inquiries. Together these would be known as *The Victoria Climbié Report*. The first inquiry was established under section 81 of the Children Act 1989 and was concerned with the functions of local authority social services committees and the way they relate to children. The second inquiry was established under section 84 of the National Health Service Act 1977 and was concerned with matters arising under that Act. The third inquiry was established under section 49 of the Police Act 1996 and was concerned with policing.

Chapter 3   From Maria Colwell to Victoria Climbié: The Emergence of Late Modernity

1   As Hobsbawm (1994, p. 408) has argued:

> The central fact about the crisis decades [1973–93] is not that capitalism no longer worked as well as it had done in the Golden Age, but that its operations had become uncontrollable. Nobody knew what to do about the vagaries of the world economy or possessed instruments to manage them ... the crisis decades were the era when the national state lost its economic powers.

2   By the early 1990s in Britain, just four large media groups controlled around 92 per cent of the circulation of national daily newspapers and 89 per cent of the circulation of Sunday papers (Thompson, 1996, p. 77).

3   The cultural revolution of the later twentieth century can thus best be understood as the triumph of the individual over society, or rather, the breaking of the threads which in the past had woven human beings into social textures. For such textures had consisted not only of the actual relations between human beings and their

forms of organization but also the general models of such relations and the expected patterns of people's behaviour towards each other; their roles were prescribed, though not always written. (Hobsbawm, 1994, p. 334)

4   In 1951 women formed 29 per cent of the active workforce and around 50 per cent by the mid-1990s (Walby, 1997). According to the General Household Survey, in 1975, 81 per cent of men aged 16–64 were economically active and 62 per cent of women, but by 1996 the figure had become 70 per cent for both (ONS, 1998, Tables 5.8 and 5.9). During the 1980s, employment for women with children increased faster than among women without children, and the most dramatic increases were for women with children under five years old; the difference in the activity rates between women with and without dependent children halved between 1973 and 1996 (Lewis, 2001). However, almost half of women workers were employed part time.

5   The patriarchal family, the cornerstone of patriarchalism, is being challenged at the end of the millennium by the inseparably related processes of the transformation of women's work and the transformation of women's conscious-ness. Driving forces behind these processes are the rise of an informational global economy, technological changes in the reproduction of the human species, and the powerful surge of women's struggles, and of a multifaceted feminist movement. (Castells, 1997, p. 135)

6   Young (1999, pp. 114–15) outlines some of the key processes which, he argues, can be seen to feed into and encourage 'the manufacture of monsters':

● their 'wickedness' is clear cut so that there is little or no debate about their guilt and culpability

● their acts are 'unbelievable' and on the 'edge of human comprehension and empathy'

● their background is essentially different from 'our own' and is often seen as a product of a highly disorganised, violent or abusive family

● they are beyond redemption and cannot change

● they pose an extraordinary risk and threat which cannot be managed through 'normalising' methods

● the mass media plays a key role in the process of demonisation by active campaigning and searching out 'the monster' and holding the police and other criminal justice agencies responsible for failing to 'protect the public' such that the criminal justice system is placed on the defensive

● there is a growing coverage, sale and demand for a wide range of cultural artefacts particularly in the form of films, books, TV and the internet which sell highly sexualised and violent pornography and which the popular media, particularly tabloid newspapers, can both simultaneously condemn and cite widely.

Chapter 4   Rethinking Child Protection and Family Support

1   Jonathan Bradshaw (1990, p. 51) concluded his survey of child poverty and deprivation in the UK by writing:

> During the 1980s children have borne the brunt of the changes that have occurred in the economic conditions, demographic structure and social policies of the UK. More children have been living in low income families and the number of children living in poverty has doubled. Inequalities also became wider.

The situation was further confirmed by Kumar (1993) in an exhaustive survey of the effects of increased poverty and inequality on children resulting from increases in unemployment, debt, housing repossessions and general increased hardship and insecurity. The situation had been made worse by changes in the social security system which had left claimants with greater financial responsibility and reduced access to additional sources of financial support from the state (Graham, 1994).

2   Drawing on a similar methodology, Ferguson and O'Reilly (2001), investigating child protection processes and outcomes in Ireland in 1996/7, found a similar pattern to that identified by Thorpe (1994) and Gibbons et al. (1995), and they emphasised that 'neglect is the most common form of abuse, and the biggest single deficit in meeting identified need lies in the area of parenting' (Ferguson and O'Reilly, 2001, p. 22).

3   In September 1996 the Department of Health launched 'the refocusing children's services initiative' to fund small-scale, concrete projects to identify innovative approaches. The whole initiative cost just £700k which covered the costs of the 45 projects, an evaluation and a conference. The range of funding was from £500 to an upper limit of £25k, with a maximum end date of March 1998 (Robbins, 1999).

4   At the core of the 'refocusing debate', the LAC project and, more generally, the arguments being developed for the need for early intervention to forestall a range of problems in later life was a particular model of child development which has continued to underpin many of the developments I will discuss in Chapters 6 and 8. As we saw in Chapter 2, the concept of a 'child in need' in the Children Act 1989 was defined primarily in terms of a child's physical, intellectual, emotional, social and behavioural development. Within this standardised model of development, childhood is seen as a period of dependency in which adults are the dominant providers and children are the passive recipients. It is parents who, therefore, carry the prime responsibility for the child's development. This standardised model of child development is based on many of the ideas promulgated earlier in the twentieth century, which I discussed in Chapter I, and has been at the core of the post-war period.

Ironically, just at the time when this standardised model of child development has increasingly taken on the guise of received wisdom and its influence on

policy and practice has become ever more pervasive, its central premises have
been subject to increasing critiques from a wide variety of disciplines, including
history, philosophy, sociology, anthropology and psychology itself (Walkerdine
1984, 1993; Ingleby, 1986; Woodhead, 1988, 1997, 1999; Burman, 1994, 1997;
Taylor, 2004). The model is seen as overly normative in ways which do not
recognise the diversity of developmental pathways and is liable to pathologise
deviations, a particular problem when increasing emphasis is placed upon early
intervention in order to avoid later abnormalities. The model is seen as
historically and culturally specific, overly individualised and construes children
as being in the process of 'becoming' adults rather persons in their own right
(James and Prout, 1997; Lee, 2001).

Chapter 5   Governing Childhood under New Labour

1   The initiative was originally led by Norman Glass, who was then at the Public
Services Directorate at the Treasury and who described Sure Start as

> a radical cross-departmental strategy to raise the physical, social, emotional and
> intellectual status of young children through improved services. It is *targeted* at
> *children under four* and their families *in areas of need*. It is part of the government's
> policy to *prevent social exclusion* and aims to improve the life chances of younger
> children through better access to early education and play, health services for
> children and parents, family support and advice on nurturing. It will be *locally led*
> and *locally delivered* but will be based on evidence from the United Kingdom and
> elsewhere on 'what works' in terms of improving the life chances of children
> and their parents. (Glass, 1999, p. 257, emphases added)

2   In order to emphasise the cross-cutting nature of the programme, David Blunkett,
the secretary of state for education and employment, would speak for the
programme in Cabinet while the minister of public health would continue to
have day-to-day responsibility and chair the steering group. Similarly, questions
in the House of Commons would be tabled during education question time but
the answers would be given by the minister of public health.

Chapter 6   'Working Together to Safeguard Children'

1   For example, in relation to the first objective 'to ensure that children are securely
attached to carers capable of providing safe and effective care for the duration of
childhood', it was stated that 'this objective applies to family support work as well
as children looked after' (DH, 1998b, p. 12).

2   For example, the decision to deregister a case from the child protection register 'must be based on a careful and thorough analysis of current risk' (Home Office et al., 1991, para. 6.44). Following *Protecting Children: A Guide for Social Workers Undertaking a Comprehensive Assessment in Cases of Child Protection* (DH, 1988), and published on the same day as the 1988 Working Together, the assessment of risk to the child was seen as continuing to play an important role for long-term planning in child protection cases after 1991.

3   These were identified as:

    (i)   referral and recognition;
    (ii)   immediate protection and planning the investigation;
    (iii)   investigation and initial assessment;
    (iv)   child protection conference and decision making about the need for registration;
    (v)   comprehensive assessment and planning;
    (iv)   implementation, review and, where appropriate, de-registration. (Home Office et al., 1991, Part 5, para. 5.10)

4   The key elements of this 'integrated approach' were laid out in para. 1.9:

    Effective measures to safeguard children should not be seen in isolation from the wider range of support and services available to meet the needs of children and families:

    •   many of the families who become the subject of child protection concerns suffer from multiple disadvantages. Providing services and support to children and families under stress may strengthen the capacity of parents to respond to the needs of their children before problems develop into abuse

    •   child protection enquiries may reveal severe unmet needs for support and services among children and families. These should always be explicitly considered, even where concerns are not substantiated about significant harm to a child if the family so wishes

    •   if child protection processes are to result in improved outcomes for children, then effective plans for safeguarding children and promoting their welfare should be based on a wide-ranging assessment of the needs of the child and their family circumstances

    •   all work with children and families should retain a clear focus on the welfare of the child. Just as child protection processes should always consider the wider needs of the child and family, so broad-based family support services should always be alert to, and know how to respond quickly and decisively to potential indicators of abuse and neglect. (DH et al., 1999, para. 1.9)

5   Area review committees had been established by the 1974 DHSS circular, as policy-making bodies for the management of 'non-accidental injury to children'

cases, to 'advise on the formulation of local practice and procedures to be followed in the detailed management of cases' to be run jointly by the local authority and health authority in each area. The committee should be at a senior level and should include the chief executives of the local authority, education, housing, social services and the health authority, plus representatives from the police, the probation service and the NSPCC.

In the 1999 version of Working Together, Part 4 of the document outlines the 'role and responsibilities' of area child protection committees (ACPCs) as 'an inter-agency forum for agreeing how different services and professional groups should co-operate to safeguard children in that area, and for making sure that arrangements work effectively to bring about good outcomes for children' (DH et al., 1999, para. 4.1).

While ACPC membership

> should be determined locally, it should include as a minimum representation from: local authorities (education and social services); health services (covering both managerial and professional expertise and responsibilities); the police; the probation service; NSPCC (when active in the area); the domestic violence forum (when active in the area); the armed services (where appropriate, and especially where there is a large service base in the area). (DH et al., 1999, para. 4.11)

> The ACPC should make appropriate arrangements to involve others in its work as needed. Those with relevant interest may include (the following list is not intended to be comprehensive): adult mental health services, including forensic mental health services; the coroner; the Crown Prosecution Service; dental health services; drug and alcohol misuse services; education establishments not maintained by the local authority; Guardian Ad Litem panels; housing, cultural and leisure services: the judiciary; local authority legal services; prisons and youth detention centres; representatives of service users; voluntary agencies providing help to parents and children; witness support services; and Youth Offending Teams. (para. 4.12)

This is a long list which dwarfs that in the 1974 circular and reflects the growing complexity of the potential organisations, professionals and systems involved, together with the increased complexity and broadening of the concerns involved over the intervening 25 years.

6 Paragraph 2.18 continues that:

> To understand and establish significant harm, it is necessary to consider:
>
> - the family context;
> - the child's development within the context of their family and wider social and cultural environment;
> - any special needs, such as a medical condition, communication difficulty or disability that may affect the child's development and care within the family;
> - the nature of harm, in terms of ill-treatment or failure to provide adequate care;

- the impact on the child's health and development; and

- the adequacy of parental care.

It is important always to take account of the child's reactions, and his or her perceptions, according to the child's age and understanding.

7   Thereafter, agencies should consider whether there were:

any lessons to be learned from the tragedy about the ways in which they work together to safeguard children. Consequently when a child dies in such circumstances, the ACPC should always conduct a review into the involvement with the child and family of agencies and professionals. Additionally, ACPCs should always consider whether a review should be conducted where a child sustains a potentially life-threatening injury or serious and permanent impairment of health and development, or has been subjected to particularly serious sexual abuse; and the case gives rise to concerns about inter-agency working to protect children. (DH et al., 1999, para. 8.1)

Chapter 7   Policing the Paedophile

1   See also Philip Jenkins' (1998) study of the changing concepts of the child molester from the late nineteenth century to the modern day, and his analyses of paedophiles and the church (Jenkins, 2001).

2   Sally Clark, their mother, was found guilty of their murder and the case was seen as an example of Munchausen's syndrome by proxy (now often referred to as 'fabricated' or 'induced' illness). However, in January 2003, she was released from prison after her conviction was quashed. This was followed by two other convictions being quashed, against Trupti Patel in June 2003 and Angela Canning in December 2003, so that in January 2004 the attorney general announced a review of the 258 cases in the previous ten years in which parents were convicted of killing a child under two, and 15 pending prosecutions involving unexplained infant deaths. The evidence of 'experts', and Sir Roy Meadows in particular, who was seen as the main protagonist of Msbp, was to be subject to increasing scrutiny and scepticism. The cases received huge media coverage.

3   Often, however, it emerged in many of the cases that the child had been killed by a parent, step-parent, foster carer or another relative or close friend. But because of the 'stranger' element, press conferences were quickly organised by the police.

4   See Thomas (2000, Chapter 7) for a detailed analysis of the Bill, how it differed from the consultation document, its passage through Parliament and the major criticisms that were raised about it.

5   The 1998 Crime and Disorder Act also aimed to protect the public further by giving the courts the power to add a period of extended post-release supervision

to the sentence normally imposed upon a person convicted of a sexual or violent offence (section 58). These extended licences could only apply to sex offenders for up to ten years, and to violent offenders for up to five years, but could not be extended unless the custodial sentence was for four years or more.

6   It was notable that while the consultation document *Working Together to Safeguard Children* (DoH, 1998d) had a section (3.7–3.10) on the Sex Offenders Act 1997 which recognised that the new Working Together would need to 'be consistent with, and build upon, these arrangements' and that the role of the ACPC would need to be clarified, the final version of Working Together published in late 1999 had no mention of this. Harmonisation was clearly not straightforward.

7   As Terry Thomas has pointed out, a factor prompting police and probation collaboration and risk assessments was the so-called 'North Wales decision'. In the summer of 1997 two sex offenders sought a judicial review of the police decision to disclose information on them to their neighbours; the court upheld the right of the police to do this but only when there was 'good reason', that is, 'high risk', which thereby implied more 'risk assessment' (see Thomas, 2000, pp. 118–19).

8   The Scouts Association files on convicted paedophiles provided the basis for the campaign.

9   See Ashenden (2002); Bell (2002); Critcher (2002a, 2002b, 2003, Chapter 7); Thomas (2001), and Silverman and Wilson (2002, Chapter 8) for more detailed analyses of the *News of the World* campaign and the political and public responses.

10 In fact the poll and the way the results were manipulated by the *News of the World* was heavily criticised in an article in the *Guardian* (see A Travis, 'Figure it out', 23 August 2000).

11 Under the proposals:

   - a duty would be placed on the probation service to ask victims or their families if they wished to be consulted about the release arrangements for sex and violent offenders sentenced for twelve months or more

   - the operation of the register would be tightened so that initial registration would be within 72 hours rather than 14 days

   - there would be new powers for the police to photograph and fingerprint on initial registration and an increase in the penalty for non-compliance from a maximum of six months' imprisonment to five years

   - the secretary of state would have the power to make regulations concerning notification to the police and probation service by those responsible for the detention and release of sex offenders liable to registration including hospitals as well as prisons and the courts

- and a new sex offender restraining order would be introduced, which a crown court could impose, placing restrictions on an offender coming out of custody, in relation to approaching former victims.

12 It was revealed in court that five years previously, and therefore too early to be on the register, Whiting had been convicted of abducting and sexually assaulting a nine-year-old girl. Sentenced to four years, he had served just two and a half. The examining psychiatrist and the judge of the original trial were interrogated about the apparently lenient sentence, based on the contradictory judgement that while Whiting posed a 'high risk', he did not have 'paedophile tendencies'.

13 The role of the media is not straightforward. While at one level, as far as public policy is concerned, it can be seen that the focus by late 2000 had become increasingly concerned with the need to provide an exceptional response to the paedophile, its impact in other respects can be seen as quite different. More specifically, in helping to bring the issue of child sexual abuse into the public domain, it allowed people, particularly women, to talk about experiences which had previously been virtually impossible to discuss.

Jenny Kitzinger (2001, 2004), in comparing the transcripts of interviews and focus groups in two research projects she carried out in 1984 and 1995 with women aged 14–79, has shown how the dramatic changes in media recognition which occurred between the two projects transformed public knowledge. But the transcripts also demonstrated how the media were implicated in 'private' knowledge by helping to make sense of intimate experiences of violence and providing a framework for personal interaction and reference points for building a sense of identity.

In the mid-1980s, there seemed to be a cultural vacuum, in that those who were interviewed struggled to articulate the literally unspeakable; however, the increasing recognition of child sexual abuse in the following ten years seemed to have profound personal ramifications. Abuse survivors, who had grown up without their experiences being recognised by the dominant culture, began to find words and images for what had happened to them and 'it was media coverage, rather than comments from friends or family, which was most often identified as a trigger for confronting childhood abuse' (Kitzinger, 2001, p. 96). While this might be news coverage of events, it was much more likely to be related to a TV drama or soap (Henderson, 1996).

Recognition on TV and radio, in newspapers, magazines and films became a vital part of women's process of naming and making sense of their experiences. Women referred to the importance of representation in every form – from the 'agony' column in magazines to TV news reports, from soap opera to current affairs discussions (Kitzinger, 2001, p. 97).

14 Additionally, for those whose risk was assessed as being particularly high and for whom it might be difficult to establish satisfactory arrangements, for example accommodation, MAPPPs might refer a case in exceptional circumstances to the public protection group of the National Probation Service, who would enlist the cooperation of the police and probation in other parts of the country and

CRITICAL

provide short-term additional resources where necessary. In cases where an offender was not subject to statutory licence conditions and supervision, the police might take special surveillance measures and/or apply for a sex offender order. In 2001/2, 173 cases were referred to the public protection group (National Probation Service, 2003).

15 This included, among other things, that children under the age of 13 were deemed to be incapable of giving legally significant consent to any form of sexual activity. It also introduced the new offences of

- adult sexual activity with a child
- sexual activity between minors
- sexual grooming
- familial sexual abuse of a child
- prohibited sexual relationships between certain adult blood relatives
- abuse of a position of trust
- the commercial sexual exploitation of a child.

The sexual offender order was also combined with restraining orders to form the new sexual offences prevention orders (SOPOs).

16 The Criminal Justice Act 2003 made the prison service part of the 'responsible authority' with the police and the National Probation Service. Section 325 also imposed a statutory duty to cooperate on those agencies which, although not part of the criminal justice system, work with offenders. The legislation enabled the home secretary to appoint two 'lay advisors' to participate in the work of the MAPPA in each area. The precise nature of the 'duty to cooperate' was to be determined by the bodies on which the duty was imposed in agreement with the responsible authority.

17 It is important to note that while the media and much of the public and political debate about the case assumed that he was a caretaker at the same school that was attended by Holly Wells and Jessica Chapman, he was not. He worked at a different school; it was his girlfriend, Maxine Carr, who worked at their school. Knowing his history of alleged offences could only have stopped him working at that school but would not have changed his girlfriend's contact with the girls and hence his knowing them. This important fact was glossed over among fears about protecting children from paedophiles. (Many thanks to Eileen Munro for pointing this out.)

18 The number of adults working with children is estimated at 3.3 million and there are many more working with adults (Sale, 2004).

19 As the report identified, there were a number of features of this review which distinguished it from most other case reviews:

- Most serious case reviews relate to one child or young person. In this review there were seven main cases, plus a further two which needed to be considered.

- Most serious case reviews followed the death or serious injury of a child. In this case two children did die, in tragic circumstances, but the focus was not on them but on a completely different set of young people, not all of whom were reported to have considered themselves, at the time, to have suffered harm at the hands of Ian Huntley, although some may have felt differently subsequently.

- Most serious case reviews took place shortly after the death or injury suffered by their subjects. In this case the events had taken place some time in the past. In the intervening period some of the records had been lost or destroyed and many of the staff had moved to other jobs or retired. (Kelly, 2004, pp. 6–7)

Chapter 8   'Every Child Matters'

1   David Blunkett, the home secretary, similarly told chief constables to review their police child protection units.

2   While included in the overall Joint Chief Inspectors' Report, a separate report was also produced by Her Majesty's Chief Inspectorates of Probation and Constabulary (HMIP and HMIC, 2002).

3   The principles and overall rationale for the introduction of IRT and sharing information across government generally were considerably advanced in April 2002 with the publication of a document by the Cabinet Office Performance and Innovation Unit, which saw such initiatives as providing a major challenge but also constituting a major way forward for public services. It argued that the ability of the public sector to deliver high-quality services, develop well-targeted policies and ensure efficient government depended on the effective use of knowledge and information – including personal information about citizens. In the process, the handling of such data raised a wide range of issues about privacy and the balance between individual rights and the common good. While perhaps requiring statutory backing and resources, the document identified specific opportunities for progressing such developments. The first area was 'identifying and supporting children at risk of social exclusion', but the options also included ex-offenders, improving services for families, for example Sure Start, helping children in need, the better use of statistical and management information and better access to health records.

   At the same time a number of commentators were beginning to raise concerns that policies primarily developed for addressing youth crime were being applied more broadly to help realign services for children in need. As a leader in the December 2002 issue of *Zero2Nineteen* commented: 'the IRT initiative itself emerged from the government's determination to curb street crime and there is a danger that the direction of policy will be dictated by the desire to win votes rather than the interests of young people'. That the interests of children may come off second best is suggested by the almost total absence of consultation with children and families before the IRT initiative was announced 'despite the Children and Young People's Unit's mission to promote the participation of children and young people in policy making' (p. 3).

4 She would hold the responsibility for early years development, Sure Start, the CYPU and the Children's Fund, and the careers advice service Connexions. The remit included children's social services and child protection and the teenage pregnancy strategy, formerly the responsibility of the Department of Health, and would also cover family policy, formerly the responsibility of the Home Office, together with family and parenting law which was previously part of the Lord Chancellor's Office.

5 While the Green Paper differed from the Laming Report in a number of key respects, Lord Laming gave the government proposals his clear and broad support. He said that he was delighted with the government's map for the future of children's services and hoped ministers would maintain the commitment and provide the resources to complete the journey:

> It was my hope that the dreadful things that happened to Victoria Climbié would be a turning point in the way in which we organise services for children in our society. I wanted to ensure we had in place not just protection for children but a different vision about the priority to be given to the well-being of children and furthering their proper development. I was not looking for an urgent reaction with flashing blue lights, but an approach to children that identified their needs at an earlier stage and responded to them ... if this vision is to be carried through, key services will have to change fundamentally. Our commitment must be preventive work, not corrective work. (Lord Laming, quoted in Carvel, 2003, p. 7)

6 The Green Paper referenced an article by John Bynner (2001), which had been developed from a paper he had presented to one of the original Treasury seminars, which had contributed to the 1998 Comprehensive Spending Review and which had provided the original impetus for the Sure Start programme (see Chapter 5).

7 To achieve this, the Green Paper (para. 4.3) said it wanted to see a local 'information hub' developed in every authority consisting of a list of all the children living in the area. The basic details would include: name, address and date of birth; school attended or if excluded or refused access; GP; a flag stating whether the child was known to agencies such as education welfare, social services, police and youth offending teams and, if so, the contact details of the professional dealing with the case; where a child was known to more than one specialist agency, the lead professional who would take overall responsibility for the case. To reflect the broader remit, from 1 December 2003 the IRT project became the information sharing and assessment (ISA) project.

8 The development of the integrated children's system (ICS) was built upon previous developments, such as the Assessment Framework and the LAC materials, and aimed to offer a single approach to undertaking the key process

of assessment, planning, intervention and review, based on an understanding of children's developmental needs in the context of their families and communities. While the system was developed initially to help social service managers and practitioners to improve the outcomes of their work with children and families, it was being taken forward in association with other government departments in recognition that these were common processes for all agencies. The development was first signalled, formally, in *Learning the Lessons, The Government's Response to* Lost in Care (DH, 2000c), and was also to be integral to the development of the National Service Framework for Children (DH, 2003a). The National Service Framework for Children was being developed alongside other similar frameworks in order to 'drive up standards of services' in the context of change in the NHS and local government. It aimed to establish national standards, while recognising there could be flexibility at the local level as to how the standards would be met. In particular, it was felt that such a framework would ensure that the tragic failures in care management for children subjected to heart surgery in Bristol and exposed in the public inquiry led by Sir Ian Kennedy (2001; Alaszewski, 2002) would not be repeated.

It was argued that no single agency could be responsible for meeting the needs of all children and families and that the government had introduced a number of initiatives, such as Connexions, the Children's Fund, Sure Start and youth offending teams, which cut across the boundaries of traditional service-based departments. The scope of the ICS was thus widened to take these new developments into account, in the belief that all providers of services for children and families would benefit from a common approach to assessment, planning, intervention and review and from being able to share relevant information with each other. The ICS thus comprised a framework for assessment planning, intervention and review, and core data requirements which would set out the information essential for effective multi-agency practice with children and families, and form part of the overall information required to deliver and plan services.

Key features of the ICS were that:

- it aimed to provide common terms for understanding and describing the developmental needs of children, which could be used by all those who work with children and families

- it would enable information gathered during assessments to be used more effectively in making plans and deciding on the best interventions

- it would provide the basis for reviewing whether a child was making progress in important areas of their development, such as health and education

- common use of the framework by local agencies and programmes would enable them to work better together, share information more easily and facilitate referrals between organisations

- it would benefit children and families by enabling them to understand what information agencies were seeking and why, and would help them judge whether they were getting the help they needed.

For social services the ICS was designed:

- to generate the core information about 'children in need' and their families required by central government

- to provide a set of exemplars which would demonstrate how relevant information could be used to generate reports for particular purposes, such as child protection conferences or reviews

- to form the basis for designing front-end software to assist social workers to collect, organise, retrieve and analyse information about cases

- to constitute the e-social care record required by government (originally by 2005) (see DH, 2003b; Walker and Scott, 2004).

The ICS was clearly a highly ambitious project in terms of its internal complexity and potential span of application.

9   The recommendation rejected from the Laming Report was number 72: 'No child about whom there are concerns about deliberate harm should be discharged from hospital back into the community without an identified GP. Responsibility for ensuring this happens rests with the hospital consultant under whose care the child has been admitted.' The government rejected this because 'it cannot be the responsibility of the hospital consultant to force anyone to register with a GP. However, the revision of the Children Act 1989 would include two volumes of core guidance accompanied by additional supplements. The core guidance to organisations included in this 'will cover safe transfer from hospital to community in the context of interagency working and follow up' (p. 49).

The rejected recommendation from the Joint Chief Inspectors' Report was number 2.21: 'ACPCs with their constituent agencies should ensure that reviews of serious cases are undertaken on all appropriate cases within the timescales and expectations of Chapter 8 of Working Together to Safeguard Children, that reports are circulated appropriately and action plan recommendations are implemented.' The government response was:

> the Government agrees that the process for serious case reviews needs to be changed, and is consulting on proposals for a new system. Under this, all unexpected child deaths would be screened by local 'screening groups'. These would decide which cases should be subject to a serious case review. In addition, there will be a national overview to ensure serious case reviews are carried out on the right cases, to the correct standards, and a periodic overview report on these reviews will be published. (p. 64)

10   When the Laming Report was published, government ministers sent a checklist of all the recommendations that were about good professional practice to chief executives of all NHS bodies and councils with social services responsibilities and the chief constables of all police forces. They were asked to guarantee, within three months, that this good practice was in place. The checklist was followed up with a self-audit tool from the SSI for councils and CHI for NHS

bodies to assist senior managers and elected members in assessing whether or not their organisations were meeting all the necessary standards. ACPO followed up the checklist with a letter to all forces, asking them about their practice. The response to these audit tools and checklists would give a picture of the priority given to child protection across the NHS, social services and the police.

The findings were published in October 2003 (CHI, HMIC and SSI, 2003) and stated that while performance was found to be improving, it was dangerously patchy, with 45 per cent of social services departments failing to serve most children well. There was confusion about what information on children at risk should be shared between different agencies, partly due to differing views about human rights legislation, data protection and patient confidentiality.

The audit also had a direct and very public impact in the way the SSI judged performance in 2003. In carrying out its work, the SSI uses a wide variety of evidence to assess a council's performance, including performance indicators, inspections and twice-yearly performance monitoring. From 2002, it gave each council a performance rating from zero to three stars. In 2003 this included a performance indicator on child protection review conferences and the audit results. However, how the results fed into the overall performance assessment was far from clear (Dobson, 2003).

11 While the Children Bill was going to legislate for the new role of director of children's services, who would be accountable for both local authority education and children's social services, *Next Steps* (DfES, 2004a) allowed for local determination around organisational structure, delegation and line management structures. There was reference to the possibility of the role encompassing adult social services alongside other responsibilities and even to the potential, at least initially, for the local authority chief executive to be the designated director (see, for example, Thompson and Coughlan, 2004).

12 The children's commissioner would be a voice for all children and young people, especially the most vulnerable. The commissioner would:

- draw on children's views and make sure that they were fed into policy making and service delivery, both locally and nationally

- advise government and engage with others, such as the media and business, whose decisions and actions affect children's lives

- work with relevant ombudsmen and statutory bodies to ensure complaints systems are in place and are effective and child friendly

- at the direction of the secretary of state, investigate individual cases that have wider relevance for children

- be independent of government and report annually to Parliament via the secretary of state.

However, it was clear that the commissioner would have much less independence than commissioners in other countries, including Wales and Scotland, and this was heavily criticised by a wide range of children's charities.

Chapter 9   Towards 'the Preventive State'

1   The idea of prevention is crucially based on the idea of prediction, that is, it is possible to anticipate and thereby intervene to change the future. Invariably, the evidence drawn upon is based on aggregate data derived from studies that compare populations and the statistical differences between them. In the area of children this means that, for example, children reared in circumstances of multiple disadvantages do worse at school, fall into crime and become socially excluded in adult life. The problem is that factors which are derived from an aggregate population do not necessarily apply in each case where those factors are present. These are particularly evident in the broad areas of child abuse.

Work by Kevin Browne clearly demonstrates the problems. He prospectively evaluated a typical checklist completed by midwives and health visitors around the time of birth. The checklist was developed from a number of demographic and epidemiological studies he had previously carried out in the UK with special reference to non-accidental injury to children (Browne and Saqi, 1987, 1988). Health visitors in conjunction with professional colleagues completed the checklist on all children born in 1985 and 1986 in three health districts in Surrey, England. In total, 14,252 births were screened and 964 (7 per cent) were identified as 'high risk'. The full population of 14,252 children was then followed up for five years and, in 1991, 106 families had been the subject of a child protection case conference for suspected or actual abuse of their newborn child, giving an incidence of seven children in every thousand. The screening procedure was sensitive to 68 per cent of abusing families and correctly specified 94 per cent of non-abusing families. However, nearly a third of the abusing families had few risk factors and were incorrectly identified as 'low risk'. Similarly 6 per cent of the non-abusing families were incorrectly identified as 'high risk'. As Browne pointed out, 'the checklist detection rate would mean that for every 14,252 births screened it would be necessary to distinguish between 72 true risk cases and 892 false positives in the 964 cases identified as high risk' (1993, p. 29). The problems associated with the 'false negatives' and the 'false positives' are endemic to any attempts at prediction/early intervention and hence will miss some with tragic consequences and will falsely identify others with different tragic consequences, including those of the inappropriate infringement of civil liberties. See Parton et al. (1997, Chapter 3) for a more extensive discussion of these issues.

Ruth Sinclair and Roger Bullock (2002) carried out a review of serious case review reports. Forty cases were randomly selected for analysis, 31 where a child had died, and 9 where there had been serious injury. While there were some common features in the children's circumstances, including poor standards of care, emotional neglect, domestic violence and mental health problems, overall their circumstances varied greatly. In some cases the abuse occurred 'out of the blue', in others it occurred in a context of low level need and occasionally it arose in situations where it seemed to have been 'waiting to happen'. A similar level of diversity was apparent in terms of the prior involvement of the child and family with welfare agencies. Some were virtually unknown to anyone, others were long-standing cases, often with parents being known since their childhood. In only 6 out of the 40 cases had there been enduring concerns about risks of harm to the child. Sinclair and Bullock concluded that the factors common to these cases had limited value in helping to predict, with any accuracy, which children would become the victims of abuse.

2 Foucault (1977) drew on the 'panopticon' as the increasingly dominant metaphor for understanding surveillance in the late eighteenth and nineteenth centuries. The panopticon was a proposed prison design by the eighteenth-century reformer Jeremy Bentham (1995). What distinguished this structure was its design to maximise the visibility of inmates who were isolated in individual cells such that they were unaware moment to moment whether they were being observed by guards in a central tower. More than a simple device for observation, the panopticon worked in conjunction with explicitly articulated norms as established by the emerging social sciences, in an effort to transform the prisoner's relation to him or herself. This disciplinary aspect of panoptic observation involved a productive soul training which encouraged inmates to reflect upon the minutiae of their own behaviour in subtle and ongoing efforts to transform themselves. Foucault proposed that the panopticon served as a diagram for a new model of power which extended beyond the prison to take hold in other disciplinary institutions characteristic of the era, such as the factory, hospital, military and school.

3 However, while the notion of risk gives the impression of calculability and objectivity, it is inherently contingent upon and open to differing and sometimes conflicting interpretations, as recent arguments about the nature of 'shaken baby syndrome' and 'Munchausen's syndrome by proxy' testify.

References

Abel-Smith, B. and Townsend, P. (1965) *The Poor and the Poorest*. London, Bell and Hyman.

Abrams, P. (1968) *The Origins of British Sociology 1834–1914*. Chicago, University of Chicago Press.

Alaszewski, A. (2002) 'The Impact of the Bristol Royal Infirmary Disaster and Inquiry on Public Services in the UK', *Journal of Interprofessional Care*, **16**(4), pp. 371–8.

Alderson, P. and Morrow, V. (2004) *Ethics, Social Research and Consulting with Children and Young People*. Harlow, Barnardo's.

Aldgate, J. (2002) 'Evolution Not Revolution: Family Support, Services and the Children Act 1989', in H. Ward and W. Rose (eds) *Approaches to Needs Assessment in Children's Services*. London, Jessica Kingsley.

Aldgate, J. and Tunstill, J. (1995) *Making Sense of Section 17: Implementing Services for Children in Need within the 1989 Children Act*. London, Stationery Office.

Archard, D. (1993) *Children: Rights and Childhood*. London, Routledge.

Aries, P. (1962) *Centuries of Childhood: A Social History of Family Life*. New York, Jonathan Cape.

Armstrong, C., Hill, M. and Secker, J. (1998) *Listening to Children and Young People*. London, Mental Health Foundation.

Ashenden, S. (1996) 'Reflective Governance and Child Sexual Abuse: Liberal Welfare Rationality and the Cleveland Inquiry', *Economic Society*, **25**(1), pp. 64–88.

Ashenden, S. (2002) 'Policing Perversion: The Contemporary Governance of Paedophilia', *Cultural Values*, **6**(1/2), pp. 197–222.

Ashenden, S. (2004) *Governing Child Sexual Abuse: Negotiating the Boundaries of Public and Private, Law and Science*. London, Routledge.

Audit Commission (1994) *Seen But Not Heard: Coordinating Community Health and Social Services for Children in Need*. London, HMSO.

BASPCAN (1981) *Child Sexual Abuse*. York, BASPCAN.

Baher, E.C., Hyman, C., Jones, C., Jones, R., Kerr, A. and Mitchel, R. (1976) *At Risk: An Account of the Work of the Battered Child Research Department*. London, Routledge & Kegan Paul.

Balding, J., Regis, D. and Wise, A. (1998) *No Worries? Young People and Mental Health*. Exeter, Schools Health Education Unit.

Barrett, M. and McIntosh, M. (1982) *The Anti-Social Family*. London, NLB.

Bauman, Z. (1989) *Modernity and the Holocaust*. Oxford, Basil Blackwell.

Bauman, Z. (1992) *Intimations of Postmodernity*. London, Routledge.

Bauman, Z. (1998) *Globalization: The Human Consequences*. Cambridge, Polity Press.

Beck, U. (1992a) *Risk Society: Towards a New Modernity*. London, Sage.

Beck, U. (1992b) 'From Industrial Society to Risk Society: Questions of Survival, Social Structure and Ecological Enlightenment', *Theory, Culture and Society*, **9**(1), pp. 97–123.

Beck, U. and Beck-Gernsheim, E. (1995) *The Normal Chaos of Love*. Cambridge, Polity Press.

Beck, U. and Beck-Gernsheim, E. (2002) *Individualization: Institutionalized Individualism and its Social and Political Consequences*. London, Sage.

Behlmer, G.K (1982) *Child Abuse and Moral Reform in England, 1870–1908*. Stanford, CA, Stanford University Press.

Bell, S. (1988) *When Salem Came to the Boro: The True Story of the Cleveland Child Abuse Crisis*. London, Pan Books.

Bell, V. (2002) 'The Vigilant(e) Parent and the Paedophile: The *News of the World*'s Campaign 2000 and the Contemporary Governmentality of Child Sexual Abuse', *Feminist Theory*, **3**(1), pp. 83–102.

Bentham, J. (1995) *The Panoptican Writings*. London, Verso.

Berridge, D. and Brodie, I. (1996) 'Residential Care in England and Wales: The Inquiries and After', in M. Hill and J. Aldgate (eds) *Child Welfare Services: Developments in Law, Policy, Practice and Research.* London, Jessica Kingsley.

Besharov, D.J. (1991) 'Child Abuse Reporting and Investigation: Policy Guidelines for Decisionn-Making', in M. Robin (ed.) *Assessing Child Maltreatment Reports.* New York, Haworth Press.

Bibby, P.C. (ed.) (1996) *Organised Abuse: The Current Debate.* Aldershot, Arena.

Bichard Inquiry Report (2004) *A Public Inquiry Report on Child Protection Procedures in Humberside Police and Cambridgeshire Constabulary, particularly the Effectiveness of Relevant Intelligence-based Recording, Vetting Practices since 1995 and Information Sharing with Other Agencies; HC653,* London, Stationery Office.

Blair, T. (1993) 'Why Crime is a Socialist Issue', *New Statesman,* **29**(12), pp. 27–8.

Blair, T. (1995) 'The Rights We Enjoy Reflect the Duties We Owe', *The Spectator Lecture,* 22 March.

Blair, T. (1996) *New Britain: My Vision of a Young Country.* London, Fourth Estate.

Blair, T. (1998) *The Third Way: New Politics for the New Century.* Fabian Pamphlet 588. London, The Fabian Society.

Blair, T. (1999) 'Beveridge Revisited: Welfare State for the 21st Century', in R. Walker (ed.) *Ending Child Poverty: Popular Welfare for the 21st Century.* Bristol, Policy Press.

Blair, T. (2001) Foreword in Social Exclusion Unit, *Preventing Social Exclusion.* London, Stationery Office.

Boateng, P. (1999) 'The Government's Role in Early Intervention' (speech at a conference on the importance of early interventions held in London 12 March 1998) in R. Bayley (ed.) *Transforming Children's Lives: The Importance of Early Intervention. Occasional Paper 25.* London, Family Policy Studies Centre.

Bottoms, A.E. (1995) 'The Philosophy and Politics of Punishment and Sentencing', in M.V. Clarkson and R. Morgan (eds) *The Politics of Sentencing Reform.* Oxford, Oxford University Press.

Bowlby, J. (1951) *Maternal Care and Mental Health.* Geneva, World Health Organization.

Bowlby, J. (1973) *Attachment and Loss,* volume II: *Separation, Anxiety and Anger.* London, Hogarth Press.

Bowlby, J. (1979) *The Making and Breaking of Affectional Bonds.* London, Tavistock.

Bowlby, J. (1980) *Attachment and Loss,* volume III: *Loss, Sadness and Depression.* London, Hogarth Press.

Bradshaw, J. (1990) *Child Poverty and Deprivation in the UK.* London, National Children's Bureau.

Brandon, M., Thoburn, J., Lewis, A. and Wade, J. (1999) *Safeguarding Children with the Children Act 1989.* London, Stationery Office.

Brannan, C., Jones, J. and Murch, J. (1993) *Castle Hill Report.* Shrewsbury, Shropshire County Council.

Brannen, J. and Moss, P. (eds) (2003) *Rethinking Children's Care.* Buckingham, Open University Press.

Bright, J. (1997) *Turning the Tide: Crime, Community and Prevention.* London, Demos.

Brown, G. (2001) Foreword in HM Treasury, *Tackling Child Poverty: Giving Every Child the Best Possible Start in Life.* London, HM Treasury, www.hm-treasury.gov.uk.

Browne, K. (1993) 'Home Visitation and Child Abuse: The British Experience', *American Professional Society on the Abuse of Children,* **6**(4), pp. 11–31.

Browne, K. and Saqi, S. (1987) 'Parent-Child Interaction in Abusing Families: Its Possible Causes and Consequences', in P. Maher (ed.) *Child Abuse: The Educational Perspective.* Oxford, Basil Blackwell.

Browne, K. and Saqi, S. (1988) 'Approaches to Screening Families at High Risk for Child Abuse', in K. Browne, C. Davies and P. Stratton (eds) *Early Prediction and Prevention of Child Abuse.* Chichester, John Wiley.

Buckingham, D. (2000) *After the Death of Childhood: Growing Up in the Age of Electronic Media.* Cambridge, Polity Press.

Bullock, R. (1998) 'The Use of *Looked After Children* in Child Protection', *Children & Society,* **12**(3), pp. 234–5.

Burman, E. (1994) *Deconstructing Developmental Psychology,* London, Routledge.

Burman, E. (1997) 'Developmental Psychology and its Discontents', in D. Fox and I. Prilleltensky (eds) *Critical Psychology: An Introduction*. London, Sage.

Butler, I. and Drakeford, M. (2003) *Social Policy, Social Welfare and Scandal: How British Public Policy is Made*. Basingstoke, Palgrave Macmillan.

Butler, I. and Williamson, H. (1994) *Children Speak: Children, Trauma and Social Work*. London, NSPCC/Longman.

Butler, I. and Williamson, H. (1996) ' "Safe?" Involving Children in Child Protection', in I. Butler and I. Shaw (eds) *A Case of Neglect? Children's Experiences and the Sociology of Childhood*. Aldershot, Avebury.

Bynner, J. (2001) 'Childhood Risks and Protective Factors in Social Exclusion', *Children & Society*, **15**(5), pp. 285–301.

Byrne, D. (1999) *Social Exclusion*. Buckingham, Open University Press.

Cabinet Office (1999) *Modernising Government* (Cm 4310). London, Stationery Office.

Cabinet Office Performance and Innovation Unit (2002) *Privacy and Data Sharing: The Way Forward for Public Services*. London, Cabinet Office.

Calder, M.C. (ed.) (2004) *Child Sexual Abuse and the Internet: Tackling the New Frontier*. Lyme Regis, Russell House Publishing.

Campbell, B. (1988) *Unofficial Secrets: Child Sexual Abuse The Cleveland Case*. London, Virgo.

Campbell, B. (1993) *Goliath: Britain's Dangerous Places*. London, Methuen.

Canavan, J., Dolan, P. and Pinkerton, J. (eds) (2000) *Family Support: Direction from Diversity*. London, Jessica Kingsley.

Carvel, J. (2003) 'It was my hope that the dreadful things that happened to Victoria would be a turning point: Climbié inquiry chairman looks to new dawn in child care services', *Guardian*, 9 September, p. 7.

Castel, R. (1991) 'From Dangerousness to Risk', in G. Burchell, C. Gordon and P. Miller (eds) *The Foucault Effect: Studies in Governmentality*. London, Harvester-Wheatsheaf.

Castells, M. (1996) *The Rise of the Network Society*. Oxford, Blackwell.

Castells, M. (1997) *The Power of Identity*. Oxford, Blackwell.

Castells, M. (2000) 'Materials for an Exploratory Theory of Network Society', *British Journal of Sociology*, **51**(1), pp. 5–24.

Catalano, R.F. and Hawkins, J.D. (1996) 'The Social Development Model: A Theory of Anti-Social Behaviour', in J.D. Hawkins (ed.) *Delinquency and Crime: Current Theories*. Cambridge, Cambridge University Press.

Cawson, P. (2002) *Child Maltreatment in the Family*. London, NSPCC.

Cawson, P., Wattam, C., Brooker, S. and Kelly, G. (2000) *Child Maltreatment in the United Kingdom: A Study of the Prevalence of Child Abuse and Neglect*. London, NSPCC.

Chief Secretary to the Treasury (2003) *Every Child Matters* (Cm 5860). London, Stationery Office.

Clarke, J. (1980) 'Social Democratic Delinquents and Fabian Families: A Background to the 1969 Children and Young Persons Act', in The National Deviancy Conference (eds) *Permissiveness and Control: The Fate of the Sixties Legislation*. London, Macmillan.

Clarke, J. (2004) *Changing Welfare Changing States: New Directions in Social Policy*. London, Sage.

Clarke, J. and Langan, M (1993) 'The British Welfare State: Foundation and Modernisastion', in A. Cochrane and J. Clarke (eds) *Comparing Welfare States: Britain in International Context*. London, Sage.

Clarke, J. Gewirtz, S. McLaughlin, E. (eds) (2000) *New Managerialism: New Welfare*. London, Sage.

Clarke, J. and Glendinning, C. (2002) 'Partnership and the Remaking of Welfare Governance', in C. Glendinning, M. Powell and K. Rummery (eds) *Partnerships, New Labour and the Governance of Welfare*. Bristol, Policy Press.

Cleaver, H. and Walker, S. with Meadows, P. (2004) *Assessing Children's Needs and Circumstances: The Impact of the Assessment Framework*. London, Jessica Kingsley.

Cleaver, H., Unell, I. and Aldgate, J. (1999) *Children's Needs – Parenting Capacity: The Impact of Parental Mental Illness, Problem Alcohol and Drug Use, and Domestic Violence on Children's Development*. London, Stationery Office.

Clyde, J. (1992) *The Report of the Inquiry into the Removal of Children from Orkney in February 1991*. Edinburgh, HMSO.

Cobley, C. (2000) *Sex Offenders: Law, Policy and Practice*. Bristol, Jordans.

Cohen, S. (1973) *Folk Devils and Moral Panics*. St Albans, Paladin.

Cohen, S. (1979) 'The Punitive City: Notes on the Dispersal of Social Control', *Contemporary Crises*, **3**(4), pp. 339–63.

Cohen, S. (1983) 'Social-Control Talk: Telling Stories about Correctional Chance', in D. Garland and P. Young (eds) *The Power to Punish*. London, Heinemann.

Cohen, S. (1985) *Visions of Social Control: Crime, Punishment and Classification*. Cambridge, Polity Press.

Collier, R. (2001) 'Dangerousness, Popular Knowledge and the Criminal Law: A Case Study of the Paedophile as Sociocultural Phenomenon', in P. Alldridge and C. Brants (eds) *Personal Autonomy, the Private Sphere and the Criminal Law: A Comparative Study*. Oxford/Portland, OR, Hart Publishing.

Colton, M., Drury, C. and Williams, M. (1995) *Children in Need: Family Support under the Children Act 1989*. Aldershot, Avebury.

CHI, HMIC and SSI (Commission for Health Improvement, Her Majesty's Inspectorate of Constabulary and the Social Services Inspectorate) (2003) *The Victoria Climbié Report: Key Findings from the Self Audits of NHS Organisations, Social Services Departments and Police Forces*. London, CHI.

Comprehensive Spending Review (1998) *Cross Departmental Review of Provision for Young Children: Supporting Papers Vol 1 and 2*. London, HM Treasury. (Copies available from the Public Enquiry Unit, HM Treasury, Parliament Street, London, SW1 3AG.)

Cooper, A. and Hetherington, R. (1999) 'Negotiation', in N. Parton and C. Wattam (eds) *Child Sexual Abuse: Responding to the Experiences of Children*. Chichester, Wiley.

Cooper, A. and Hetherington, R. (2001) 'Child Protection: Lessons from Abroad', in L. Cull and J. Roche (eds) *The Law and Social Work*. Buckingham, Open University Press.

Cooper, A., Hetherington, R., Bairstow, K., Pitts, J. and Spriggs, A. (1995) *Positive Child Protection: A View from Abroad*. Lyme Regis, Russell House Publishing.

Cooper, A., Hetherington, R. and Katz, I. (2003) *The Risk Factor: Making the Child Protection System Work*. London, Demos.

Cooper, J. (1983) *The Creation of the British Personal Social Services 1962–74*. London, Heinemann.

Corby, B. (1990) 'Making Use of Child Protection Statistics', *Children & Society* **4**(4), pp. 304–14.

Corby, B., Doig, A. and Roberts, V. (1998) 'Inquiries into Child Abuse', *Journal of Social Welfare and Family Law*, **20**(4), pp. 377–95.

Corby, B., Doig A. and Roberts, V. (2001) *Public Inquiries into Abuse of Children in Residential Care*. London, Jessica Kingsley.

Court, J. (1969) 'The Battered Child: (1) Historical and Diagnostic Reflection; (2) Reflection on Treatment', *Medical Social Work*, **22**, pp. 11–20.

Cowburn, M. and Dominelli, L. (2001) 'Making Hegemonic Masculinity: Reconstructing the Paedophile as the Dangerous Stranger', *British Journal of Social Work*, **31**(3), pp. 399–415.

Critcher, C. (2002a) 'Media, Government and Moral Panic: the Politics of Paedophilia in Britain', *Journalism Studies*, **3**(4), pp. 521–35.

Critcher, C. (2002b) 'Government, Media and Moral Crisis: Paedophilia in the British Press', in a cura di Rossella Savarese (ed.) *Comunicazione e crisi: Media, conflitti e società*, Milan, Franco Angeli.

Critcher, C. (2003) *Moral Panics and the Media*. Buckingham, Open University Press.

Cunningham, H. (1995) *Children and Childhood in Western Society Since 1500*. London, Longman.

Curtis Committee (1946) *Report of the Care of Children Committee* (Cmnd 6922) London, HMSO.

CYPU (Children and Young People's Unit) (2001a) *Tomorrow's Future: Building a Strategy for Children and Young People*. London, DfEE.

CYPU (Children and Young People's Unit) (2001b) *Children's Fund: Guidance for Applicants*. London, DfEE.

CYPU (Children and Young People's Unit) (2002) *Local Preventative Strategy: Interim Guidance for Local Authorities and Other Local Agencies (Statutory and Non-statutory) Providing Services to Children and Young People*. www.cypu.gov.uk/corporate/services/preventative.cfm, accessed 04/06/04.

CYPU (Children and Young Persons' Unit) (2003) *Coordinating Children's Services: Information Sharing and Assessment.* www.cypu.gov.uk/corporate/irt/inde, accessed 04/06/04.

Dahlberg, G., Moss, P. and Pence, A. (1999) *Beyond Quality in Early Years Education and Care: Postmodern Perspectives.* London, Falmer Press.

Dandecker, C. (1990) *Surveillance, Power and Modernity: Bureaucracy and Discipline from 1700 to the Present Day.* Cambridge, Polity Press.

Davies, G.M. and Westcott, H.C. (1999) *Interviewing Child Witnesses under the Memorandum of Good Practice: A Research Review Policy Research Series Paper 115.* London, Stationery Office.

Deakin, N. (1994) *The Politics of Welfare: Continuities and Change* (2nd edn) Hemel Hempstead, Harvester-Wheatsheaf.

Deleuze, G. (1990) 'Postscript on Control Societies', in G. Deleuze *Negotiations: 1970–1990.* Chichester, Columbia University Press.

Dencik, L. (1989) 'Growing up in the Postmodern Age', *Acta sociologica*, **32**(2), pp. 155–180.

Department for Education and Skills (2004a) *Every Child Matters: Next Steps.* London, DfES.

Department for Education and Skills (2004b) *Common Assessment Framework; Consultation.* London, DfES.

Department for Education and Skills, Department of Health, and the Home Office (2003) *Keeping Children Safe: The Government's Response to the Victoria Climbié Inquiry Report and Joint Chief Inspectors' Report for Safeguarding Children* (Cm 5861). London, Stationery Office.

Department of Health (1988) *Protecting Children: A Guide for Social Workers Undertaking a Comprehensive Assessment in Cases of Child Protection.* London, HMSO.

Department of Health (1994) *Children Act Report 1993.* London, HMSO.

Department of Health (1995a) *Child Protection: Messages from Research.* London, HMSO.

Department of Health (1995b) *Looking After Children: Good Parenting, Good Outcomes Training Guide.* London, HMSO.

Department of Health (1998a) *Modernising Social Services: Promoting Independence, Improving Protection, Raising Standards* (Cm 4169). London, Stationery Office.

Department of Health (1998b) *The Quality Protects Programme: Transforming Children's Services,* LDC (98) 28.

Department of Health (1998c) *Caring for Children Away from Home: Messages from Research.* Chichester, Wiley.

Department of Health (1998d) *Working Together to Safeguard Children: New Government Proposals for Inter-Agency Cooperation.* Consultation Paper.

Department of Health (2000a) *Assessing Children in Need and their Families: Practice Guidance.* London, Stationery Office.

Department of Health (2000b) *Studies which Inform the Development of the Framework for the Assessment of Children in Need and their Families.* London, Stationery Office.

Department of Health (2000c) *Learning the Lessons: The Government's Response to* Lost in Care*: The Report of the Tribunal of Inquiry into the above of Children in Care in the Former County Council Areas of Gwynedd and Clwyd since 1974.* London, Stationery Office.

Department of Health (2001) *The Children Act Now: Messages from Research.* London, Stationery Office.

Department of Health (2002a) *Safeguarding Children: A Joint Chief Inspectors' Report on Arrangements to Safeguard Children.* London, Department of Health.

Department of Health (2002b) *Time to Break up Old, Monolithic Social Services Milburn: Local Council Care Must Change to Reflect Changes in Society.* Press release ref 2002/0432, available at www.info.doh.gov.uk/doh/intpress.nsf/2002–04openDocument, accessed 21/10/02.

Department of Health (2003a) *Getting the Right Start: The National Service Framework for Children, Young People and Maternity Services Emerging Findings.* London, Crown Copyright.

Department of Health (2003b) *About the Integrated Children's System,* www.children.doh.gov.uk/integratedchildrenssystem/about.htm, accessed 4/6/04.

Department of Health and Cleaver, H. (2000) *Assessment Recording Forms.* London, Stationery Office.

Department of Health, Cox, A. and Bentovim, A. (2000a) *The Family Assessment Pack of Questionnaires and Scales.* London, Stationery Office.

Department of Health, Department of Education and Employment, Home Office (2000b) *Framework for the Assessment of Children in Need and their Families*. London, Stationery Office.

Department of Health, Home Office, and Department of Education and Employment (1999) *Working Together to Safeguard Children: A Guide to Inter-Agency Working to Safeguard and Promote the Welfare of Children*. London, Stationery Office.

Department of Health, Home Office, Department for Education and Skills, DCMS, Office of the Deputy Prime Minister, and the Lord Chancellor's Department (2003) *What to Do if You're Worried a Child is Being Abused*. London, DH.

DHSS (1970) *The Battered Baby* (CM022/70).

DHSS (1972) *Battered Babies* (LASSL, 26/72).

DHSS (1974) *Non-Accidental Injury to Children* (LASSL (74) (13)).

DHSS (1976a) *Non-Accidental Injury to Children: Area Review Committees* (LASSL (76) (2)).

DHSS (1976b) *Non-Accidental Injury to Children: The Police and Case Conferences* (LASSL (76) (26)).

DHSS (1978) *Child Abuse: The Register System* (LA/C396/23D).

DHSS (1980) *Child Abuse: Central Register Systems* (LASSL (80)4, HN (80)).

DHSS (1982) *Child Abuse: A Study of Inquiry Reports 1973–1981*. London, HMSO.

DHSS (1985) *Review of Child Care Law: Report to Ministers of an Interdepartmental Working Party*. London, HMSO.

DHSS (1988) *Working Together: A Guide to Inter-Agency Co-operation for the Protection of Children from Abuse*. London, HMSO.

Department of Health and Social Security (Northern Ireland) (1985) *Report of the Committee of Inquiry into Children's Homes and Hostels*. Belfast, HMSO.

Dicks, H.V. (1970) *Fifty Years of the Tavistock Clinic*. London, Routledge & Kegan Paul.

Dingwall, R. (1986) 'The Jasmine Beckford Affair', *Modern Law Review*, **49**(4), pp. 488–518.

Dingwall, R. (1989) 'Some Problems about Predicting Child Abuse and Neglect', in O. Stevenson (ed.) *Child Abuse: Public Policy and Professional Practice*. Hemel Hempstead, Harvester-Wheatsheaf.

Dingwall, R., Eekelaar, J. and Murray, T. (1995) 'Postscript', in *The Protection of Children: State Intervention and Family Life* (2nd edn). Oxford, Basil Blackwell.

Dobson, A. (2003) 'Finding the Right Tool', *Care and Health Magazine*, (50): 17–18.

Dominelli, L. (1986) 'Father-Daughter Incest: Patriarchy's Shameful Secret', *Critical Social Policy*, **16**, pp. 8–22.

Dominelli, L. (1989) 'Betrayal of Trust: A Feminist Analysis of Power Relationships in Incest Abuse and its Relevance for Social Work Practice', *British Journal of Social Work*, **19**(4), pp. 291–307.

Donnison, D. and Stewart, M. (1958) *The Child and the Social Services*. London, The Fabian Society.

Donzelot, J. (1980) *The Policing of Families: Welfare Versus the State*. London, Hutchinson.

Donzelot, J. (1988) 'The Promotion of the Social', *Economy and Society*, **17**(3), pp. 395–427.

Douglas, M. (1992) *Risk and Blame: Essays in Cultural Theory*. London, Routledge & Kegan Paul.

Dryfoos, J.G. (1990) *Adolescents at Risk: Prevalence and Prevention*. Oxford, Oxford University Press.

Ermisch, J. and Francesconi, M. (1998) *Cohabitation in Great Britain: Not for Long, but Here to Stay*. Working Paper 81-1, University of Essex, ESRC Research Centre on Micro-Social Change.

Esping-Anderson, G. (1999) *Social Foundations of Postindustrial Economics*. Oxford, Oxford University Press.

Esping-Anderson, G. with Gallie, D., Hemerijck, A. and Muyles, J. (2002) *Why We Need a New Welfare State*. Oxford, Oxford University Press.

Etzioni, A. (1993) *The Spirit of Community: Rights, Responsibilities and the Communitarian Agenda*. New York, Simon & Schuster.

Etzioni, A. (1997) *The New Golden Rule: Community and Morality in a Democratic Society*. New York, HarperCollins.

Evans, J. (2003) 'Vigilance and Vigilantes: Thinking Psychoanalytically about Anti-paedophile Action', *Theoretical Criminology*, **7**(2), pp. 163–89.

Ewald, F. (1991) 'Insurance and Risk', in G. Burchell, C. Gordon and P. Miller (eds) *The Foucault Effect: Studies in Governmentality*. London, Harvester-Wheatsheaf.

Farrell, C. and Morris, J. (2003) 'The "Neo-Bureaucratic" State: Professionals, Managers and Professional managers in Schools, General Practices and Social Work', *Organization*, **10**(1), pp. 129–56.

Farrington, D. (1995) 'The Development of Offending and Anti-social Behaviour from Childhood: Key Findings from the Cambridge Study in Delinquent Development', *Journal of Child Psychology and Psychiatry*, **360**, pp. 929–64.

Farrington, D. (1996) *Understanding and Preventing Youth Crime*. York, Joseph Rowntree Foundation.

Farrington, D.P. and West, D. (1990) 'The Cambridge Study in Delinquent Development: A Long-term Follow-up of 411 London Males', in G. Kaiser and H.J. Kerner (eds) *Criminality: Personality, Behaviour, Life History*. Berlin, Springer-Verlag.

Fawcett, B., Featherstone, B. and Goddard, J. (2004) *Contemporary Child Care Policy and Practice*. Basingstoke, Palgrave Macmillan.

Featherstone, B. (2004) *Family Life and Family Support: A Feminist Analysis*. Basingstoke, Palgrave Macmillan.

Featherstone, B. and Evans, H. (2004) *Children Experiencing Maltreatment: Who Do They Turn To?* London, NSPCC.

Feeley, M. and Simon, J. (1994) 'Actuarial Justice: The Emerging New Criminal Law', in D. Nelken (ed.) *The Futures of Criminology*. London, Sage.

Ferguson, H. (1990) 'Rethinking Child Protection Practices: A Case for History', in The Violence Against Children Study Group, *Taking Child Abuse Seriously*. London, Unwin Hyman.

Ferguson, H. (1996) 'The Protection of Children in Time', *Child and Family Social Work*, **1**(4), pp. 205–18.

Ferguson, H. (1997) 'Protecting Children in New Times: Child Protection and the Risk Society', *Child and Family Social Work*, **2**(4), pp. 221–34.

Ferguson, H. (2004) *Protecting Children in Time: Child Abuse, Child Protection and the Consequences of Modernity*. Basingstoke, Palgrave Macmillan.

Ferguson, H. and O'Reilly, M. (2001) *Keeping Children Safe: Child Abuse, Child Protection and the Promotion of Welfare*. Dublin, A and A Farmar.

Ferri, E., Bynner, J. and Wadsworth, M. (eds) (2003) *Changing Britain, Changing Lives: Three Generations at the Turn of the Century*. London, Institute of Education, University of London.

Finch, J. and Groves, D. (eds) (1983) *A Labour of Love*. London, Routledge & Kegan Paul.

Foley, P., Parton, N., Roche, J. and Tucker, S. (2003) 'Contradictory and Convergent Trends in Law and Policy affecting Children in England', in C. Hallett and A. Prout (eds) *Hearing the Voices of Children: Social Policy for a New Century*. London, Routledge Falmer.

Foucault, M. (1973) *The Birth of the Clinic: An Archeology of Medical Perception*. London, Tavistock.

Foucault, M. (1977) *Discipline and Punish: The Birth of the Prison*. Harmondsworth, Penguin.

Foucault, M. (1979) *The History of Sexuality* volume 1: *An Introduction*. Harmondsworth, Penguin.

Foucault, M. (1991) 'Governmentality', in G. Burchell, C. Gordon and P. Miller (eds) *The Foucault Effect: Studies in Governmentality*. London, Harvester-Wheatsheaf.

Fox-Harding, L. (1996) *Family, State and Social Policy*. Basingstoke, Macmillan – now Palgrave Macmillan.

France, A. and Utting, D. (2005) 'The Paradigm of "Risk and Protection-focused Prevention" and Its Impact on Services for Children and Families', *Children & Society*, **19**(2), pp. 77–90.

Franklin, B. (ed.) (1986) *The Rights of Children*. Oxford, Basil Blackwell.

Franklin, B. (1989) 'Wimps and Bullies: Press Reporting of Child Abuse', in P. Carter, T. Jeffs and M. Smith (eds) *Social Work and Social Welfare Yearbook One*. Milton Keynes, Open University Press.

Franklin, B. (1994) *Packaging Politics: Political Communication in Britain's Media Democracy*. London, Arnold.

Franklin, B. (ed.) (1995) *A Comparative Handbook of Children's Rights*. London, Routledge.

Franklin, B. (1997) *Newszak and News Media*. London, Arnold.

Franklin, B. (ed.) (2002) *The New Handbook of Children's Rights: Comparative Policy and Practice*. London, Routledge.

Franklin, B. and Parton, N. (2001) 'Press-ganged! Media Reporting of Social Work and Child Abuse', in M. May, R. Payne and E. Brunsdon (eds) *Understanding Social Problems: Issues in Social Policy*. Oxford, Blackwell.

Franklin, B. and Petley, J. (1996) 'Killing the Age of Innocence: Newspaper Reporting of the Death of James Bulger', in J. Pilcher and S. Wagg (eds) *Thatcher's Children? Politics, Childhood and Society in the 1980s and 1990s*. London, Falmer Press.

Freeman, M.D.A. (1983) *The Rights and Wrongs of Children*. London, Francis Pinter.

Freeman, R. (1992) 'The Idea of Prevention: A Critical Review', in S. Scott, G. Williams, S. Platt and H. Thomas (eds) *Private Risks and Public Dangers*. Aldershot, Avebury.

Freeman, R. (1999) 'Recursive Politics: Prevention, Modernity and Social Systems', *Children & Society*, **13**(4), pp. 232–41.

Froggett, L. (2002) *Love, Hate and Welfare: Psychosocial Approaches to Policy and Practice*. Bristol, Policy Press.

Frost, N. (1992) 'Implementing the Children Act 1989 in a Hostile Climate', in P. Carter, T. Jeffs and M.K. Smith (eds) *Changing Social Work and Welfare*. Buckingham, Open University Press.

Frost, N. and Stein, M. (1989) *The Politics of Child Welfare*. Hemel Hempstead, Harvester-Wheatsheaf.

Gallagher, B., Bradford, M. and Pease, K. (2002) 'The Sexual Abuse of Children by Strangers: Its Extent, Nature and Victims' Characteristics', *Children & Society*, **16**(5), pp. 346–59.

Gamble, A. (1988) *The Free Economy and the Strong State: The Politics of Thatcherism*. Basingstoke, Macmillan – now Palgrave Macmillan.

Garland, D. (1985) *Punishment and Welfare: A History of Penal Strategies*. Aldershot, Gower.

Garland, D. (1996) 'The Limits of the Sovereign State: Strategies of Crime Control in Contemporary Society', *British Journal of Criminology*, **36**(4), pp. 445–71.

Garland, D. (2001) *The Culture of Control: Crime and Social Order in Contemporary Society*. Oxford, Oxford University Press.

Garland, D. (2003) 'The Rise of Risk', in R. Ericson and A. Doyle (eds) *Risk and Morality*. Toronto, University of Toronto Press.

Garnham, N. (2001) Opening Statement to the Victoria Climbié Inquiry, www.victoria-climbie-inquiry.org.uk/Evidence/Archive/Sept01/260901, accessed 20/02/03.

Garrett, P.M. (1999a) 'Mapping Child-Care Social Work in the Final Years of the Twentieth Century: A Critical Response to the "Looking After Children" System', *British Journal of Social Work*, **29**(1), pp. 27–47.

Garrett, P.M. (1999b) 'Producing the Moral Citizen: the "Looking After Children" System and the Regulation of Children and Young People in Public Care', *Critical Social Policy*, **19**(3), pp. 291–311.

Garrett, P.M. (2002) 'Yes Minister: Reviewing the "Looking After Children" Experience and Identifying the Messages for Social Work Research', *British Journal of Social Work*, **32**(7), pp. 832–46.

Garrett, P.M. (2003) *Remaking Social Work with Children and Families: A Critical Discussion on the 'Modernisation' of Social Care*. London, Routledge.

Garrett, P.M. (2004) 'The Electronic Eye: Emerging Surveillant Practices in Social Work with Children and Families', *European Journal of Social Work*, **7**(1), pp. 57–71.

Geach, H. and Szwed, E. (eds) (1983) *Providing Civil Justice for Children*. London, Arnold.

Ghate, D. and Daniels, A. (1997) *Talking About My Generation: A Survey of 8–15 year olds Growing up in the 1990's*. London, NSPCC.

Ghate, D. and Hazel, N. (2002) *Parenting in Poor Environments: Stress, Support and Coping*. London, Jessica Kingsley.

Gibbons, J., Conroy, S. and Bell, C. (1995) *Operating the Child Protection System*. London, HMSO.

Giddens, A. (1990) *The Consequences of Modernity*. Cambridge, Polity Press.

Giddens, A. (1991) *Modernity and Self Identity: Self and Society in the Late Modern Age*. Cambridge, Polity Press.

Giddens, A. (1992) *The Transformation of Intimacy: Sexuality, Love and Eroticism in Modern Societies*. Cambridge, Polity Press.

Giddens, A. (1994) *Beyond Left and Right: The Future of Radical Politics*. Cambridge, Polity Press.

Giddens, A. (1998) *The Third Way: The Renewal of Social Democracy*. Cambridge, Polity Press.

Giddens, A. (2000) *The Third Way and its Critics*. Cambridge, Polity Press.

Gilbert, N. (ed.) (1997) *Combating Child Abuse: International Perspectives and Trends*. Oxford, Oxford University Press.

Glasgow Media Group (2001) *Reporting Child Deaths: The Role of the Media*. London, NSPCC.

Glass, N. (1999) 'Sure Start: The Development of an Early Intervention Programme for Young Children in the United Kingdom', *Children & Society*, **13**(4), pp. 257–74.

Glendinning, C., Powell, M. and Rummery, K. (eds) (2002) *Partnerships, New Labour and the Governance of Welfare*. Bristol, Policy Press.

Goldberg, S., Muir, R. and Kerr, J. (eds) (1996) *Attachment Theory: Social, Developmental and Clinical Perspectives*. Hillside, NY, Analytic Press.

Gough, D. (1996) 'The Literature on Child Abuse and the Media', *Child Abuse Review*, **5**(5), pp. 363–76.

Gough, I. (1979) *The Political Economy of the Welfare State*. Basingstoke, Macmillan.

Graham, H. (1994) 'The Changing Financial Circumstances of Households with Children', *Children & Society*, **8**(2), pp. 98–113.

Graham, J. and Utting, D. (1996) 'Families, Schools and Criminality Prevention', in T. Bennett (ed.) *Preventing Crime and Disorder: Targeting Strategies and Responsibilities*. Cambridge, Cropwood.

Graham, S. and Wood, D. (2003) 'Digitizing Surveillance; Categorization, Space, Inequality', *Critical Social Policy*, 23(2), pp. 227–48.

Gray, J. (2002) 'National Policy on the Assessment of Children in Need and their Families', in H. Ward and W. Rose (eds) *Approaches to Needs Assessment in Children's Services*. London, Jessica Kingsley.

Green, J. (1997) *Risk and Misfortune: The Social Construction of Accidents*. London, UCL Press.

Greer, C. (2003) *Sex Crime and the Media: Sex Offending and the Press in a Divided Society*. Cullompton, Willan Publishing.

Grubin, D. (1998) *Sex Offending Against Children: Understanding the Risk. Police Research Series Paper 99*. London, The Home Office.

Gwent County Council (1992) *Ty Mawr Community Home Inquiry*. Gwent County Council.

Hacking, I. (1988) 'The Sociology of Knowledge about Child Abuse', *Nous*, **2**, pp. 53–63.

Hacking, I. (1990) *The Taming of Chance*. Cambridge, Cambridge University Press.

Hacking, I. (1991a) 'How Should We Do the History of Statistics', in G. Burchell, C. Gordon and P. Miller (eds) *The Foucault Effect: Studies in Governmentality*. Hemel Hempstead, Harvester-Wheatsheaf.

Hacking, I. (1991b) 'The Making and Moulding of Child Abuse', *Critical Inquiry*, 17 (Winter), pp. 253–88.

Hacking, I. (1992) 'World-making by Kind-making: Child Abuse for Example', in M. Douglas and D. Hull (eds) *How Classification Works: Nelson Goodman among the Social Sciences*. Edinburgh, Edinburgh University Press.

Haggerty, K.D. and Ericson, R.V. (2000) 'The Surveillant Assemblage', *British Journal of Sociology*, **51**(4), pp. 605–22.

Hall, P. (1976) *Reforming the Welfare*. London, Heinemann.

Hallett, C. and Birchall, E. (1992) *Coordination and Child Protection: A Review of the Literature*. London, HMSO.

Hallett, C., Murray, C. and Punch, S. (2003) 'Young People and Welfare: Negotiating Pathways', in C. Hallett and A. Prout (eds) *Hearing the Voices of Children: Social Policy for a New Century*. London, Routledge Falmer.

Harder, M.H. and Pringle, K. (eds) (1997) *Protecting Children in Europe: Towards a New Millennium*. Aalborg, Aalborg University Press.

Hardiker, P., Exton, K. and Barker, M. (1991) *Policies and Practices in Preventive Child Care*. London, Avebury/Gower.

Harlow, E. and Webb, S.A. (eds) (2003) *Information and Communication Technologies in the Welfare Services*. London, Jessica Kingsley.

Hartley, P. (1985) *Child Abuse, Social Work and the Press: Towards the History of Moral Panic*. Warwick Critical Studies No.4, Department of Applied Social Studies, University of Warwick.

Hayden, C., Goddard, J., Gorin, S. and Van der Spek, N. (1999) *State Child Care: Looking After Children?* London, Jessica Kingsley.

Hebenton, B. and Thomas, T. (1996) 'Tracking Sex Offenders', *Howard Journal*, **35**(2), pp. 97–112.

Hebenton, B. and Thomas, T. (1997) *Keeping Track? Observations on Sex Offender Registers in the US*. Crime Detection and Prevention Series, Paper 83, Police Research Group, London, Home Office.

Hellinckx, W., Colton, A. and Williams, M. (eds) (1997) *International Perspectives on Family Support*. Aldershot, Arena.

Henderson, L. (1996) *The Issue of Child Sexual Abuse in TV Fiction: Audience Reception of Channel 4's "Brookside"*. London, Channel 4.

Hendrick, H. (1994) *Child Welfare: England 1872–1989*. London, Routledge.

Hendrick, H. (2003) *Child Welfare: Historical Dimensions, Contemporary Debate*. Bristol, Policy Press.

Her Majesty's Inspectorate of Probation and Her Majesty's Inspectorate of Constabulary (2002) *Protecting Children from Potentially Dangerous People: An Inter-Agency Inspection on Children's Safeguards*. London, HMIP and HMIC.

Hetherington, R., Cooper, A., Smith, P. and Wilford, G. (1997) *Protecting Children: Messages from Europe*. Lyme Regis, Russell House Publishing.

Heywood, J. (1978) *Children in Care: The Development of the Service for the Deprived Child*. London, Routledge & Kegan Paul.

Hill, M., Davis, J., Prout, A. and Tisdall, K. (eds) (2004) 'Children, Young People and Participation', *Children & Society*, Special Issue, **18**(2).

HM Treasury, Department for Education and Skills, Department for Work and Pensions and Department for Trade and Industry (2004) *Choice for Parents, The Best Start for Children: A Ten Year Strategy for Childcare*. London, Stationery Office.

HM Treasury (2002) *2002 Spending Review: Opportunity and Security for All Investing in an Enterprising Society: New Public Spending Plans 2003–2006*. London, Stationery Office.

Hobsbawm, E. (1994) *The Age of Extremes: The Short Twentieth Century 1914–1991*. London, Michael Joseph.

Hodgson, L. (2004) 'Manufactured Civil Society: Counting the Cost', *Critical Social Policy*, **24**(2), pp. 139–64.

Hollway, W. and Jefferson, T. (1997) 'The Risk Society in an Age of Anxiety: Situating the Fear of Crime', *British Journal of Sociology*, **48**(2), pp. 255–66.

Holman, B. (1996) 'Fifty Years Ago: The Curtis and Clyde Reports', *Children & Society*, **10**(3), pp. 197–209.

Home Office (1967) *Administration of Punishment at Court Lees Approved School*. (Cmnd 3367). London, HMSO.

Home Office (1989) *Report of the Advisory Group on Video Evidence* (Pigot Report). London, HMSO.

Home Office (1996) *Sentencing and Supervision of Sex Offenders – A Consultation Document*. (Cm 3304). London, HMSO.

Home Office (1997a) *Community Protection Order – A Consultation Paper*. London, HMSO.

Home Office (1997b) *Sex Offenders Act 1997*. Circular 39/97, London.

Home Office (1998a) *Crime and Disorder Act 1998, Introductory Guide, Anti-Social Behaviour Orders and Sex Offender Orders*. London, Home Office.

Home Office (1998b) *Supporting Families: A Consultation Document*. London, Stationery Office.

Home Office (2000) *Government Proposals to Better Protect Children from Sex and Violent Offenders*. Press Release 15 September. London, Home Office.

Home Office (2001) *Initial Guidance to the Police and Probation Services on Section 67 and 68 of the Criminal Justice and Court Services Act*. London, Stationery Office.

Home Office (2002) *Protecting the Public: Strengthening Protection against Sex Offenders and Reforming the Law on Sexual Offences*. (Cm 5668). London, Stationery Office.

Home Office (2003) *MAPPA Guidance*. London, Crown Copyright.

Home Office and Department of Health (1992) *Memorandum of Good Practice on Video Recorded Interviews with Child Witnesses for Criminal Proceedings*. London, HMSO.

Home Office, Department of Health, Department of Education and Science, and the Welsh Office (1991) *Working Together Under the Children Act 1989: A Guide to Arrangements for Interagency Co-operation for the Protection of Children from Abuse.* London, HMSO.

Home Office PSTU (Police Science and Technology Unit) (1999) *Draft Guidance on the Disclosure of Information about Sex Offenders who may Present a Risk to Children and Vulnerable Adults.* August, London.

Horton, S. and Farnham, D. (eds) (1999) *Public Management in Britain.* Basingstoke, Palgrave – now Palgrave Macmillan.

Howe, D. (1992) 'Child Abuse and the Bureaucratisation of Social Work', *Sociological Review*, **40**(3), pp. 491–508.

Hutchby, I. and Moran-Ellis, J. (eds) (2001) *Children, Technology and Culture.* London, Routledge Falmer.

Ingleby Report (1960) *Report of the Committee on Children and Young Persons* (Cmnd 1191). London, HMSO.

Ingleby, D. (1986) 'Development in Social Context', in M. Richards and P. Light (eds) *Children of Social Worlds: Development in a Social Context.* Cambridge, Polity Press.

Jackson, S. and Kilroe, S. (eds) (1996) *Looking After Children: Good Parenting, Good Outcomes Reader.* London, HMSO.

Jackson, S. and Scott, S. (1999) 'Risk Anxiety and the Social Construction of Childhood', in D. Lupton (ed.) *Risk and Sociocultural Theory: New Directions and Perspectives.* Cambridge, Cambridge University Press.

James, A.L. and James, A. (2001) 'Tightening the Net: Children, Community, and Control', *British Journal of Sociology*, **52**(2), pp. 211–28.

James, A. and James, A.L. (2004) *Constructing Childhood: Theory, Policy and Social Practice.* Basingstoke, Palgrave Macmillan.

James, A. and Prout, A. (eds) (1997) *Constructing and Reconstructing Childhood: Contemporary Issues in the Sociological Study of Childhood* (2nd edn). London, Falmer Press.

James, G. (1994) *Study of Working Together 'Part 8' Reports.* London, Department of Health.

Jamieson, L. (1998) *Intimacy: Personal Relationships in Modern Society.* Cambridge, Polity Press.

Jenkins, P. (1992) *Intimate Enemies: Moral Panics in Contemporary Great Britain.* New York, Aldine de Gruyter.

Jenkins, P. (1998) *Moral Panic: Changing Concepts of the Child Molester in Modern America.* London, Yale University Press.

Jenkins, P. (2001) *Paedophiles and Priests: Anatomy of a Contemporary Crisis.* Oxford, Oxford University Press.

Jenks, C. (1996) *Childhood*, London, Routledge.

Jenson, J. and Saint-Martin, D. (2001) 'Changing Citizenship Regimes: Social Policy Strategies in the Investment State', Paper prepared for the workshop on Fostering Social Cohesion: A Comparison of New Political Strategies. Université de Montreal, June 21–22.

Jenson, J. and Saint-Martin, D. (2002) 'Building Blocks for a New Welfare Architecture: From Ford to LEGO?' Paper prepared for the annual meeting of the American Political Science Association, Boston, August.

Jerrom, C. (2002) 'Prime Minister Signals Overhaul of Services for Children at Risk', *Community Care*, 7–13 November, p. 12.

Jordan, B. (1996) *A Theory of Poverty and Social Exclusion.* Cambridge, Polity Press.

Jordan, B. (1998) *The New Politics of Welfare: Social Justice in New Global Context.* London, Sage.

Jordan, B. (1999) 'Bulger: "Back to Basics" and the Rediscovery of Community', in B. Franklin (ed.) *Social Policy, the Media and Misrepresentation.* London, Routledge.

Jordan, B. and Düvell, F. (2003) *Migration: The Boundaries of Equality and Justice.* Cambridge, Polity Press.

Kamerman, S. and Kahn, A. (1990) 'If CPS is driving child welfare – where do we go from here?' *Public Welfare*, 48, Winter, pp. 9–13.

Katz, I. and Pinkerton, J. (eds) (2003) *Evaluating Family Support: Thinking Internationally, Thinking Critically.* Chichester, John Wiley.

Kelly, C. (2004) *Serious Case Review: Ian Huntley; North East Lincolnshire 1995–2001. Report of Sir Christopher Kelly.* North East Lincolnshire Area Child Protection Committee.

Kempe, C.H., Silverman, F.N., Steel, B.F., Droegemueller, W. and Silver, H.K. (1962) 'The Battered Child Syndrome', *Journal of the American Medical Association*, **181**, pp. 17–24.

Kemshall, H. (1996) *Risk in Probation Practice*. Aldershot, Ashgate.

Kemshall, H. (2001) *Risk Assessment and Management of Known Sexual and Violent Offenders: A Review of Current Issues*. Police Research Series, Paper 140. London, Home Office.

Kemshall, H. (2003) 'The Community Management of High-Risk Offenders', *Prison Service Journal*, (146), pp. 2–5.

Kemshall, H. and Maguire, M. (2001) 'Public Protection, Partnership and Risk Penality', *Punishment and Society*, **3**(2), pp. 237–64.

Kemshall, H. and Maguire, M. (2003) 'Sex Offenders, Risk Penality and the Problem of Disclosure to the Community', in A. Matravers (ed.) *Sex Offenders in the Community: Managing and Reducing Risks*. Cullumpton, Willan Publishing.

Kemshall, H. and McIver, G. (eds) (2004) *Managing Sex Offender Risk*. London, Jessica Kingsley.

Kendall, L. and Harker, L. (eds) (2002) *From Welfare to Wellbeing: The Future of Social Care*. London, Institute of Public Policy Research.

Kennedy, I. (2001) *Learning from Bristol: The Report of the Public Inquiry into Children's Heart Surgery at the Bristol Royal Infirmary 1984–1995* (Cm 5207). London, Stationery Office.

Khoo, E.G., Hyvönen, U. and Nygren, L. (2002) 'Child Welfare Protection: Uncovering Swedish and Canadian Orientations to Social Intervention in Child Maltreatment', *Qualitative Social Work*, **1**(4), pp. 451–71.

Kiernan, K. and Estaugh, V. (1993) *Cohabitation, Extra-Marital Childbearing and Social Policy*. London, Family Policy Studies Centre.

Kilgallon, W. (1995) *Report of the Independent Review into Allegations of Abuse at Meadowdale Children's Home and Related Matters*. Morpeth, Northumberland County Council.

King, M. (1995) 'The James Bulger Murder Trial: Moral Dilemmas and Social Solutions', *The International Journal of Children's Rights*, **3**(1), pp. 1–21.

Kirkwood, A. (1993) *The Leicestershire Inquiry 1991*. Leicester, Leicestershire County Council.

Kitzinger, J. (1996) 'Media Representations of Sexual Abuse Risks', *Child Abuse Review*, **5**(5), pp. 319–33.

Kitzinger, J. (1999) 'The Ultimate Neighbour from Hell? Stranger Danger and the Media Framing of Paedophiles', in B. Franklin (ed.) *Social Policy, the Media and Misrepresentation*. London, Routledge.

Kitzinger, J. (2001) 'Transformations of Public and Private Knowledge: Audience Reception, Feminism and the Experience of Childhood Sexual Abuse', *Feminist Media Studies*, **1**(1), pp. 91–104.

Kitzinger, J. (2004) *Framing Abuse: Media Influence and Public Understanding of Sexual Violence Against Children*. London, Pluto Press.

Kitzinger, J. and Skidmore, P. (1995) 'Playing Safe: Media Coverage of Child Sexual Abuse Prevention Strategies', *Child Abuse Review*, **4**(1), pp. 47–56.

Knight, T. and Caveney, S. (1998) 'Assessment and Action Records: Will They Promote Good Parenting?' *British Journal of Social Work*, **28**(1), pp. 29–43.

Kumar, V. (1993) *Poverty and Inequality in the UK: The Effects on Children*. London, National Children's Bureau.

La Fontaine, J. (1990) *Child Sexual Abuse*. Cambridge, Polity Press.

La Fontaine, J. (1994) *The Extent and Nature of Organised and Ritual Abuse*. London, HMSO.

La Fontaine, J. (1998) *Speak of the Devil: Tales of Satanic Abuse in Contemporary England*. Cambridge, Cambridge University Press.

Laming Report (2003) *The Victoria Climbié Inquiry: Report of an Inquiry by Lord Laming* (Cm 5730). London, Stationery Office.

Lancashire County Council (1992) *The Scotforth House Inquiry*. Lancaster, Lancashire County Council.

Lasche, C. (1977) *Haven in a Heartless World*. New York, Basic Books.

Leadbeater, C. (1996) *The Self-policing Society*. London, Demos.

LeBlanc, M. and Frechette, M. (1989) *Male Criminal Activity from Childhood through Youth: Multi-level and Developmental Perspectives*. New York, Springer-Verlag.

Lee, N. (2001) *Childhood and Society: Growing Up in an Age of Uncertainty*. Buckingham, Open University Press.

Levitas, R. (ed.) (1986) *The Ideology of the New Right*. Cambridge, Polity Press.

Levitas, R. (1996) 'The Concept of Social Exclusion and the New Durkheimian Hegemony', *Critical Social Policy*, **16**(1), pp. 5–20.

Levitas, R. (1998) *The Inclusive Society*. Basingstoke, Macmillan – now Palgrave Macmillan.

Lewis, J. (2001) *The End of Marriage? Individualism and Intimate Relations*. Cheltenham, Edward Elgar.

Lindsey, M. (1994) *The Welfare of Children*. New York, Oxford University Press.

Lister, R. (2003) 'Investing in the Citizen-workers of the Future: Transformations in Citizenship and the State under New Labour', *Social Policy and Administration*, **37**(5), pp. 427–43.

Local Government Association, National Health Service Confederation, and the Association of Directors of Social Services (2002) *Serving Children Well – A New Vision for Services to Children*. London, LGA.

Loeber, R. and Stouthamer-Loeber, M. (1986) 'Family Factors as Correlates and Predictors of Juvenile Conduct Problems and Delinquency', in M. Tonty and N. Morris (eds) *Crime and Justice – An Annual Review of Research*. Chicago, University of Chicago.

London Borough of Brent (1985) *A Child in Trust: Report of the Panel of Inquiry Investigating the Circumstances Surrounding the Death of Jasmine Beckford*. London, London Borough of Brent.

London Borough of Greenwich (1987) *A Child in Mind: Protection in a Responsible Society; Report of the Commission of Inquiry into the Circumstances Surrounding the Death of Kimberley Carlile*. London, London Borough of Greenwich.

London Borough of Lambeth (1987) *Whose Child? The Report of the Panel Appointed to Inquire into the Death of Tyra Henry*. London, London Borough of Lambeth.

London Borough of Lewisham (1985) *The Leeways Inquiry Report*. London, London Borough of Lewisham.

Lovell, E. (2001) *Megan's Law: Does it Protect Children? A Review of Evidence on the Impact of Community Notification as Legislated Through Megan's Law in the United States*. London, NSPCC.

Lyon, D. (1994) *The Electronic Eye: The Rise of Surveillance Society*. Cambridge, Polity Press.

Lyon, D. (2001) *Surveillance Society: Monitoring Everyday Life*. Buckingham, Open University Press.

Maclean, M. (2002) 'The Green Paper *Supporting Families* 1998', in A. Carling, S. Duncan and R. Edwards (eds) *Analysing Families: Morality and Rationality in Policy and Practice*. London, Routledge.

MacLeod, M. (1996) *Talking with Children about Child Abuse*. London, ChildLine.

Maguire, M. and Kemshall, H. (2004) 'Multi-Agency Public Protection Arrangements: Key Issues', in H. Kemshall and G. McIver (eds) *Managing Sex Offender Risk*. London, Jessica Kingsley.

Maguire, M., Kemshall, H., Noaks, L., Wincup, E. and Sharpe, K. (2001) *Risk Management of Sexual and Violent Offenders: The Work of Public Protection Panels*. Police Research Series, Paper 139. London, Home Office.

Malaguzzi, L. (1993) 'History, Ideas and Basic Philosophy', in C. Edwards, L. Gandini and G. Forman (eds) *The Hundred Languages of Children*. Norwood, NJ, Ablex.

Marsh, A., McKay, S., Smith, A. and Stephenson, A. (2001) *Low Income Families in Britain: Work, Welfare and Social Security in 1999. DSS Report No. 138*. London, Stationery Office.

Marshall, P. (1997) *The Prevalence of Conviction for Sexual Offending: Research Finding No. 55*. Research and Statistics Directorate, London, Home Office.

Marx, G.T. (2002) 'What's New About the "New Surveillance"? Classifying for Change and Continuity', *Surveillance and Society*, **1**(1), pp. 9–29.

Mathiesen, T. (ed.) (1997) 'The Viewer Society: Michel Foucault's "Panopticon Revisited"', *Theoretical Criminology*, **1**(2), pp. 215–33.

Matravers, A. (2003) *Sex Offenders in the Community: Managing and Reducing the Risks*. Cullompton, Willan Publishing.

Matthews, R. and Young, J. (eds) (2003) *The New Politics of Crime and Punishment*. Cullompton, Willan Publishing.

May, M. (1978) 'Violence in the Family: An Historical Perspective', in J.P. Martin (ed.) *Violence and the Family*. Chichester, Wiley.

May-Chahal, C. and Herczog, M. (eds) (2003) *Child Sexual Abuse in Europe*. Strasbourg, Council of Europe Publishing.

Midgeley, J. (1999) 'Growth, Redistribution and Welfare: Toward Social Investment', *Social Services Review*, **74**(1), pp. 3–31.

Miliband, R. (1978) 'A State of Desubordination', *British Journal of Sociology*, **29**(4), pp. 394–409.

Millar, J. and Ridge, T. (2002) 'Parents, Children, Families and New Labour: Developing Family Policy?', in M. Powell (ed.) *Evaluating New Labour's Welfare Reforms*. Bristol, Policy Press.

Monckton, Sir W. (1945) *Report on the Circumstances which Led to the Boarding-out of Dennis and Terence O'Neil at Bank Farm, Minsterley, and the Steps Taken to Supervise their Welfare* (Cmd 6636). London, HMSO.

Morris, A., Giller, H., Szwed, E. and Geach, H. (1980) *Justice for Children*. London, Macmillan.

Morrison, B. (1997) *As If*. London, Granta Books.

Moss, P. and Petrie, P. (2002) *From Children's Services to Children's Spaces: Public Policy, Children and Childhood*. London, Routledge Falmer.

Moss, P., Dillon, J. and Statham, J. (2000) 'The "Child in Need" and the "Rich Kid": Discourses, Constructions and Practices', *Critical Social Policy*, **20**(2), pp. 233–55.

Mrazek, P.J. and Haggerty, R.J. (eds) (1994) *Reducing Risks for Mental Disorders: Frontiers for Preventive Intervention Research*. Washington, DC, Institute of Medicine/National Academy Press.

Mrazek, P.B., Lynch, M. and Bentovim, A. (1981) 'Recognition of Sexual Abuse in the United Kingdom', in P.B. Mrazek and C.H. Kempe (eds) *Sexually Abused Children and their Families*. Oxford, Pergamon Press.

Munro, E. (2004a) 'The Impact of Child Abuse Inquiries since 1990', in N. Stanley and J. Manthorpe (eds) *The Age of Inquiry: Learning and Blaming in Health and Social Care*. London, Routledge.

Munro, E. (2004b) 'State Regulation of Parenting', *Political Quarterly*, **75**(2), pp. 180–4.

Munro, E. (2004c) 'Can "Tracking" Children Reduce the Harm of Poverty?', *Poverty*, **119**, pp. 7–10.

Myers, J. (1994) *The Backlash: Child Protection under Fire*. Thousand Oaks, CA, Sage.

Nash, M. (1999) *Police, Probation and Protecting the Public*. London, Blackstone Press.

National Health Service Executive (1997) *Guidance to Hospital Managers and Local Authority Social Services Departments on the Sex Offenders Act 1997*. Circular HSG (97)37, London, NHSE.

National Probation Service (2003) *Multi-Agency Public Protection Arrangements: Annual Report 2001–2*. London, Home Office.

NSPCC/University of Sheffield (2000) *The Child's World: Assessing Children in Need, Training and Development Pack*. London, NSPCC.

Nelson, S. (1987) *Incest: Fact and Myth*. Edinburgh, Stramullion.

Newburn, T. (1996) 'Back to the Future? Youth Crime, Youth Justice and the Rediscovery of "Authoritarian Populism"', in J. Pilcher and S. Wagg (eds) *Thatcher's Children? Politics, Childhood and Society in the 1980's and 1990's*. London, Falmer Press.

Newman, J. (2001) *Modernising Governance: New Labour, Policy and Society*. London, Sage.

O'Carroll, T. (1980) *Paedophilia: The Radical Case*. London, Peter Owen.

Office for National Statistics (1998) *Living in Britain: Results from the 1996 General Household Survey*. London, Stationery Office.

Office of National Statistics (2002) *Social Trends*. London, Stationery Office.

Okell, C. and Butcher, C.H.H. (1969) 'The Battered Child Syndrome', *Law Society Gazette*, **66**, p. 9.

O'Malley, P. (ed.) (1998) *Crime and the Risk Society*. Aldershot, Ashgate.

O'Malley, P. (1999) 'Volatile and Contradictory Punishment', *Theoretical Criminology*, **2**(1), pp. 5–28.

Oppenheim, C. and Lister, R. (1996) 'The Politics of Child Poverty 1979–1995', in J. Pilcher and S. Wagg (eds) *Thatcher's Children? Politics, Childhood and Society in the 1980's and 1990's*. London, Falmer Press.

Packman, J. (1981) *The Child's Generation* (2nd edn). Oxford, Basil Blackwell and Martin Robertson.

Packman, J. (1993) 'From Prevention to Partnership: Child Welfare Services Across Three Decades', *Children & Society*, **7**(2), pp. 183–95.

Packman, J. and Jordan, B. (1991) 'The Children Act: Looking Forward, Looking Back', *British Journal of Social Work*, **21**(2), pp. 315–27.

Parker, R. (1991) 'Introduction. Why Assess Outcomes?', in R. Parker, H. Ward, S. Jackson, J. Aldgate and P. Wedge (eds) *Looking After Children: Assessing Outcomes in Child Care: The Report of an Independent Working Party established by the Department of Health*. London, HMSO.

Parker, R. (1995) 'A Brief History of Child Protection', in E. Farmer and M. Owen (eds) *Child Protection Practice: Private Risks and Public Remedies*. London, HMSO.

Parker, R, Ward, H., Jackson, S., Aldgate, J. and Wedge, P. (eds) *Looking After Children: Assessing Outcomes in Child Care: The Report of an Independent Working Party established by the Department of Health*. London, HMSO.

Parton, C. (1990) 'Women, Gender Oppression and Child Abuse', in The Violence Against Children Study Group *Taking Child Abuse Seriously: Contemporary Issues in Child Protection Theory and Practice*. London, Unwin Hyman.

Parton, N. (1985a) *The Politics of Child Abuse*. Basingstoke, Macmillan – now Palgrave Macmillan.

Parton, N. (1985b) 'Children in Care: Recent Changes and Debates', *Critical Social Policy*, Summer, **13**, pp. 107–17.

Parton, N. (1986) 'The Beckford Report: A Critical Appraisal', *British Journal of Social Work*, **16**(5), pp. 511–30.

Parton, N. (1991) *Governing the Family: Child Care, Child Protection and the State*. Basingstoke, Macmillan – now Palgrave Macmillan.

Parton, N. (1992) 'The Contemporary Politics of Child Protection', *Journal of Social Welfare and Family Law*, May, pp. 100–13.

Parton, N. (1995) 'Neglect as Child Protection: The Political Context and the Practical Outcomes', *Children & Society*, **9**(1), pp. 67–89.

Parton, N. (1996a) 'Child Protection, Family Support and Social Work: A Critical Appraisal of the Department of Health Studies in Child Protection', *Child and Family Social Work*, **1**(1), pp. 3–11.

Parton, N. (1996b) 'Social Work, Risk and "the Blaming System"', in N. Parton (ed.) *Social Theory, Social Change and Social Work*. London, Routledge.

Parton, N. (ed.) (1997) *Child Protection and Family Support: Tensions, Contradictions and Possibilities*. London, Routledge.

Parton, N. (1998) 'Risk, Advanced Liberalism and Child Welfare: The Need to Rediscover Uncertainty and Ambiguity', *British Journal of Social Work*, **28**(1), pp. 5–27.

Parton, N. (1999) 'Ideology, Politics and Policy', in O. Stevenson (ed.) *Child Welfare in the United Kingdom 1948–1998*. Oxford, Blackwell Science.

Parton, N. (2004) 'From Maria Colwell to Victoria Climbié: Reflections on Public Inquiries into Child Abuse a Generation Apart', *Child Abuse Review*, **13**(2), pp. 80–94.

Parton, N. and Matthews, R. (2001) 'New Directions in Child Protection and Family Support in Western Australia: A Policy Initiative to Refocus Child Welfare Practice', *Child and Family Social Work*, **6**(2), pp. 97–113.

Parton, N. and Thomas, T. (1983) 'Child Abuse and Citizenship', in B. Jordan and N. Parton (eds) *The Political Dimensions of Social Work*. Oxford, Basil Blackwell.

Parton, N., Thorpe, D. and Wattam, C. (1997) *Child Protection: Risk and the Moral Order*. Basingstoke, Macmillan – now Palgrave Macmillan.

Pascall, G. (1986) *Social Policy: A Feminist Analysis*. London, Tavistock.

Patterson, G.R. (1994) 'Some Characteristics of a Developmental Theory for Early Onset Delinquency', in J.J. Haugaard and M.F. Lenzenweger (eds) *Frontiers of Developmental Psychopathology*. Oxford, Oxford University Press.

Pawson, R. (2002) *Does Megan's Law Work? A Theory-Driven Systematic Review*. ESRC UK Centre for Evidence Based Policy and Practice, Working Paper 8; Queen Mary College, University of London.

Payne, L. (2004) 'Information Sharing and Assessment (ISA): Can Data Management Reduce Risk?', *Children & Society*, **18**(5), pp. 383–6.

Payne, M. (1992) 'Psychodynamic Theory within the Politics of Social Work Theory', *Journal of Social Work Practice*, **6**(2), pp. 141–9.

Pease, K. (2002) 'Crime Reduction', in M. Maguire, R. Morgan and R. Reiner (eds) *The Oxford Handbook of Criminology*. Oxford, Oxford University Press.

Perkin, H. (1989) *The Rise of Professional Society: England since 1880*. London, Routledge.

Phillips, M. (1993) 'Tough Love', *Observer*, 13 June.

Philp, A.F. and Timms, N. (1962) *The Problem of the Problem Family*. London, Family Service Units.

Pitts, J. (2001) *The New Politics of Youth Crime: Discipline or Solidarity*. Lyme Regis, Russell House.

Pitts, J. (2003) 'Youth Justice in England and Wales', in R. Matthews and J. Young (eds) *The New Politics of Crime and Punishment*. Cullompton, Willan Publishing.

Plotnikoff, J. and Woolfson, R. (2000) *Where are They Now? An Evaluation of Sex Offender Registration in England and Wales*. Police Research Series Paper 126. London, Home Office.

Plummer, K. (1995) *Telling Sexual Stories: Power, Change and Social Worlds*. London, Routledge.

Pollock, L.A. (1983) *Forgotten Children: Parent–Child Relations from 1500 to 1900*. Cambridge, Cambridge University Press.

Polsky, A.J. (1991) *The Rise of the Therapeutic State*. Princeton, Princeton University Press.

Power, H. (2003) 'Disclosing Information on Sex Offenders: The Human Rights Implications', in A. Matravers *Sex Offenders in the Community: Managing and Reducing the Risks*. Cullompton, Willan Publishing.

Power, M. (1994) 'The Audit Society', in A.G. Hopwood and P. Miller (eds) *Accounting as Social and Institutional Practice*. Cambridge, Cambridge University Press.

Power, M. (1997) *The Audit Society: Rituals of Verification*. Oxford, Oxford University Press.

Pratt, J. (1997) *Governing the Dangerous*. Sydney, Federation Press.

Pratt, J. (2000) 'Emotive and Ostentatious Punishment: Its Decline and Resurgence in Modern Society', *Punishment and Society*, **2**(4), pp. 417–39.

Pringle, K. (1998) *Children and Social Welfare in Europe*. Buckingham, Open University Press.

Pritchard, C. and Bagley, C. (2001) 'Suicide and Murder in Child Murderers and Child Sexual Abusers', *Journal of Forensic Psychiatry*, **12**(2), pp. 269–86.

Prout, A. (2000) 'Children's Participation: Control and Self-realisation in British Late Modernity', *Children & Society*, **14**(4), pp. 304–15.

Prout, A. (2003) 'Participation, Policy and the Changing Conditions of Childhood', in C. Hallett and A. Prout (eds) *Hearing the Voices of Children: Social Policy for a New Century*. London, Routledge Falmer.

Pugh, G. and Parton, N. (eds) (2003) 'New Labour Policy and its Outcomes for Children', *Children & Society Special Issue*, 17(3), June.

Queensland Ombudsman (2003) *An Investigation into the adequacy of the Actions of Certain Government Agencies in Relation to the Safety, Well Being and Care of the late Baby Kate, who Died aged 10 weeks*. Brisbane, Queensland Ombudsman.

Qvortrup, J. (1994) 'Childhood Matters: An Introduction', in J. Qvortrup, M. Bardy, G. Sgritta and H. Wintersberger (eds) *Childhood Matters: Social Theory, Practice and Politics*. Aldershot, Avebury.

Raynor, P. and Vanstone, M. (2002) *Understanding Community Penalties: Probation, Policy and Social Change*. Buckingham, Open University Press.

Reder, P. and Duncan, S. (1999) *Lost Innocents: A Follow-up Study of Fatal Child Abuse*. London, Routledge.

Reder, P. and Duncan, S. (2004a) 'From Colwell to Climbié: Inquiring into Fatal Child Abuse', in N. Stanley and J. Manthorpe (eds) *The Age of the Inquiry: Learning and Blaming in Health and Social Care*. London, Routledge.

Reder, P. and Duncan, S. (2004b) 'Making the Most of the Victoria Climbié Inquiry Report', *Child Abuse Review*, **13**(2), pp. 95–104.

Rhodes, R. (1997) *Understanding Governance*. Buckingham, Open University Press.

Rhodes, R. (2000) *The Governance Narrative: Key Findings and Lessons from the ESRC's Whitehall Programme*. London, Public Management and Policy Association.

Rickford, F. (2002) 'Denham signals move to use crime as the hook for children's policies', *Community Care*, 21–27 November, pp. 20–1.

Robbins, D. (1999) 'The Refocusing Children's Services Initiative: An Overview of Practice', in R. Bayley (ed.) *Transforming Children's Lives: The Importance of Early Intervention. Occasional Paper 25*. London, Family Policy Studies Centre.

Rose, N. (1985) *The Psychological Complex: Psychology, Politics and Society in England 1869–1939*. London, Routledge & Kegan Paul.

Rose, N. (1999a) *Governing the Soul: The Shaping of the Private Self* (2nd edn). London, Free Assocation.

Rose, N. (1999b) *Powers of Freedom: Reframing Political Thought*. Cambridge, Cambridge University Press.

Rose, N. and Miller, P. (1992) 'Political Power beyond the State: Problematics of Government', *British Journal of Sociology*, **43**(2), pp. 173–205.

Rose, W. (1994) 'An Overview of the Development of Services – the Relationship between Protection and Family Support and the Intentions of the Children Act 1989', *Department of Health Paper for Sieff Conference*, 5 September, Cumberland Lodge.

Rush, F. (1980) *The Best Kept Secret: Sexual Abuse of Children*. New York, McGraw-Hill.

Rutter, M. (1981) *Maternal Deprivation Re-assessed*. Harmondsworth, Penguin.

Rutter, M. (1985) 'Resilience in the Face of Adversity: Protective Factors and Resistance to Psychiatric Disturbance', *British Journal of Psychiatry*, **147**, pp. 598–611.

Rutter, M. (1990) 'Psychosocial Resilience and Protective Mechanisms', in J. Rolf, A.S. Masten, D. Cichetti, K.H. Nuechterlein and S. Weintraub (eds) *Risk and Protective Factors in the Development of Psychopathology*. Cambridge, Cambridge University Press.

Sale, A. (2004) 'Are You on the A-List?' *Community Care*, 29 July–4 August, (1533), pp. 34–5.

Scott, J.C. (1998) *Seeing Like a State: How Certain Schemes to Improve the Human Condition have Failed*. London, Yale University Press.

Scott, S., Jackson, S. and Backett-Milburn, K. (1998) 'Swings and Roundabouts: Risk Anxiety and the Everyday Worlds of Children', *Sociology*, **32**(4), pp. 689–705.

Scottish Executive (2002) *'It's everyone's job to make sure I'm alright': Report of the Child Protection Audit and Review*. Edinburgh, Scottish Executive.

Scottish Office (1997a) *Sex Offenders Act 1997 Guidance on Implementation*. (Circular HD12/97 2154). Edinburgh, Scottish Office.

Scottish Office (1997b) *Implementation of the Sex Offenders Act 1997 – Implications for Local Authorities* (Circular SWSG 11/97). Edinburgh, Scottish Office.

Scraton, P. (ed.) (1997) *'Childhood' in 'Crisis'*. London, UCL Press.

Secretary of State for Social Services (1974) *Report of the Inquiry into the Care and Supervision Provided in Relation to Maria Colwell*. London, HMSO.

Secretary of State for Social Services (1988) *Report of the Inquiry into Child Abuse in Cleveland* (Cm 412). London, HMSO.

Shearer, A. (1979) 'The Legacy of Maria Colwell', *Social Work Today*, **9**(4), pp. 12–19.

Sheller, M. and Urry, J. (2003) 'Mobile Transformations of "Public" and "Private" Life', *Theory, Culture and Society*, **20**(3), pp. 107–25.

Shorter, E. (1976) *The Making of the Modern Family*. London, Collins.

Silverman, J. and Wilson, D. (2002) *Innocence Betrayed: Paedophilia, the Media and Society*. Cambridge, Polity Press.

Simon, J. (1998) 'Managing the Monstrous: Sex Offenders and the New Penology', *Psychology, Public Policy and Law*, **4**(1/2), pp. 452–67.

Sinclair, R. (2004) 'Participation in Practice: Making it Meaningful, Effective and Sustainable', *Children & Society*, **18**(2), pp. 106–18.

Sinclair, R. and Bullock, R. (2002) *Learning from Past Experience: A Review of Serious Case Reviews*. London, Department of Health.

Sinclair, R., Hearn, B. and Pugh, G. (1997) *Preventive Work with Families: The Role of Mainstream Services*. London, National Children's Bureau.

Skidmore, P. (1995) 'Telling Tales: Media Power, Ideology and the Reporting of Child Sexual Abuse in Britain', in D. Kidd-Hewitt and R. Osborne (eds) *Crime and the Media: The Post-Modern Spectacle*. London, Pluto Press.

Skidmore, P. (1998) 'Gender and the Agenda: News Reporting of Child Sexual Abuse', in C. Carter, G. Branston and S. Allan (eds) *News, Gender and Power*. London, Routledge.

Skinner, C. (2003) 'New Labour and Family Policy', in M. Bell and K. Wilson (eds) *The Practitioner's Guide to Working with Families*. Basingstoke, Palgrave Macmillan.

Sleeman, J.F. (1979) *Resources of the Welfare State: An Economic Introduction*. London, Longman.

Smart, C. (2000) 'Reconsidering the Recent History of Child Sexual Abuse', *Journal of Social Policy*, **29**(1), pp. 55–72.

Smart, C. and Neale, B. (1999) *Family Fragments?* Cambridge, Polity Press.

Smith, C. (2001) 'Trust and Confidences: Possibilities for Social Work in High Modernity', *British Journal of Social Work*, **31**(2), pp. 287–305.

Smith, J.M. (1999) 'Prior Criminality and Employment of Social Workers with Substantial Access to Children: A Decision Board Analysis', *British Journal of Social Work*, **29**(1), pp. 49–68.

Smith, R. (2003) *Youth Justice: Ideas, Policy and Practice*. Cullompton, Willan Publishing.

Social Exclusion Unit (2000) *Report of Policy Action Team 12. Young People, National Strategy for Neighbourhood Renewal*. London, Stationery Office.

Social Exclusion Unit (2001) *Preventing Social Exclusion*. London, Stationery Office.

Social Services Committee (1984) *Children in Care (HC 360)* (Short Report). London, HMSO.

SSI (Social Services Inspectorate) (1988) *Report of the Inspection of Melanie Klein House CHE by the Social Services Inspectorate*. London, Department of Health.

SSI (Social Services Inspectorate) (1990) *Inspection of Child Protection Services in Rochdale*. London, Department of Health.

SSI (Social Services Inspectorate) (1991a) *Report of an Inspection of Grove Park Community Park by the Social Services Inspectorate*. London, Department of Health.

SSI (Social Services Inspectorate) (1991b) *Report of an Inspection of St Charles Youth Treatment Centre by the Social Services Inspectorate*. London, Department of Health.

SSI (Social Services Inspectorate) (1994) *The Child, the Court and the Video: A Study of the Implementation of the Memorandum of Good Practice on Video Interviewing of Child Witnesses*. London, Department of Health.

SSI (Social Services Inspectorate) (1995) *Learning Lessons: A Report Based on the Information Drawn from Three Seminars Organised by the Social Services Inspectorate, North of England Policy and Business Division looking at the Part 8 Review Process*. London, Department of Health.

Staffordshire County Council (1991) *The Pindown Experience and the Protection of Children*. Stafford, Staffordshire County Council.

Stanley, N. (1999) 'The Abuse of Children: an Overview of Policy and Practice', in N. Stanley, J. Manthorpe and B. Penhale (eds) *Institutional Abuse: Perspectives Across the Life-Course*. London, Routledge.

Staples, W. (1997) *The Culture of Surveillance: Discipline and Social Control in the United States*. New York, St Martin's Press.

Statham, J. and Aldgate, J. (2003) 'From Legislation to Practice: Learning from the Children Act 1989 Research Programme', *Children & Society*, **17**(2), pp. 149–56.

Stedman Jones, G. (1971) *Outcast London*. Oxford, Clarendon Press.

Steiker, C.C. (1998) 'Foreword: The Limits of the Preventive State', *Journal of Criminal Law and Criminology*, **88**(3), pp. 771–808.

Stenson, K. (2001) 'The New Politics of Crime Control', in K. Stenson and R.R. Sullivan (eds) *Crime, Risk and Punishment: The Politics of Crime Control in Liberal Democracies*. Cullompton, Willan Publishing.

Sullivan, M. (1992) *The Politics of Social Policy*. Hemel Hempstead, Harvester-Wheatsheaf.

Swaan, A. de (1988) *In Care of the State*. Cambridge, Polity Press.

Taylor, C. (2004) 'Underpinning Knowledge for Child Care Practice: Reconsidering Child Development Theory', *Child and Family Social Work*, **9**(3), pp. 225–35.

Taylor, L., Lacey, R. and Bracken, D. (1980) *In Whose Best Interests?* London, Cobden Trust/Mind.

Thane, P. (1981) 'Childhood in History', in M. King (ed.) *Childhood, Welfare and Society*. London, Batsford.

Thoburn, J., Wilding, J. and Watson, J. (2000) *Family Support in Cases of Emotional Maltreatment and Neglect.* London, Stationery Office.

Thomas, T. (2000) *Sex Crime: Sex Offending and Society*. Cullompton, Willan Publishing.

Thomas, T. (2001) 'Sex Offenders, the Home Office and the Sunday Papers', *Journal of Social Welfare and Family Law*, **23**(1), pp. 103–8.

Thomas, T. (2003) 'Sex Offender Community Notification: The American Experience', *Howard Journal of Criminal Justice*, **42**(3), pp. 217–28.

Thomas, T. (2004a) 'Should We Have Known?' *Community Care*, **1509** (12–18 February), pp. 32–3.

Thomas, T. (2004b) 'Sex Offender Registers and Monitoring', in H. Kemshall and G. McIver (eds) *Managing Sex Offender Risk*. London, Jessica Kingsley.

Thompson, J.B. (1990) *Ideology and Modern Culture*. Cambridge, Polity Press.

Thompson, J.B. (1996) *The Media and Modernity: A Social Theory of the Media*. Cambridge, Polity Press.

Thompson, J.B. (2000) *Political Scandal: Power and Visibility in the Media Age*. Cambridge, Polity Press.

Thompson, P. and Coughlan, J. (2004) 'Children Bill: Time for a Focused Approach', *ADSS Inform*, April, pp. 7–9.

Thomson, R. and Holland, J. (2002) 'Young People, Social Change and the Negotiation of Moral Authority', *Children & Society*, **16**(2), pp. 103–15.

Thorpe, D. (1994) *Evaluating Child Protection*. Buckingham, Open University Press.

Timms, N. (1964) *Social Casework: Principles and Practice*. London, Routledge & Kegan Paul.

Tomlinson, S. (2003) 'New Labour and Education', *Children & Society*, **17**(3), pp. 195–204.

Townley, B. (2002) 'Managing with Modernity', *Organisation*, **9**(4), pp. 549–73.

Townsend, P. (1970) *The Fifth Social Service: A Critical Analysis of the Seebohm Proposals*. London, The Fabian Society.

Toynbee, P. and Walker, D. (2001) *Did Things Get Better? An Audit of Labour's Successes and Failures*. London, Penguin.

Tunstill, J. and Aldgate, J. (2000) *Services for Children in Need: From Policy to Practice*. London, Stationery Office.

Utting, D. (1995) *Family and Parenthood: Supporting Families, Preventing Breakdown*. York, Joseph Rowntree Foundation.

Utting, D. (ed.) (1998a) *Children's Services: Now and in the Future*. London, National Children's Bureau.

Utting, D. (1998b) 'Children's Services: Now and in the Future', in D. Utting (ed.) *Children's Services: Now and in the Future*. London, National Children's Bureau.

Utting, D., Bright, J. and Henricson, C. (1993) *Crime and the Family: Improving Child-Rearing and Preventing Delinquency*. London, Family Policy Studies Centre.

Utting, Sir William (1991) *Children in the Public Care: A Review of Residential Child Care*. London, HMSO.

Utting, Sir William (1997) *People Life Us: The Report of the Review of the Safeguards for Children Living Away from Home*. London, HMSO.

Van Loon, J. (2002) *Risk and Technological Culture: Towards a Sociology of Virulence*. London, Routledge.

Veit-Wilson, J. (1998) *Setting Adequate Standards*. Bristol, Policy Press.

Wagner, P. (1992) 'Liberty and Discipline: Making Sense of Postmodernity, or, once again, Toward a Sociohistorical Understanding of Modernity', *Theory and Society*, 22, pp. 467–92.

Wagner, P. (1994) *A Sociology of Modernity: Liberty and Discipline*. London, Routledge.

Walby, S. (1997) *Gender Transformations*. London, Routledge.

Waldfogel, J. (2001) *The Future of Child Protection*. Cambridge, MA, Harvard University Press.

Walkerdine, V. (1984) 'Developmental Psychology and the Child-Centred Pedagogy: The Insertion of Piaget's Theory into Primary School Practice', in J. Henriques, W. Hollway, C. Urwin, C. Venn and V. Walkerdine (eds) *Changing the Subject: Psychology, Social Regulation and Subjectivity*. London, Methuen.

Walkerdine, V. (1993) 'Beyond Developmentalism?' *Theory and Psychology*, 3, pp. 451–70.

Walker, S. and Scott, J. (2004) in collaboration with members of the ICS multidisciplinary research team led by Professor Hedy Cleaver at Royal Holloway, University of London *Implementing the Integrated Children's System – a Phased Approach: Briefing Paper 6*. London, DfES.

Walton, R.G. (1975) *Women and Social Work*. London, Routledge & Kegan Paul.

Walvin, J. (1982) *A Child's World: A Social History of English Childhood, 1800–1914*. Harmondsworth, Penguin.

Ward, H. (ed.) (1995) *Looking After Children: Research into Practice*. London, Stationery Office.

Ward, H. (1998) 'Using a Child Development Model to Assess the Outcomes of Social Work Interventions with Families', *Children & Society*, **12**(3), pp. 202–11.

Ward, H. (2002) 'Introduction', in H. Ward and W. Rose (eds) *Approaches to Needs Assessment in Children's Services*. London, Jessica Kingsley.

Waterhouse, Sir R. (2000) *Lost in Care: Report of the Tribunal of Inquiry into the Abuse of Children in Care in the Former Council Areas of Gwynedd and Clwyd since 1974, HC201*. London, Stationery Office.

Wattam, C. (1999) 'Confidentiality and the Social Organisation of Telling', in N. Parton and C. Wattam (eds) *Child Sexual Abuse: Responding to the Experiences of Children*. Chichester, Wiley.

Wattam, C. (2002) 'Making Enquiries under Section 47 of the Children Act 1989', in K. Wilson and A. James (eds) *The Child Protection Handbook* (2nd edn). London, Baillière Tindall.

Wattam, C. and Woodward, C. (1996) 'And do I abuse my children? ... No! – learning about prevention from people who have experienced child abuse', *Childhood Matters: The Report of the National Commission of Inquiry into the Prevention of Child Abuse*. volume 2, *Background Papers*. London, HMSO.

Weiss, H.B. (2003) 'Foreword', in I. Katz and J. Pinkerton (eds) *Evaluating Family Support: Thinking Internationally, Thinking Critically*. Chichester, John Wiley.

West, D.J. (1982) *Delinquency: Its Roots, Careers and Prospects*. London, Heinemann.

West, D. (2000) 'Paedophilia: Plague or Panic?', *The Journal of Forensic Psychiatry*, **11**(3), pp. 511–31.

West, D. and Farrington, D. (1973) *Who Becomes Delinquent?* London, Heinemann.

Wheeler, S. (ed.) (1969) *On Record*. New York, Russell Sage Foundation.

White, I. and Hart, K. (1995) *Report of the Management of Child Care in the London Borough of Islington*. London, Borough of Islington.

White, M. and Wintour, P. (2003) 'The New Routes to Social Justice', *Guardian*, 28 November, p. 4.

White, S. (1998) 'Interdiscursivity and Child Welfare: The Ascent and Durability of Psycho-legalism', *Sociological Review*, **46**(2), pp. 264–92.

Wilkinson, H. (2001) 'The Family Way: Navigating a Third Way in Family Policy', in A. Giddens (ed.) *The Global Third Way*. Cambridge, Polity Press.

Williams, F. (1989) *Social Policy: A Critical Introduction*. Cambridge, Polity Press.

Williams, J. (2002) 'Child Protection and the Criminal Justice System', in K. Wilson and A. James (eds) *The Child Protection Handbook* (2nd edn). London, Baillière Tindall.

Williamson, E., Goodenough, T., Kent, J. and Ashcroft, R. (forthcoming) 'Conducting Research with Children: The Limits of Confidentiality and Child Protection Protocols', *Children & Society*.

Wilson, E. (1977) *Women and the Welfare State*. London, Tavistock.

Winnicott, D.W. (1964) *The Child, the Family and the Outside World*. Harmondsworth, Penguin.

Woodhead, M. (1988) 'When Psychology Informs Public Policy: the Case of Early Childhood Intervention', *American Psychologist*, **43**(6), pp. 443–54.

Woodhead, M. (1997) 'Psychology and the Cultural Construction of Children's Needs', in A. James and A. Prout (eds) *Constructing and Reconstructing Childhood: Contemporary Issues in the Sociological Study of Childhood* (2nd edn). London, Falmer.

Woodhead, M. (1999) 'Reconstructing Developmental Psychology – Some First Steps', *Children & Society*, **13**(1), pp. 3–19.

Worrall, A. (1997) *Punishment in the Community: The Future of Criminal Justice*. London, Longman.

Wroe, A. (1988) *Social Work, Child Abuse and the Press*: Social Work Monograph 66. Norwich, University of East Anglia.

Young, J. (1999) *The Exclusive Society: Social Exclusion, Crime and Difference in Late Modernity*. London, Sage.

Index